W9-BGP-500

Praise for

Murder City

"Bowden is a gifted writer; the book reads like a lyrical ode to arid despair. The literary quality of the writing, and its relentless fatalism, bring to mind Gabriel García Márquez's *Chronicle of a Death Foretold*, except in this case it is not the protagonist's death in question, but an entire city's."
—*Washington Monthly*

"Dreamlike and haunting, beautifully poetic yet brutally savage—and difficult to put down once you've started."
—*San Diego Union Tribune*

"Alarming and strangely compelling." —*Minneapolis Star-Tribune*

"Bowden is advancing a theory of human nature, a gesture more typical of art than of reporting. We understand that *Murder City* aspires to poetry, with the singular voice and tragic bent that implies."
—*Austin Chronicle*

"Enormously affecting." —*San Francisco Chronicle*

"Bowden sees Juárez as a harbinger of planetary chaos, a vision of a world undone by inequality and ravenous appetites . . . he has a very important story to tell . . . you will find some vital and powerful reporting."
—*The New Republic*

"Bowden is at his best describing the fearful atmosphere of that city . . . [Bowden] trods where few American writers venture."
—Paul Salopek, *The American Scholar*

"There is something apocalyptic going on there according to this lone voice many want silenced, making this book both compelling and important." —*The Buffalo News*

"Bowden uses his tremendous talents to tell a haunting, darkly poetic story of a city's horrifying descent into madness and anarchy. A potent book that readers won't soon forget, and a warning of what can come of an insatiable market that knows no borders."
—*Kirkus* (starred review)

"Bowden's prose (and at times poetry) has a way of stabbing at the soul, making this the book for anyone who wants to get underneath the truth and into the heart of the matter." —*Library Journal*

"The druglords kill with style and nothing happens to them. Bowden tells of one killing after another with wonderful clarity; he keeps his voice low and comes up with scene-enders that stop you cold."
—Elmore Leonard

"Writers who cover the border have stolen from Charles Bowden for years. They skirt the abyss in their books, but in *Murder City* Bowden plunges in headfirst, without a parachute. There are moments when the book threatens to burst into flames and burn your hands. Crawling with ghosts and demons, dripping blood, howling with rage and terror, it's go-for-broke apocalyptic prophecy. Forget Baghdad, forget Kandahar: Hell is only fifty yards away from your back porch, and Bowden is going to make you look or die trying."
—Luis Alberto Urrea, author of *The Devil's Highway*

"Charles Bowden is a great writer. *Murder City* is proof. The work is non-fiction. It reads like a dream."
—William Langewiesche, International Correspondent, *Vanity Fair*

"Journalists from the world over have written about the violence wracking today's Mexico. Charles Bowden, who has forgotten more about that tragic country than most of them will ever know, has gone far beyond mere reportage in this extraordinary account. He has plunged into the heart of the bloodshed, absorbed it into his very cells, and exhaled it back to us in a troubling breath of truth. And the truth is that what's happening on our southern border isn't a battle in the war of drugs; nor is it a war between drug cartels. It's nothing less than the collapse of civil society, a Hobbesian state of nature, a war of every man against every other man."
—Philip Caputo, author of *A Rumor of War*

"Charles Bowden's *Murder City* takes readers into the heart of darkness that is Ciudad Juárez, the vertically collapsing city across the river from El Paso. A compelling work of immersion journalism that reads like a novel—if fiction could be so terrifying—and provides some measure of dignity for the dead in a place where murder has become background noise."
—Lou Dubose, co-author with Molly Ivins of
Bushwhacked: Life in George W. Bush's America

MURDER CITY

Also by Charles Bowden

MURDER CITY

CIUDAD JUÁREZ AND THE GLOBAL ECONOMY'S NEW KILLING FIELDS

Charles Bowden

Photographs by Julián Cardona

NATION
BOOKS

New York

Copyright © 2010, 2011 by Charles Bowden

Hardcover first published in 2010 by Nation Books,
A Member of the Perseus Books Group
116 East 16th Street, 8th Floor
New York, NY 10003
Paperback first published in 2011 by Nation Books

Nation Books is a co-publishing venture of the Nation Institute and the
Perseus Books Group.

All rights reserved. Printed in the United States of America. No part of this book
may be reproduced in any manner whatsoever without written permission except
in the case of brief quotations embodied in critical articles and reviews. For
information, address the Perseus Books Group, 387 Park Avenue South,
New York, NY 10016-8810.

Books published by Nation Books are available at special discounts for bulk
purchases in the United States by corporations, institutions, and other
organizations. For more information, please contact the Special Markets
Department at the Perseus Books Group, 2300 Chestnut Street, Suite 200,
Philadelphia, PA 19103, or call (800) 810-4145, ext. 5000, or e-mail
special.markets@perseusbooks.com.

Photographs copyright © 2010 by Julián Cardona. Reprinted by permission of
Anderson Literary Management, LLC. All Rights Reserved. Research Assistance
was provided by the Documentary Photography Fund at The Nation Institute.

Photo section designed by Brenda Muñoz.

The Library of Congress has cataloged the hardcover as follows:
Bowden, Charles, 1945–
Murder city : Ciudad Juárez and the global economy's new killing fields /
Charles Bowden; photographs by Julian Cardona.
p. cm.

ISBN 978-1-56858-449-2 (alk. paper)
1. Drug traffic—Mexico—Ciudad Juárez. 2. Narco-terrorism—Mexico—
Ciudad Juárez. 3. Murder—Mexico—Ciudad Juárez. 4. Ciudad Juárez
(Mexico)—Social conditions.
I. Title.

HV5840.M42C5826 2010

364.152'3097216—dc22

2010001716

Paperback ISBN: 978-1-56858-645-8

E-book ISBN: 978-1-56858-622-9

10 9 8 7 6 5 4 3 2 1

His name was never in the paper. He's not the finest character that ever lived. But he's a human being, and a terrible thing is happening to him. So attention must be paid. He's not to be allowed to fall into his grave like an old dog. Attention, attention must finally be paid to such a person.

—ARTHUR MILLER, *Death of a Salesman*

But you see that line there moving through the station?
I told you, I told you, told you, I was one of those.

—LEONARD COHEN, "FIRST WE TAKE MANHATTAN"

Death solves all problems. No man, no problem.

—ANATOLY RYBAKOV, *Children of the Arbat,*
FICTITIOUSLY QUOTING JOSEPH STALIN

I shot a man in Reno
Just to watch him die.

—JOHNNY CASH, "FOLSOM PRISON BLUES"

Thank you for waiting.

—ANONYMOUS, THE FINAL WORDS OF THE FOURTH DEATH LIST OF COPS POSTED IN CIUDAD JUÁREZ, JUNE 2008. THIS ONE WAS LEFT OUTSIDE THE STATION.

DEAD MAN IN CANAL
WAS A STREET CORNER CLOWN

Armando Rodriguez, *El Diario*, Ciudad Juárez,
November 13, 2008

The man assassinated
Tuesday night in the Diaz Ordaz viaduct
was
a street clown,
according to the state authority.
Nevertheless, this person has not been identified,
but it was reported
that he was between 25 and 30 years old,
1.77 meters tall,
delicate,
light brown complexion,
short black hair.
The victim's face was painted as a clown,
green with a red nose,
reported the State Prosecutor's office.
He wore a red polo shirt,
a navy blue sweatshirt, blue jeans,
white underwear,
gray socks labeled USA,
gray and white Converse tennis shoes
and a dark, cherry red beret.
The body was found in the Diaz Ordaz viaduct,
at Norzagaray Blvd in the colonia Bellavista,
on November 11 at 9:40 pm.
The body was found on its side,
with bullet wounds in the right side,
chest
and head.
At this time, the motive for the murder is unknown as well as the
identities of the murderers.

For Armando Rodriguez, who was gunned down on November 13, 2008, after filing 907 stories on the murders of that calendar year.

Like the rest of us, he was a dead man walking.

His last story appeared hours after he was killed.

BLANCA MARTÍNEZ RAISES THE PHOTOGRAPH OF HER HUSBAND, ARMANDO RODRÍGUEZ, WHILE REPORTERS AND EMPLOYEES OF EL DIARIO PAY THEIR LAST RESPECTS TO THEIR MURDERED COLLEAGUE. SHE IS ACCOMPANIED BY ROCIO GALLEGOS.

PROLOGUE

GET IN THE CAR

Here's the deal.

We're gonna take us a ride.

Now be quiet.

Time's up, you gotta ride.

We brought the duct tape—do you prefer gray or tan? No matter, get your ass in.

We have the plastic bag, the loaded guns.

You have been waiting?

Everyone is waiting, but our list is so long.

Everyone pretends we will never come.

But everyone is on somebody's list.

Well, for you, the wait is over.

Let me tell you about a killing season.

What?

You don't like violence?

I understand.

But get in the car.

You say it hard to see because of the darkly tinted windows?

You will learn darkness.

Miss Sinaloa is a detail. She was special, so fine.

Of course, she took the ride, my God, what a ride.

Okay, yes, there is the matter of cocaine and whiskey and sanity that might undercut her standing in the community.

See those people on the street pretending you don't exist and this big machine with tinted windows doesn't exist, pretending that none of this is happening to you?

That was you until just a few minutes ago.

The killings?

Murder itself is simply a little piece of life and so it can be dismissed as exceptional or irrational or extreme.

Though it is curious how, if you kill with style, it does get everyone's attention.

Surely, we know that even at our best we can only know little pieces of life.

What, you are uncomfortable? The tape binding your hands behind your back is too tight?

Shut your fucking mouth.

You want this pistol cracked over your ugly face?

No?

That's better.

Now shut up before I have to tape your mouth.

What was I saying?

Oh, yes.

We can still believe that destroying another human life is an extreme act.

Unless of course, the slaughter is done by governments. Or the killing is done to some vague group variously dubbed as terrorists or gangsters or drug dealers or people—and this varies with location—of other color or religious notions.

Still, you can see, there is really nothing to worry about since people know how to ignore whatever interferes with the way people want to think about the world.

Yes. I mean this. People can have murders all around them and have people vanish in broad daylight and still go on just fine and say, well, those people were bad, or it doesn't happen that often.

What?

Stop shaking your head. You say nothing and do nothing.

You understand?

You are simply along for the ride. And all those things you said didn't matter, well, now maybe you will change your mind, just a little bit.

The trick is to leave, fade away and stop thinking about the killings.

In the first eleven days of August, seventy-five go down. On Monday, August 11, fifteen are murdered.

Let it go, fade away, turn the page, change the music.

Let me tell you of an incident.

I come back from the shadows against my will.

What?

You don't believe me?

Believe me.

This incident, yes, this incident. There is this woman, and she is very nice-looking, and a friend invites her to a party being hosted by men who apparently work in the drug industry. The woman, the one I am talking about, and damn you, listen as if your fucking life depended on it, well, this woman lives in southern Chihuahua and so she has little to do with Juárez just as Juárez has little to do with the real world, you know, the United States, Europe, all those kind of places where the real world exists.

When the car comes and she gets in it, her friend takes money from the men but does not come along for the ride.

For the next few days, she is gang-raped.

When she returns to the workaday world, she gives a deposition to the authorities, and suddenly she is on the front page of the newspaper. She goes into hiding, though she is still bleeding from her vagina and rectum. She remembers that at the hospital, she was shunted aside because her case was not considered an emergency.

And so she becomes a detail. That is the way of life. Everything becomes a detail if it interferes with the big picture.

She has never met Miss Sinaloa, but now, they truly know each other and they talk throughout the dark hours of the night, I can hear them, and this makes sleep difficult for me.

But I hide from such matters. I am a coward by nature and I do not like cities, loud sounds, guns, violence, or open sewage systems.

Twice I was at a fresh kill, and the freshness does matter, and flies buzzed up into my face from the blood. I cannot remember the names of the dead, hardly anything about them, but the flies buzz in my face all the time, follow me into good restaurants, trail me to fine venues where people read poems or play serious music in the calm air of the fortresses of culture.

Perhaps you think I am mad? I can see that look in your eyes, and yes, I understand why you have your reservations. But then you do not have to listen to those two women talking into the night. I cannot decide what is worse: when they are crying or when they are laughing.

And something has changed inside, something in a deep part, near that place we can never locate but often claim is the core of our being. In the past, I have covered kidnappings, murders, financial debacles, the mayhem that my species is capable of committing. I spent three years mired in reporting sex crimes. There is little within me that has not been battered or wrenched or poisoned. But the path I followed with Miss Sinaloa proved all my background to be so much nothing. I have not entered the country of death, but rather the country of killing. And I have learned in this country that killing is good.

For years, I toyed with a history of my earth, and I found that the way I could understand my earth was through its elemental fury.

Freeman Dyson, a major physicist, once tried to express the allure of power and killing. "I have felt it myself," he warned. "The glitter of nuclear weapons. It is irresistible if you come to them as a scientist. To feel it's there in your hands, to release this energy that fuels the stars, to let it do your bidding. To perform these miracles, to lift a million tons of rock into the sky. It is something that gives people an illusion of illimitable power, and it is, in some ways, responsible for all our troubles—this, what you might call technical arrogance, that overcomes people when they see what they can do with their minds."

I think Dyson erred in one detail: This attraction to slaughter and power is not simply a temptation of the mind.

I found this glitter in a room with flies buzzing off the fresh blood on the floor and walls. A candle glittered in the corner by a crucifix. The bodies had been taken out, the machine gun fire had died. There was nothing left but the flies and the flame.

Imagine living in a place where you can kill anyone you wish and nothing happens except that they fall dead. You will not be arrested. Your name will not be in the newspapers. You can continue on with your life. And your killing. You can take a woman and rape her for days and nothing will happen. If you choose, if in some way that woman displeases you, well, you can kill her after raping her. Rest assured, nothing will happen to you because of your actions.

Enough. I can barely speak of this change within me. I can hardly expect others to understand.

How did this change come to pass?

It began with a woman.

In the beginning, I was not looking for Miss Sinaloa. In fact, I had never heard of her and had no reason, no reason at all, to think she even existed. I remember clearly, it was a bright winter day, the sun poured down on me, and the desert seemed so kind and generous after spending time in the colonias and bad bars of the border city.

Suddenly, she appeared in my life.

Miss Sinaloa is . . . waiting.

Relax.

This is a nice car, no?

We're gonna have us a time.

I have been to the far country with her and now I am back.
The air of morning tastes fresh, the sunrise murdered the night,
and now the light caresses my face. I chew on ash and bone, this has become
my customary breakfast. I drink the glass of blood for my health.

She does not speak. I no longer listen.

The far country lingers on my clothes and in my hair.
I can still smell it here in the morning light. I have brought her
with me and now we will live together for the rest of my days.

Her lips gleam a ripe red and fragrance
floats from her white skin.

Ernesto Romero Adame is thirty-three years old on New Year's Day, 2008. He sits in his 2005 black Jetta Volkswagen. Bullet holes mark his neck, throat, and chest as he waits stone dead at Paseo Triunfo de la Republica Avenue. He is the first official kill of the season.

It is twenty minutes after midnight on Sunday, January 20, when Julián Cháirez Hernández is found dead by gunshot. He is a lieutenant in the municipal police and thirty-seven years old. Seven hours and ten minutes later, Mirna Yesenia Muñoz Ledo Marín is found inside her own home. She is naked and has been stabbed several times. She is ten years old. On Monday, January 21, at 7:50 A.M., Francisco Ledesma Salazar is killed in his SUV. He is thirty-five years old and the coordinator of operations for the municipal police. The gunshots come from men in a minivan. At 9:30 A.M., the body of Erika Sonora Trejo is found by police in the bathroom of her home. She is thirty-eight and eight months pregnant, and officers think her father-in-law has had at her with an axe. Later that Monday, at 5 P.M., a year-old skeleton turns up in the desert. That evening around 8:40 P.M., Fernando Lozano Sandoval is cut down in his SUV by a barrage of fifty-one rounds. He is fifty-one and the commander of the Chihuahua Bureau of Investigations. Two vehicles, a red SUV and a gray car, figure in the attack. Later, Lozano is transported to an El Paso hospital since Juárez has had recent incidents of killers visiting the wounded in hospitals in order to finish their work.

A list appears on a Juárez monument to fallen police officers. Under the heading THOSE WHO DID NOT BELIEVE are the names of five recently murdered cops. And under the heading FOR THOSE WHO CONTINUE NOT BELIEVING are seventeen names.

As the killings increase in early 2008, rumors begin to spread of Mexican army troops suddenly increasing in Ciudad Juárez and northern Chihuahua. On February 13, the soldiers go to a house and find twenty-five big guns, five small arms, seven fragmentation grenades, 3,494 rounds of various calibers, a bunch of bulletproof vests, eight radios, and five cars with Sinaloa plates. On February 16, they find twenty-one men, ten AK-47s, more than 13,000 hits of cocaine, 2.1 kilos of cocaine base, various uniforms—some of the Mexican army, some of AFI (Agencia Federal de Investigación, the Mexican equivalent of the FBI), 401 cartridges, 760 grams of marijuana, and three vehicles with Sinaloa plates. On February 21, they seize a helicopter.

On the twentieth, seven men are picked up by the army. Later, they say the soldiers beat them with cables, among other gestures.

Around 8 P.M. on Wednesday night, March 5, he crawls across the white tile floor of a small bakery near central Juárez. He has been gone two days and is a member of the city's traffic cops. Juán Rodriguez, sixty-five, looks down from his counter of bread, sweet rolls, and candies and sees that the man is barefoot and beaten and that all the insignia have been ripped from his tattered traffic-cop uniform.

Then, he hears Carlos Adrián De Anda Doncel say, "No! No police, please! Do not call the police!"

Instead, he calls his wife and says, "My love, I am well."

Within five minutes, members of his own unit arrive and whisk him away. Two days later, he flees the city. His commander says that since he is absent from duty, he will lose his job. He has three children.

Four days after the kidnapped and beaten cop appeared in the bakery, Rodriguez offers me a roll and refuses payment. When I ask him about the frightened cop begging that he not call the police, he says softly, "I can no longer say that."

Silence has returned again to this city of two million souls. The governor of Chihuahua has been in seclusion since January—they say his face is frozen due to some mysterious medical condition. The city police have announced they will no longer be answering calls but prefer to stay in their station houses.

The newspaper account of that night notes that the cop's safe return was a miracle, a historic act, because his captors—never named or identified, and they most likely never will be—"pardoned his life."

Over the previous weekend, seven men died in executions, one of them a Mexican army captain who worked in intelligence and died driving his car on Sunday morning down a Juárez avenue. By Monday, March 3, eighty-nine murders had been tallied since New Year's Day.

In 1999, Juárez went a solid year without public evidence of an execution—meaning 365 days without a corpse being left on the street in the customary style of hands bound with duct tape, mouth taped shut, and a bullet through the brain. Then, on the 366th day, the bodies began appearing again. Locals think the year of silent murder came as greeting to the newly elected governor, Patricio Martinez. And the return to executed bodies being left on the street also came as a message to this governor after his first year in office.

Juárez has long supplied Americans with what they wanted—booze during Prohibition, women at all times, opiates when they were outlawed in the

United States, quick divorces when the marriages soured—and like the rest of Mexico, the city has operated as a partnership between criminal organizations and government. Geography has made the city the link between the center of Mexico and the transportation arteries of the United States. But in the 1980s, major cocaine routes shifted from Florida to Mexico, and Juárez became the beneficiary of this change. Profits increased manyfold, and by 1995, the Juárez cartel was taking in $250 million a week, according to the U.S. Drug Enforcement Administration (DEA). Violence grew accordingly, as did corruption of the local government to protect this money. But nothing in this past of vice, drugs, corruption, and money prepared the city for the violence it was suddenly experiencing. Juárez had tasted two hundred to three hundred murders a year in the 1990s and most of the new century. Suddenly, a month of forty or fifty executions seemed quiet—the previous record slaughter for the city was thirty-nine in September 1995. A new day had begun and it looks like night.

I sit on a curb on a heavily rutted dirt street. About ten blocks away rises a new Catholic church, a huge edifice with red-tiled domes etched with yellow tiles, fine new wooden doors, the walls gleaming with stained-glass windows. The church is encircled by new pickup trucks and SUVs, all with deeply tinted windows. Inside, people pray. Set against the surrounding dirt streets and general poverty, the new huge church seems like a miracle. But in this city, it is not. Like the huge discos and fine restaurants of Juárez, it is built not of bricks and mortar but of narco-dollars.

No one speaks of this.

No one doubts this.

But where I sit on the curb, the world is linked to the church and the people praying there this Sunday. Across the street is a two-story home painted yellow and green with iron trim and a satellite dish. Up and down the dirt street, men in dark uniforms with flak jackets and machine guns stand around and watch for something. They are busy digging for bodies in a building just down the street. I can hear the soft voices of people, the bark of dogs, the swish of clothes drying on a line. Overhead, the sun hunts through the clouds. In the yard behind me, there is a shrine to the Virgin of Guadalupe, grape vines, and a large rose bush.

The digging goes on and on for days. There is much to uncover.

I am standing in the desert. A crazy man is talking to me. He says, "Someone is attacking me. I was contracted to make a killing. My family is American."

He wears a pink sport shirt.

I am sitting in a café.

The waiter asks, "Why did you come back? Aren't you finished yet?"

I tell him the people of the city keep killing each other.

He laughs.

I am in the crazy place when a retarded man hands me a children's book.

It reads, "One windy day during the harvest time, Quail sings a song—just as Coyote walks by.

"'Teach me your song, or I shall eat you up,' cries Coyote.

"But Quail's song is no ordinary song, and Coyote may end up swallowing more than he bargained for. . . . "

That is clearly the risk.

On a Sunday, a man in a Dodge Neon is gunned down.

On Wednesday, two beaten and tortured cops are found under a bridge near the cemetery.

On Wednesday night, that cop crawls into the bakery.

On Thursday, another man is executed.

On Friday, seven men are slaughtered in a house in the state capital by the authorities.

On Saturday, a man in a car is machine-gunned near the crazy place.

On Sunday, a police bodyguard is cut down.

At first, I keep a list, try to see things in sequence, search for cause and effect.

Then I learn and give up.

The kidnapped and beaten cops that turn up, well, they were never reported as kidnapped until they suddenly reappeared.

The cop cut down, his name is not printed, nor the fact that the comandante he was guarding had his name on a certain list.

The names of the seven men killed in the state capital are also never made public.

When I cross from El Paso to Juárez in January, the river is dry. Nine thousand jobs have vanished in the past few months as the economy sinks. It is thirty-three degrees and very still. Air presses down like Jell-O and has a gunmetal blue cast from the wood fires of the poor. A vendor walks with a stack of newspapers on his head and carefully plods between the puddles.

Everything has already begun, but at this moment it has not yet been said out loud. The beginning will come later, when the dead get so numerous we can no longer silence them.

He is really unimportant. He seems to move in and out of jail in New Mexico. He is in the United States illegally, that is true, but he has a list of injustices he wishes to state, injustices that cover thirteen years in the country.

For example, U.S. authorities try to interview him when he is too tired to talk. Also, he suffers from gastrointestinal problems and he is seldom given the right medication at the right time. He has an infection in his right arm, and he does not get proper treatment for that, either. Detention officers have pounded on him and dislocated his shoulder. He says the guards mess with his medications so that he will go crazy. Also, once a dentist drilled his tooth and that tooth disappeared.

He has been drinking fairly hard since age seventeen. Yes, there have been blackouts. When he was young, he did marijuana and inhalants.

As for his family members, they have no history of suicide. True, his dad drank a lot and was violent and his mom got violent also and once tried to choke him when he was a boy.

The examining doctor notes that he has a poorly groomed beard and sometimes does not make sense. He can't quite figure out what is wrong with him, but the physician does not think the man can represent himself before the authorities. Eventually, the United States kicks him back into Mexico.

And then he winds up at the crazy place in the desert outside Juárez.

He is part of a story that never gets told.

There is a rhythm of casual violence in the city that almost always goes unmentioned. The mayor of Juárez lives in El Paso so that he can keep his hand on the pulse of the city. The publisher of the daily paper in Juárez also lives in El Paso. The publisher of the daily paper in the capital of Chihuahua lives in New Mexico. A growing number of the businesspeople of Juárez live in El Paso. Leaders in the drug industry also keep homes in El Paso.

But for the average citizen of Juárez, such a remove is not a possibility. They lack the money and the legal documents to live in the United States. As winter slides into spring and the killing season accelerates, the poor continue their lives in Juárez and often find their deaths there. The new violence is simply an increase in the volume of their tired lives.

A woman and her boyfriend sit in a car drinking and arguing. Her young daughter is in the car, also. Then the man sends the girl to a nearby Laundromat. When she comes back, she notices her mother is not moving. The boyfriend says that she is sleeping. He takes the girl home. Later, the authorities determine the woman died from a laceration to her liver. She was forty-seven when her boyfriend paused in his drinking to beat her to death. It is early March.

On Sunday, March 15, a violent dust storm sweeps the city. In the past thirty hours, there have been six reported murders. People fly kites all over the city.

There is a report of a woman who is beaten by her husband. And she flees for her life with her two daughters. He follows. Her Mercedes is found empty.

The daily paper reports that local citizens are complaining of traffic delays because streets get suddenly shut down as police investigate and do forensic investigations at kill sites.

Far down the road, long after the killings splattered across the city, the mayor of Juárez gives an interview. It is June and he says now that he knew in very early January that the killing season was coming—he does not explain how he came to possess this gift of prophecy. He says he was informed that the murders would begin on January 6, but actually, he learned they began January 5. No matter, because you see, the killings are really between two criminal organizations and do not actually involve the decent citizens of Juárez. He is the man in charge and he says, don't worry.

There is a comforting system here. No one really knows who the bad people are in Juárez. Until they are murdered, and once they are murdered, then everyone knows they are bad because good people have nothing to fear. The mayor says only 5 innocents can be found among the 500 people that have been murdered so far. Which means the killers, whoever they are, have revealed to the city 495 bad people that no one really knew about until the gunfire unmasked them.

He does admit that Juárez suffers from "a lack of tranquility."

Miss Sinaloa

She came to this place in the desert to live with the other crazy people under the giant white horse. She did not belong, but then neither did the *caballo*. The half-mile-long horse was sketched on the Sierra de Juárez with whitewash by a local architect in the late 1990s. He copied the design from the Uffington horse in Great Britain, a three-thousand-year-old creation deep from the dreamtime of neolithic people. He said he was doing it as an exercise in problem solving (this horse faces right, the original faces left and is three times as large) and as a way to draw attention to the beauty of the mountains. What he did not say is what some in the city whispered, that the horse was sponsored by Amado Carrillo, then head of the Juárez cartel.

The cartel begins in the mists of time, but with the flow of cocaine starting in the mid-1980s, it becomes a colossus. In the spring of 1993, the head of the cartel is murdered while on holiday in Cancún, and Amado Carrillo takes over. He has a genius for business, and soon ten to twelve billion a year is flowing into the cartel coffers. Carrillo becomes the organizational genius who brokers cocaine shipments for the other Mexican cartels, buys the Mexican government, and lands full-bodied jets full of cocaine at the Juárez airport. By the time he is murdered in 1997, he has taken the Mexican drug world from that age of the outlaw into the era of a multinational business.

But the era of Carrillo was the golden age of peace in Juárez, when murders ran two or three hundred a year and, at any one moment, fifteen tons of cocaine was warehoused in the city and waiting to go visit American noses.

There was a time when death made sense in Juárez. You died because you lost a drug load. Or you died because you had a drug load. Or you died because you tried to do a drug deal. Or you died because you were a snitch. Or you died because you were weak and a woman and it was dark and someone thought it would be fun to rape and kill you. There was a pleasant order to death, a ritual of federal police or state police or the army taking you, then tying your hands and feet with duct tape, torturing you, and finally killing you and tossing your body into a hole with a dose of milk, the friendly term for lime. Your death would be called a *carne asada*, a barbeque. Life made sense then, even in death. Those were the good old days.

Now, the world has changed. Since the first of January 2008, El Paso, the sister city of Juárez and just across the remnants of the Rio Grande, has had one murder in two months. In the first two months of the year, Juárez has officially had ninety-five, and there is likely some slippage in these numbers. Two of the dead were Juárez police commanders, the one shot twenty-two times—a third commander somehow survived and was taken to the bridge (according to rumor, in a tank, but actually in a Humvee—every fact in this city soon succumbs to magical fraud) and transferred to an ambulance and then to an El Paso hospital, where he was guarded by local and federal agents. Now he has vanished and left no forwarding address. As of February 2008, besides the people murdered in the Juárez area, another three hundred have died in Mexico, also mainly in drug killings. Thirty thousand Mexican soldiers are said to be fighting the drug world. By 2009, there will also be twenty thousand U.S. Border Patrol agents on the line facing down Mexico. Just two governments taking care of business.

Just yesterday, a friend came upon the body of a *cholo* who had been executed and left on the street. This killing did not even merit the attention of the newspapers. But then, outside of a few mentions, the U.S. media paid little notice of the slaughter until early 2009, when it became clear that neither the change of the calendar year nor the presence of the Mexican army had done anything to decrease the death toll as the months passed. True, the commanders at Fort Bliss in El Paso declared Juárez off limits to soldiers because they might get hurt. But like almost everything else that happens in this city, the response has been silence. Amado Carrillo had a thoroughbred racehorse he named *Silencio*, Silence. It is a good trait to have in this place.

She was beautiful and they called her "Miss Sinaloa." She was a teenager when the white horse was created in the late 1990s. At that time, Miss Sinaloa knew nothing of giant horses painted on mountains, nor of the cartels or of the crazy place here in the desert. She came here very recently to visit her sister, sometime in December 2005. She stayed some months and then went home to Sinaloa, the Mexican state on the Pacific coast that is the mother of almost all the major players in the drug industry in Mexico. She was very beautiful. I know this because Elvira is telling me everything as I stand in the wind with the sand whipping around me.

Elvira is heavy with a coarse sweater, pink slacks, dark skin, and cropped hair with a blonde tint dancing through it. She is one of fifteen caretakers at the crazy place—the asylum in the desert—and receives fifty dollars a week for cooking three meals a day, six days a week. A man straddles a bicycle by her side, a boy in red overalls carrying a pink purse stares, and sitting on the ground is the lean and hungry dog of the *campo*. Smoke fills the air from a trash fire behind the asylum where they all work. The facility—a concrete block wall with various rooms inside—hosts a hundred inmates. A doctor drops by on Sunday to check on the health of the crazy people, and the whole operation is sponsored by a radio evangelist in Juárez, a man all the inmates call El Pastor.

Every five days, the staff takes the blankets from the inmates, washes them, and then comes out beyond the walls and clumps them on creosote or yucca plants for drying. They now huddle in the wind like a herd of beasts—green, red, blue, violet, and one is gray with a tiger and her kitten on it. My mind spins back to the mid-1990s, when Amado Carrillo ran Juárez and for a spell was leaving bodies wrapped in tiger blankets. He was rumored to have a private zoo with a tiger, one he fed with informants, but of course, such a custom was a common legend in the drug industry. Then for a spell, he was wrapping informants in yellow ribbons as gifts to the DEA. All this happened in the quiet days of the past, when the killing was not nearly so bad.

Elvira explains how people wind up in her care: "There are many brought here because they tried to stab a father, or they are addicts, or they have been robbed or assaulted and broken forever. Many of the women here have been raped and lost their minds forever. There is a thirty-four-year-old woman here who saw her family assaulted and then she was raped and lost her mind."

She says this in a calm voice. It is simply life. The inmates consume twelve kilos of beans a day, she continues on, and could I bring them some *frijoles*?

The wind blows, the dust chokes, the white horse watches, and suddenly, Elvira starts talking about Miss Sinaloa, her exact phrase, this Miss part, yes, Miss Sinaloa she says, a beauty queen who came to Juárez.

"Once," she says with pride, "we had a very beautiful woman, Miss Sinaloa. She was here about two years ago. The municipal police brought her here. She was twenty-four years old."

And then Elvira takes flight about her beautiful hair that hung down to her ass, and how very, very white Miss Sinaloa's skin was, oh, so white. Her eyebrows had been plucked and replaced by elegant tattooed arcs to echo the hair. The police had found her wandering around on the street one morning. She had been raped and she had lost her mind. Finally, Elvira explains, her family came up from Sinaloa and took her home.

The asylum facing the giant horse is not a place in Juárez where beautiful women with white skin tend to stay. Just down the road to the east is La Campana, the alleged site of a mass grave where Louis Freeh, then head of the FBI, and various Mexican officials gathered in December 1999 to excavate bodies. That story slowly went away because the source was a local comandante who had fled to the United States, a man known on the streets of Juárez as El Animal. And he could produce very few bodies, basically only a handful, and each and every one of them he had personally murdered. The burying ground itself was owned by Amado Carrillo. One of his killers, who worked there, now teaches English to rich students in a Juárez private high school. Of course, he continues to take murder contracts between classes. And then to the southeast of La Campana is the Lote Bravo, where dead girls have been dumped since the mid-1990s. All this history comes flowing back to me as I hear the story of Miss Sinaloa.

I have been coming to this city for thirteen years, and naturally, I have, like everyone here, an investment in the dead. And the living. Here is a story, and like all stories here, like Miss Sinaloa, it tantalizes and floats in the air, and then vanishes. A poor Mexican woman in El Paso wants drug treatment for her young teenaged son, but she cannot afford the facilities in the United States, so she checks him into a clinic in Juárez. A few days, later, he is back in the United States and housed in the very hospital where the Mexican comandante who survived assassination was briefly housed. The boy has been raped and has a torn rectum.

Then the tale erases itself from consciousness.

Jane Fonda cares, so does Sally Field, and so both have been to Juárez to protest the murder of women. *The Vagina Monologues* has been staged here, also. Over the past ten years or so, four hundred women have been found murdered, the majority of them victims of husbands and lovers and hardly mysterious cases. This number represents 10 or 12 percent of the official kill rate. Two movies have been made about the dead women. Focusing on the dead women enables Americans to ignore the dead men, and ignoring the dead men enables the United States to ignore the failure of its free-trade schemes, which in Juárez are producing poor people and dead people faster than any other product. Of course, the murders of the women in Juárez are hardly investigated or solved. Murders in Juárez are hardly ever investigated, and so in death, women finally receive the same treatment as dead men. At least eight prosecutors have claimed to tackle the murders. Last year, a forensics team from Argentina showed up to straighten things out. The team was state-of-the-art, thanks to Argentina's dirty war in the 1970s that disappeared ten thousand or twenty thousand or thirty thousand people—no one really knows the tally. The Argentineans had also worked in El Salvador, another country rich with mass graves. But none of this training prepared them for Juárez. They came to solve the mystery of murdered women in Juárez. They found the reality of the city.

They found heads sitting on the floor of the morgue, bodies without heads, bodies tossed willy-nilly into mass graves. DNA also failed them at times because the local forensic talent had boiled some of the bodies of the girls, a cooking technique that destroys DNA. At least three families, they discovered, had gotten the bodies of their loved ones back, had buried them, and now had to be told they'd been given the bodies of strangers.

But then, the local authorities can be a bit of a problem. The former police chief was busted in January 2008 for setting up a dope deal in El Paso. Two cops disappeared a week ago. Four days later, a vagrant discovered a shopping bag downtown with the uniform of one of the cops—it had his name, blood stains, and bits of duct tape, this latter being a favored shackling device of locals when they execute people. So apparently, there is a naked policeman wandering the city.

And then, there is the tale of Miss Sinaloa. She goes to a party with police, and then after the fun, the police bring her to the crazy place. A fairskinned woman is a treat for street cops. When the girls began vanishing from Juárez in 1993 and then reappearing at times as raped corpses or simply bones, the local cops referred to them as *las morenitas*—the little dark ones— because the favored prey came from the poor barrios where young women who slave in American-owned factories for next to nothing live. Miss Sinaloa hails from a different world.

But there is always one enduring fact in Juárez: There are no facts. The memories keep shifting. Miss Sinaloa is a beauty who comes to party in Juárez and is raped. Miss Sinaloa is a beauty who comes to party in Juárez and consumes enormous amounts of cocaine and whiskey and becomes crazy, so *loca*, that the people call the police and the cops come and take Miss Sinaloa away and they rape her for days and then dump her at the crazy place in the desert. She has long hair and is beautiful, and a doctor examines her and there is no question about the rapes. She has bruises on her arms and legs and ribs.

She is now almost a native of the city.

Dead Reporter Driving

There is a man driving fast down the dirt road leading to the border. A rooster tail of dust marks his passage. He is very frightened, and his fourteen-year-old son sits beside him in silence. The boy is that way—very bright, yet very quiet. They are unusually close. The father has raised him as a single parent since he was four after the relationship with the mother did not work out.

Now, father and son are fleeing to the United States. Back in their hometown of Ascensión, Chihuahua, men with automatic rifles are searching for them. These men are soldiers in the Mexican army and intend to kill the father, and perhaps the son, too. As the man drives toward the U.S. port of entry, they are ransacking his house. No one in the town will dare to lift a hand. The newspaper will not cover this event.

The man knows these facts absolutely.

His name is Emilio Gutierrez Soto, and he is the reporter covering this part of Mexico and that is why he is a dead man driving. He passes an *ejido*, one of the collective villages created by the Mexican revolution as the answer to the land hunger of the poor. Once, the army came here, beat up a bunch of peasants, and terrorized the community under the guise of fighting a war on drugs. The peasants never filed any complaints, because they are tied to the land and could not flee if there were reprisals for their protests. They also knew that any complaints would be ignored by their government. This is the kind of thing the reporter knows but does not write and publish. Like the peasants, he knows his place in the system.

It is June 16, 2008, and in two days, the man will have his forty-fifth birthday, should he live that long.

The military has flooded across Mexico since President Felipe Calderón assumed office in December 2006 with a margin so razor thin that many Mexicans think he is an illegitimate president. His first act was to declare a war on the nation's thriving drug industry and his favorite tool was the Mexican army. Now over 40,000 soldiers are marauding all over the country in this war against the nation's drug organizations. In 2008, between 5,000 and 6,000 Mexicans died in the violence, a larger loss than what the United States has endured during the entire Iraq war. Since the year 2000, 24 reporters have been officially recorded as murdered in Mexico, 7 more have vanished, and an unknown number have fled into the United States. But all numbers in Mexico are slippery because people have a way of disappearing and not being reported. The entire police force of Palomas, Chihuahua, fled in 2008, with the police chief seeking shelter in the United States, the rest of the cops simply hiding in Mexico. Between July and October 2008, at a minimum 63 people—Mexican cops, reporters, and businesspeople—sought political asylum at crossings in West Texas and New Mexico. In all of 2008, 312 Mexicans filed credible fear claims at U.S. ports of entry, up from 179 in 2007. Many more simply blended into U.S. communities. This is the wave of blood and terror suffocating the man as he heads north.

The reporter has tried to live his life in an effort to avoid this harsh reality. He has been careful in his work. His publisher has told him it is better to lose a story than to take a big risk. He does not look too closely into things. If someone is murdered, he prints what the police tell him and lets it go at that. If people sell drugs in his town or warehouse drugs in his town, he ignores this information. Nor does he inquire about who controls the drug industry in his town or anywhere else.

The man driving is terrified of hitting an army checkpoint. They are random and they are everywhere. The entire Mexican north has become a killing field. In Palomas, a border town of maybe three thousand souls, forty men have already been executed this very year, and another seventeen people have vanished in kidnappings. Some of these murders are by drug cartels. Some of these murders are by state and federal police. Some of these murders are by the Mexican army. There are now many ways to die.

The high desert is beautiful, a pan of creosote with lenses of grass in moist low spots. Here and there, volcanic remnants make black marks on the earth, and to the north and west, sierras rise. There is almost no water. Almost all the rivers flowing from the Sierra Madre die in the desert. But it is home, the place he has spent his life.

The reporter may die for committing a simple error. He wrote an accurate news story. He did not know this was dangerous, because he thought the story was very small and unimportant. He was wrong and that was the beginning of all his trouble.

This is because there are two Mexicos.

There is the one reported by the U.S. press, a place where the Mexican president is fighting a valiant war against the evil forces of the drug world and using the incorruptible Mexican army as his warriors. This Mexico has newspapers, courts, and laws and is seen by the U.S. government as a sister republic.

It does not exist.

There is a second Mexico, where the war is *for* drugs, for the enormous money to be made in drugs, where the police and the military fight for their share, where the press is restrained by the murder of reporters and feasts on a steady diet of bribes, and where the line between government and the drug world has never existed.

The reporter lives in this second Mexico.

Until very recently, he liked it just fine. In fact, he loved it because he loves Mexico and has never thought of leaving. Even though he lives near the border, he has not bothered to cross for almost ten years.

But now, things have changed. He has researched the humanitarian treaties signed by the United States, and he thinks, given these commitments by the American government, he and his boy will be given asylum. He has decided to tell the authorities nothing but the truth. His research has failed to uncover one little fact: No Mexican reporter has ever been given political asylum by the United States of America.

Suddenly, he sees a checkpoint ahead, and there is no way to escape it.

Men in uniforms pull him over.

He is frightened but discovers to his relief that this checkpoint is run by the Mexican migration service and so, maybe, they will not give him up to the army.

"Why are you driving so fast?"

"I am afraid. There are people trying to kill me."

"The narcos?"

"No, the soldiers."

"Who are you?"

He hands over his press pass.

"Oh, you are the one, they searched your house."

"I have had problems."

"Those sons of bitches do whatever they want. Go ahead. Good luck."

He roars away. When he stops at the port of entry at Antelope Wells in the boot-heel of New Mexico, U.S. Customs asks, as they always do, what he is bringing from Mexico.

He says, "We bring fear."

There is a phantom living in Juárez, and his name is on everyone's lips: *la gente*. He is the collective unconsciousness of the city, a hoodoo conjured up out of murder, rape, poverty, corruption, and deceit. Everyone in the city—man, woman, and child, professor and street alcoholic—knows what *la gente* thinks. Just as I have never met or interviewed an American politician who did not know what "the little people" think, nor have I met this army of phantom dwarfs that allegedly dominate my own nation or heard so much as a whisper from another domestic band, the Silent Majority. In the same way, I must listen to drivel about la gente.

In politer circles, la gente gives way to a different phantom, a thing called civil society. Of course, neither la gente nor civil society exists, just as in the United States there are no little people nor a Silent Majority. All these terms are useful for two reasons: They allow people to talk about things they do not know, and they allow people to pretend there is an understanding about life that does not exist. Oh, and there is a final bonus: They allow newspaper columnists to discuss people they have never met and say knowingly what the people they have never met actually think.

In Juárez, la gente—this collective mind that is wise and knowing—is a necessary crutch because the police are corrupt, the government is corrupt, the army is corrupt, and the economy functions by paying third-world wages and charging first-world prices. The Mexican newspapers dance around truth because, one, corrupt people who are rich and powerful dominate what can be printed and, two, any reporter honest enough to publish the truth dies.

And so we are left, those of us who actually entertain the possibility that facts exist and that facts matter, with rumor and this phantom called la gente. Of course, this means we have no one to talk to and can only console ourselves with the dead, their bodies leaking blood out those neat holes made by machine guns, because the dead are past lying and the dead know one real fact: Someone killed them. They often do not know who killed them. Nor do they know why they were killed. But at least they know they have been killed and are now dead.

This is more than civil society and la gente know because the television news and the newspapers do not always report murders and if they report murders they do not always give the names and if they give the names, they almost never follow up on the murders.

You live.

You die.

You vanish from public records.

And you become the talk of the phantom called la gente.

Juárez is pioneering the future again, and this is a city of achievements. It claims the invention of the margarita, it is the birthplace of the zoot suit, of velvet paintings, of the border factory era, of the most innovative and modern drug cartel, of world-class murder of women and also of men. In the short month of February alone, 1,063 cars are stolen in the city—around 36 a day. Here a vehicle is worth a hundred dollars to a junkie—the price a chop shop pays before the machine is butchered and shipped to China for the metal.

There are explanations for all this. A favorite is that it is all because of the drug world, especially a current battle the authorities claim is going on between cartels for control of the crossing into El Paso. Some blame the massive migration of the poor to the city to work in the factories. Others, especially those who focus on the murder of the girls, sense a serial killer is prowling the lonely dark lanes. Finally, some simply see the state as waning here and the violence as a new order supplanting the fading state with criminal organizations.

I am in a tiny minority on this matter. I see no new order emerging but rather a new way of life, one beyond our imagination and the code words we use to protect ourselves from life and violence. In this new way of life, no one is really in charge and we are all in play. The state still exists—there are police, a president, congress, agencies with names studded across the buildings. Still, something has changed, and I feel this change in my bones.

The violence has crossed class lines. The violence is everywhere. The violence is greater. And the violence has no apparent and simple source. It is like the dust in the air, part of life itself.

Government here and in my own country increasingly pretends to be in charge and then calls it a day. The United States beefs up the border, calls in high-tech towers, and tosses up walls, and still, all the drugs arrive on time and all the illegal people make it into the fabled heartland and work themselves into a future.

People tell me there are murders in Detroit, women are raped in Washington, D.C., the cops are on the take in Chicago, drugs are everywhere in Dallas, the government is a flop in New Orleans. And Baghdad is not safe, mortars arc through the desert sky there into the American womb of the Green Zone. People tell me Los Angeles is a jungle of gangs, that we have our own revered mafia. And that drugs flood Mexico and Juárez because of the wicked, vice-ridden ways of the United States. All of these assertions are ways to ignore the deaths on the killing ground.

According to the Mexican government and the DEA, the violence in Juárez results from a battle between various drug cartels. This makes perfect sense, except that the war fails to kill cartel members. With over two hundred fresh corpses in ninety days, there is hardly a body connected to the cartels. Nor can the Mexican army seem to locate any of the leaders of the cartels, men who have lived in the city for years. The other problem with this cartel war theory is that the Mexican army in Juárez continues to seize tons of marijuana but only a few kilos of cocaine, this in a city with thousands of retail cocaine outlets.

There are two ways to lose your sanity in Juárez. One is to believe that the violence results from a cartel war. The other is to claim to understand what is behind each murder. The only certain thing is that various groups—gangs, the army, the city police, the state police, the federal police—are killing people in Juárez as a part of a war for drug profits. So a person never knows exactly why he or she is killed but is absolutely certain that death comes because of the enormous profits attached to drug sales.

Every time I walk across the pay bridge from downtown El Paso to Juárez, I see a big portrait of Che Guevara on the concrete banks that channel the original flow of the Rio Grande. Sometimes the paint has faded, but when moments get very bad in Juárez, someone magically appears and touches up the portrait. There is also a statement in Spanish that my president is a terrorist and another message that no one is illegal and that Border Patrol are killers, and there are a fistful of revolutionary heroes whose faces scamper across a map of South America and Mexico. Such statements also insist on order because that is the ground where heroes flourish.

Often, down below on the dry soil of the river, there is a crazy man. He shouts in English, "Welcome! Hello America!" And he holds a cup in his hand for catching tossed coins.

When I cross back, often late in the night, he is on the other side of the bridge, but now he begs in Spanish.

Behind the loony, a bunch of crosses were painted on a wall to symbolize the dead girls of Juárez. The simple message in Spanish says they were actually killed by capitalism incubating in the American-owned maquiladoras, the border factories of such renown in the parlors where wine is sipped to toast the global economy.

Every day in Juárez, at least two hundred thousand people get out of bed to pull a shift in the maquilas. The number varies—right now probably twenty thousand jobs have vanished in Juárez as a chill sweeps through the global economy. Within a year, eighty to one hundred thousand jobs will vanish. Just after the millennium, about one hundred thousand maquila jobs left the city for mainland China, because as *Forbes* magazine pointed out, the Mexicans wanted four times the wages of the Chinese. A fair point. The greedy Mexicans were taking home sixty, maybe seventy dollars a week from the plants in a city where the cost of living is essentially 90 percent that of the United States. Turnover in these plants runs from 100 to 200 percent a year. The managers say this is because of the abundant opportunities of the city. Labor is still a bargain here—but so is death. Four years ago, the Chihuahua State Police were doing contract murders. They supplied their own guns and bullets with the full knowledge of the U.S. Department of Homeland Security.

But we must not talk about such matters. Juárez officially has almost no unemployment. The factories gleam in industrial parks sculpted by the local rich. The city grows. There is talk of even building a new city off to the west, where the giant white horse watches over the desert flats. That is why I like to go there.

I sit on the sand in the desert under the giant white horse by the place of the crazy people and I think of Miss Sinaloa.

She understands. And soon I think I will if I am given enough time on the killing ground.

I insist on getting out of the truck even though I know everyone in the narco neighborhood is watching me. I suck in the dusty air, feel the warmth of the sun. Across the street, a large German shepherd barks through the iron fence. He stares me down and does his work of guarding a world where only large, angry dogs go about unarmed.

There are a few basic rules about the Mexican army. If you see them, flee, because they famously disappear people. If you are part of them, desert, because they famously pay little. In the 1990s, President Ernesto Zedillo formed a new, pure force to fight drugs and had them trained by the United States. They were paid a pittance—a friend of mine in the DEA grew close to them because his agency instantly put them on the payroll and he was their pay-master. By 2000, the special antidrug force had joined the Gulf cartel and be-came known as the Zetas, U.S.-trained military killers with discipline and skill with weapons. The original Zetas are mainly dead, but their style—decapitations, military precision in attacks—spread and now they are the model for killers in many cartels. They are also an inspiration and a constant lure for Mexican soldiers who desert for the cartels—over a hundred thousand troops fled the army and joined criminal organizations in the first decade of the new century. The pay is better and so is the sense of power.

In 2000, the election of Vicente Fox ended the seventy-year reign of the In-stitutional Revolutionary Party, or PRI. The drug industry ceased to be controlled by the central government, many independents entered the business, domestic drug use skyrocketed, and federal control of the nation grew ever more feeble. The razor-thin election of Felipe Calderón in 2006 brought the very legitimacy of the president into question. He responded by unleashing the army against the drug industry ten days after his election as a show of force. And that is when the killing began to spiral to previously unimagined levels. First, he sent twenty thou-sand troops to his home state of Michoacan. Then, the military mission grew to thirty thousand nationally, and eventually forty-five to fifty thousand. With each escalation, the number of murdered Mexicans exploded. At about the same time, the United States began mumbling about Plan Mexico, a billion and a half dol-lars to help our neighbors to the south fight the good fight, with the lion's share going to the army. Put simply, the United States took a Mexican institution with long ties to the drug industry—the army was a partner in the huge marijuana plantation in Chihuahua, Rancho Bufalo, of the mid-1980s, and it was a Mex-ican general who became the drug czar in 1997 until it was discovered he worked for the Juárez cartel—and bankrolled it to fight the drug industry.

And so in Juárez tonight, the army does the killing, the United States gloats over a battle against the cartels, the president of Mexico beams as Plan

Mexico comes close to his grasp. And the street soldiers of the drug industry either duck down or die—the kills in Juárez are largely of nobodies or of their local cop allies. And the Zetas, the thousands they have trained, and their imitators get friskier. They have training camps in northern Mexico—they killed four cops from Nuevo Laredo in such a camp and then burned them in barrels. They have heavy arms, grenades, rockets, good morale, and high pay. Desertion is not an option.

By the late 1990s, the cartel in Juárez was said to have rockets. And was hiring former Green Berets to make sure its communications systems were up to snuff. But as the bodies mount in Juárez, the capos are not the ones with bullet holes. In fact, there is no evidence they are even concerned by this military exercise. It is a mystery.

During this season of gore, Francisco Rafael Arellano Felix, the former head of the Tijuana cartel, was released in El Paso in early March after doing about ten years in Mexican and U.S. prisons. He crossed the bridge into what the DEA claims is enemy territory, the turf of the Juárez cartel. By all reports, he expressed no concern as he made his way to the airport.

I sit on the patio drinking wine in a barrio named after Emiliano Zapata. The city has a statue of the murdered revolutionary hero, and he looks spindly as he holds an extended rifle with one hand. Originally, Zapata pointed his weapon toward neighboring El Paso, but then one mayor thought this impolite and turned the dead hero around. About a hundred and fifty yards away runs the drainage canal for floods in the city, a conduit that also doubles as a kind of freeway into the poor barrios that coat this hillside.

At around noon on March 10, Juán Carlos Rocha, thirty-eight, stands on an island in this freeway peddling *P.M.*, the afternoon tabloid that features murders and sells to working-class people. Two men approach and shoot him in the head. No one sees anything except that they are armed, wear masks, and move like commandos. They walk away from the killing. A city cop lives facing the murder site.

A crowd gathers and watches police clean up the murder scene.

Rocha, the people in the barrio say, sold more than *P.M.* He also offered cocaine at four to six dollars a packet. He'd been warned twice by mysterious strangers to cease this activity. He did not listen.

He allegedly earned about three hundred dollars a week as his cut of the retail cocaine business, more than three times what the neighboring factory workers, his customers, make. As he lies in a pool of blood in the bright sunlight, his brown jacket is neatly folded on the traffic island, his cap on the pavement, where it tumbled from his shattered skull. A woman in a tube top takes his photograph with her cell phone while uniformed schoolgirls stand in a pod and watch.

There are more than twenty thousand such retail outlets in this city, many employing vendors working three shifts a day. Now there is a battle going on for these small ventures in cutthroat capitalism.

A friend of mine can barely leave anything in his house, because local addicts rob it the moment he exits. He is on his third large dog. The previous two were poisoned. He has hopes for the third guard dog.

The day after the killing, the vendor is the cover story in *P.M.*, the tabloid he peddled on his traffic island. His street name was *El Cala*, The Skull.

On March 27, 2008, the army admits it is taking Juárez by force. In front of the hotel downtown, a soldier stands with a .50-caliber machine gun. Over 180 armed and armored vehicles hunt evil on the streets, plus an air wing that includes a helicopter gunship. Two thousand troops arrive, or more. Or so the government says, the press repeats, but no one is ever allowed to make a real count. The soldiers wear black masks and are short and dark. The officers have lighter skin that loses pigment steadily as the rank gets higher until there is the rarefied air of the generals who look like Europeans dropped in some colonial outpost.

Roadblocks go up everywhere, especially at night, when events are difficult to see and impossible to monitor. The authorities say this is necessary because two hundred people have been murdered since the first of year.

There will be ten patrol bases and forty-six roving units. Night life in Juárez collapses because the local citizens dread hitting a military checkpoint in the dark.

It is Palm Sunday, the beginning of Semana Santa, Holy Week, a time for families to reunite and for men to gather and drink themselves senseless as they bask in the grace of God. Two police cars convoy through the quiet of Juárez, one with a city comandante, the other with bodyguards. Suddenly, they are pinned at a traffic light by a car in front and then another car pulls alongside and machine-guns the vehicles. Customers at the nearby gas station duck as bullets plunge through metal.

The comandante's bodyguard dies and others are wounded. This bodyguard has a curious past. In January, the comandante's name—Victor Alejandro Gomez Marquez—was posted on the list that appeared on the monument to the fallen policemen as a person scheduled to die. But the bodyguard is the man who truly hears death whispering in his ear. He recently told his mother he had fifteen days to live. Then, he came over to his mother's house again and sat with a friend as they drank a liter of whisky. This time, he told his mother he had at best eight days to live.

She told him, "Be positive. Christ's blood is covering you and protecting you."

Now, he is done with living.

The mural depicts a conquistador, another wall is a collage of snapshots from the work. A sign says, "God is greater than my problems." In the corner rests a metal statue of a man in armor. This is the office of El Pastor, José Antonio Galvan, the radio evangelist who took in the battered remains of Miss Sinaloa and gave her succor in the crazy place. He is sitting right in front of me, a mop of graying hair, a fleshy body, a ready smile. He is showing me a movie of the asylum—men beaten by police and dumped half crazy on the streets, addled addicts with seeping ulcerated wounds, women who will never remember what happened to them and never want to remember.

I stare at the ruined faces in the video and ask, "Does your congregation support this work?"

He smiles, points to the crazy people on the screen, and says, "This is my congregation."

There was a bad storm in the winter of 1998, and El Pastor was driving in Juárez when he saw a mound on the street and swerved just as a man emerged from the pile of snow where he slept. God spoke to him at that moment and so El Pastor rounded up friends and for a day gathered the wounded off the streets—brain-damaged addicts, ruined gang members—everyone left at the mercy of the snows in a city without mercy.

"Oh, they smelled bad," he says, "covered with shit and all that."

The office of El Pastor once was a drug house where addicts punctured their veins and savored their dreams. He descended on this place as a street preacher raving in the *calles*. The local priest called him a devil. But he drew others to him. As for the devil, El Pastor fights him daily—he keeps a black and red punching bag near at hand and slams it with his fists as he fights Satan.

Everything about El Pastor is vital and coarse, his language often vulgar, his feel for the crazy people visceral. The world is lucky he gave up the bottle and the drugs and turned toward God.

El Pastor spent sixteen years as an illegal in Los Angeles and learned to be a crane operator, do lots of drugs and alcohol, and earn sixteen dollars an hour. He could be rough on the job—twice he threw men out of buildings and he was not on the first floor. Eventually, he went to prison and then was deported back to Mexico. He became a street addict in Juárez. Then in 1985, he was born again and began preaching on the street to drug addicts. Rough edges remain and keep him honed. On one arm he has a tattoo of a good-looking *mestiza* and on the other, a good-looking Indian woman. Before he went to work in the United States, he hated white people and despised Mexicans who crossed over. But then he married, had children and went to El Norte. And found that this country he disliked fed him and his family and now he says, "I love Mexico, but not the Mexican system." He has two kids in college in the United States, and one son has served eight years in the U.S. Army Special Forces. Now he must raise ten thousand dollars a month on the radio simply to meet the medical, food, and staff costs of this crazy place he has created.

He gives me the short course in the history of his city.

"The violence is high in Juárez," he says in a soft voice. "A lot of young people come to Juárez and have the American dream—it is so close. But now the border is closed. People come from the south, they are clean and hardworking and they don't know anything about the streets. And guys take them in, and soon they are selling their bodies and using drugs. After a year, they have gang tattoos. The capos now sell drugs here where there is a growing market because then they don't have to cross them into the United States. Now fourteen-year-olds are moving a ton of cocaine."

I ask if he remembers a patient called Miss Sinaloa.

"Oh, yes," he says. "She was at an orgy."

The Casablanca is, of course, white and has many rooms with parking beside each one and metal doors to protect the privacy of the cars and license plates from prying eyes. Men bring women here for sex and love and joy and whatever other terms they prefer. This was Miss Sinaloa's eventual destination. In front stands Valentino's, a large nightclub with red-tiled domes, the party haven that also beckoned her.

Miss Sinaloa came here from her Pacific Coast home. For days she was raped by eight policemen. Her buttocks bore the handprints of many men by the time she got to El Pastor, and there were bite marks on her breasts.

She arrives at the crazy place on December 16, 2005, after 5 P.M. The city police bring her out and dump her. They have, they say, had her in jail, but she is too much to handle. She fights and yells and is no fun at all.

She has lost her mind and now she comes to the place of kindred souls.

Everyone is not as lucky as Miss Sinaloa. Heidi Slauquet was very good-looking and made paintings. For years, she was a party girl in Mexico City, and in the early 1990s, she wound up in Juárez. For a while, she had a night-club where *narco-traficantes* liked to go. For a while, she was a lover of Amado Carrillo. And then when that wore out, she became a kind of hostess and made sure beautiful girls came to the parties, girls like Miss Sinaloa.

On November 29, 1995, she takes a cab to Juárez International Airport. The cabby eventually turns up dead. Heidi never reappears. People at the air-port say that Heidi's cab was stopped by what looked to be federal police.

Nobody talks about them, because silence means everyone can pretend they do not exist. They are on every street, sometimes asleep on the sidewalks or huddled in a doorway. No one knows their real numbers because a real count would slap reality into everyone's faces. They are the brain-damaged of the city. The mother could not get enough food when she was big with child, or she had bad habits, the booze, glue, paint sniffing, all kinds of habits. Or she managed to deliver a healthy child but then the street finally beckons and the child goes to the glue and the paint or maybe meth claws the brains out. Still, they are there, on every *calle*, legs shortened by hunger, wizened heads from malnutrition, jerky movements from the chemicals, madness in the eyes, and often there are voices, brilliant voices that speak to them even though the rest of us are not privileged enough to hear these voices.

I am on the main avenue, I have just crossed the bridge, and the morning is sunny and bright with promise. She walks up with a shuffling gait, her head rocking as she jabbers. She's wearing Capri pants, black running shoes, and a knit blouse, and her hair is clean. She has some of her teeth and is coasting somewhere in her thirties. She is a whore and from the looks of her emaciated body I guess heroin or meth, but I don't know. What I know is this: She is a product of the city, a testament to the cheap drugs and the expendable lives, and her story will never be in the newspaper, nor will she—or the army that wanders the city and is just like her—ever be counted and considered in the studies and essays about life in Juárez.

That is part of my attraction to El Pastor. He gets the rejects of the Mex-ican health system, of the Mexican jail system, and of Mexican compassion.

He also gets the people the U.S. Border Patrol apprehends who are crazy with the damage of life. The agency tosses them back in order not to take care of them. And El Pastor scoops them up and takes them to his crazy place in the desert, and for the first time in years, these people have someone touch them and not cringe.

I look at her and say, no.

She continues weaving and bobbing around me, and then, with a smile, she staggers off to find some other hope of a blow job, a few pesos and a fix in the early morning Juárez light.

But she is everywhere in this city and sometimes she is a woman and sometimes she is a man, and sometimes she is a child, but always she is a casualty of the life of this place. And a hero because simply dealing with the life here and refusing to give in takes courage that is absent among the rich and powerful of this city.

El Pastor is a small lens, and if you look through this lens, you see these invisible people because he is their last and only hope. And he has files, over a thousand files on the invisible people of Juárez.

Here is one.

He goes by a lot of names and one he really likes is Pedro Martinez. He is forty-two when American psychiatrists interview him. The agents have caught him yet again in the United States illegally and then they decide he is a crazy person and so he becomes something for American medicine to explain.

This is not easy. He says he has been in the Kansas State Penitentiary, but a search turns up no records. He says he was evaluated in the county jail in Danville, Kentucky, but these records also cannot be found. He does say this: Five years ago, he was hit on the back of the head and lost consciousness. He had a urinary infection in Florida. He had gonorrhea and injected himself with penicillin. He has also tried things. From age seven, he smoked marijuana for ten years. He has been treated four or five times, he notes, for inhaling thinner. He tried crack cocaine but this only lasted four months. He likes beer and figures he has been an alcoholic since age eleven. Actually, he offers, he lost his license in North Carolina for drunk driving. So he's been around and really toured these United States.

He was born in Tabasco, Mexico, but was raised in Veracruz. His mom is dead, his dad alive somewhere, and somehow he managed to get through the sixth grade.

Oh, and he is married to a woman from Iran, one he met in prison in Kentucky, and they had several children together. The marriage lasted two years. Here the doctors falter and find his stories from Kentucky hard to follow, something about a guy named Jim Buster and woman known as De Fannie.

He has worked. He has done gardening and manual labor and been out in those fields. He has also worked with growing tobacco.

There have been bumps on his road. In Kentucky, his girlfriend was difficult and so he was convicted of burning down a house. He tries to explain, but the doctors cannot follow the flow of words he spews—something about homosexuality, medical stuff, mental health stuff, small brains. He did a year in Mexico, he says, for selling marijuana. Six times he has been jailed for entering the United States of America. Also, he laughs as he answers the doctors' questions and they find this inappropriate.

So they decide he is suffering from a psychosis.

But Pedro Martinez insists he is not mentally ill. He is six feet two inches tall and weighs 149 pounds and his body temperature is 96.3.

The doctors notice that he has poor eye contact and sometimes he is hard to hear because he lowers his voice. Also, during one interview he asks the doctor, "Do you hear the voices?" He would turn to a corner of the room and talk to a woman named Peggy, but the doctors noted that they could not see Peggy. Besides that, he has poor grooming.

When he was told he would face a hearing on his mental competency, he said, "The judge, I am the judge."

When he saw the doctor's chart on him, he said, "I am not taking this shit. Give me the chart. Take your name off the chart."

So they douse him with pills, antipsychotic medication, and this calms him down. Now they realize he is paranoid schizophrenic. Case closed.

And then, to solve all the problems, he is booted across the bridge, and El Pastor finds him on the street and takes him out to that crazy place. His brief fling at history—those U.S. medical evaluation records—ends and he rejoins the invisible people from whom he came. He is part of that army that has brigades all over Mexico and all over Juárez, the shock troops of poverty and drugs and booze and despair. He can negotiate the United States, he just cannot convince American experts that he knows as much as they do.

This happens. The brain-damaged often fail to get serious notice from the authorities.

But time is on the side of Pedro Martinez. Each day, there are more and more like him. The world now is designed to raise up huge crops of people just like him.

Everyone here is always talking. But no one ever says a real word because that can get you dead. Some blame the language, the calculated indirection of Spanish. Some blame a lack of education. Some blame the dust that is always in the air, the endless dirt giving everyone a mild cough that they use to punctuate sentences and to accent their silence and comments. Some claim fear creates the silence. In the past few years, Mexican reporters who bother to report are sometimes murdered and so the reports are becoming rarer in this nation. A newspaper story on a killing will have an almost pornographic description of a car or a corpse—and silence on the killers. This is the sound of the growing terror, this silence.

Guns make up for the silence that coats everyone's lips. The city police lieutenant and his son get in his huge, new four-door Nissan Titan truck. The boy is eight, his dad thirty-two. About 250 rounds dance through the machine. The wife races out, sees the carnage, and tries to drive them to the hospital. But the cop dies, the boy's arm is destroyed, and he dies also. The neighbors come out and stare. Numbers help. For example, 237 rounds were fired from guns of 7.62 by 30 caliber, 16 rounds came from an AK-47, and 1 round came from a 7.62 by 39 caliber. The cop was on a list of names posted

January 26 on the police memorial monument. He was characterized under the heading FOR THOSE WHO CONTINUE NOT BELIEVING.

The neighbors say that it is terrible about the child because the boy was young and innocent and played in the street a lot. No one is willing to give the reporters their name. And after a while, no one wants to talk at all. That is the silence that graces the city. Things happen and no one says much. Then after a while, no one admits the thing even happened.

Across the river in El Paso, the daily newspaper fails for days to make any mention of the dead cop or the dead eight-year-old boy. The silence can be a great comfort. Things can be frightening and yet reduced to nothingness by silence.

At noon one day in May, I am standing in a crowd staring at a dead man on the sidewalk. He was executed twenty minutes ago. Then a call comes, there is another killing. We rumble up into the hills. The body has been taken away, and now people stroll past the blood on the dirt as if there had been no gunfire, no scream, no thud, no murder. Just the soft buzzing of flies over the puddled blood. The wind carrying dust, the cry of roosters.

Two guys are in a Honda and it is Friday night. Two vehicles pull up and machine-gun them. No one notices. A man is walking down the street at night. He is riddled with bullets. After a while, people creep carefully from the houses. And then suddenly a pickup truck appears, and six men climb out, grab the body, toss it in back, and drive away. After that the police and soldiers arrive, but of course there is nothing for them to do. Or say.

Silence.

There are two ways to be safe and to stay sane. One is silence, pretending that nothing happened and refusing to say out loud what happened. The other is magical thinking, inventing various explanations for what you refuse to say and by these explanations dismiss the very thing you cannot let pass your lips. Of course, this applies only to individuals. Newspapers, politicians, and government agencies have a third method, they cite organizations—the drug cartels—and say that whatever is happening is because of "them." This tactic is very appealing and takes one back to childhood, when the night belonged to monsters and hobgoblins. It was the tool of the cold war, when communists lurked under the bed, and is the tool of the new wars against terrorism and drugs. Like a stopped clock, it is accurate now and then. Organizations of all kinds lie, cheat, steal, and kill. But in Juárez, almost no account explaining the killings is linked to fact.

Instead, the cars driven by killers and the cars of the dead are lovingly described. Spent cartridges found at the scene are sorted by caliber and counted. The dead are sketched—the color of the skin and hair, the size of the bodies, the estimated age. But often there are no names, nor do updates appear in future editions. Three carloads of men described as commandos hit an upscale motel for lovers, one that functions almost like a gated community. They find a man and woman in a room, kill them, leave, and then nothing. The meaning beneath the skin of the word *commando* is never explored. But it is carefully reported that one hundred spent cartridges littered the room. The governor, José Reyes Baeza, announces on March 24 after a long silence, "All of the public security agencies are infiltrated—all of them, pure and simple—and we are not going to put our hands in the fire for any bad element."

He also tells the populace that he has assurances from the highest government sources that the violence will decline in the next few weeks. Apparently, there is some wizard in the ministries who has access either to the future or to the forces that have been killing wholesale since New Year's Day.

There is nothing but silence from the police forces, and not another word is said in the press.

Silence, like protest, is the drug of our time, the way we do something by doing nothing. We march, we wave placards, and we go mum, and all avoid touching the levers of power and all avoid stepping on the third rail of truth.

I sit on a tree well surrounding a scraggly shrub just down the street from one of the houses of death. Directly in front of me is a federal cop—a few minutes ago, they took my passport, examined it as a mystery object, and called it in to be recorded. I am now on notice. The street is rough and dirt, and ten yards to the west is a walled compound with a camera watching the entrance. Fifty yards down the *calle* the boys are digging, and eventually thirty-six bodies will come belching out of the ground. No one in the neighborhood ever heard, saw, or smelled a thing.

The bodies will not be shown to grieving relatives of missing people, nor will the location of the bodies be disclosed, nor will the press mention that the bodies have vanished.

The dog snarls through the steel fence. He is the only person here in the moment and refuses to be silent. The federal police wear masks.

Weeks and weeks go by, and the only mention of the bodies in the newspapers is that they have been taken off to Mexico City. Not a single sentence on who these forty-five people in the two death houses once had been, nor is the identity of their killers ever discussed in print. Nor is there any exploration of just who owned these two buildings where people were murdered and buried in gardens of bones.

Silence.

. . .

The sacred lines are being erased as the walls go up and towers slam light on the ground at night. The war flees into the sky, where machines enable the illusion of control. For over eighteen hundred miles the line between Mexico and the United States follows a river or crosses deserts or scampers up and down mountains or wallows in the wind softly singing against the green face of the grasslands.

I am sitting along the line and I am far from Juárez and Miss Sinaloa, but it is all of a package. The fabled cartels have been assigned cities, and made into boxes and arrows on organizational charts created by the U.S. agencies. But they seem reluctant to stay within these lines.

A month ago I drove a dirt road past two big work camps with piles of steel girders and rows of heavy equipment, depots where men went forth each day to weld and build car barriers to stop evil people from bringing evil things north. This is homeland security.

Then last week a semi with a loaded trailer came through the car barrier and drove north on a dirt road. And didn't quite make it. I stand where it slid off the road and down a steep slope. I can smell cow shit and the stench of death—it was officially hauling a load of steers. The new car barrier didn't stop it because someone has already cut out chunks in two places and put in gates.

No matter. Up in the sky, there are Black Hawk and A-Star helicopters, and big dirigibles looking with radar deep into the heart of Mexico, and ground sensors in the dirt and towers with magic eyes hooked to computers, and a standing army of gunmen in uniforms—more people, at least twenty thousand, under arms to police this line than the roster of the entire U.S. Army at the beginning of that long-ago Mexican War.

This is the blanket we use to wrap our nervous dreams, and we call it security. We invent special nodes of hell, cartels, cities like Juárez. We call killers drug lords as they sell industrial compounds, torture, and murder. We scan the skies and the earth, we stare with infrared lenses in the night, we bluster and weld and build walls. And we never really face what is in front of us, never face what is inside our gutless language of cartels and drug lords and homeland security, never face that forces are unleashed on the land with names like poverty, a fix, murder, and despair, and our tools cannot master these forces.

Miss Sinaloa knows this. And I am learning.

I am standing on the edge of order, a place called Palomas, Chihuahua, about an hour or so west of Juárez and on the line. Census data says seventy-five hundred people live here, but due to the economic failures of farming, then of migrant smuggling, followed by the current boom in killing and kidnapping, it may now be home to three thousand. In 1916, Pancho Villa crossed here and attacked Columbus, New Mexico, an army fort and hamlet three miles north. The United States responded by sending an army south under General John Blackjack Pershing, a military venture that never even caught a glimpse of Villa. *Palomas* means "doves," but today there is no cooing in town and little else except violence in the air. This morning, around 7 A.M., a man was found out at the town dump riddled with bullets—rounds that seem to indicate a military weapon. I wander past the big statue of Pancho Villa and walk up to the small police station. One officer is out front, and at my approach, he flees into the station.

Everyone is a bit skittish here.

On February 18, 2008, four men were cut down and two died. On February 27, two men were cut down at the gas station on the main drag. The barrage ran three minutes, and the two men tasted the force of three to four hundred rounds. Then in the middle of March, the police chief fled to the United States and his staff deserted. Temporary cops were sent in from Ascensión. After that, two corpses were found by the road south of town. And just a day or two ago, four bodies were found burned to bone in a ranch house. But then in May 2007, four guys drove up to the U.S. border crossing here with three of them dead, including the driver. The wounded guy in the front passenger seat managed to keep a foot on the gas pedal as the rolling charnel house crept into the port of entry.

Now the police hide in the station. They are new, brought in from out of town. They don't really patrol, in fact. They sleep in the jail, where it is safe.

They sell a brand of tequila here shaped like a cartridge. It is called Hijos de Villa, The Sons of Villa. By April 1, at least forty people have been murdered in the town of doves.

Two teenage girls in tube tops and slacks pose at the point on the bridge between Juárez and the United States where a plaque announces the border. A friend snaps a photograph. Just below, a Border Patrol chopper sweeps along the line. No one even looks over at it.

On the U.S. side of the bridge, a holding pen teems with Mexicans. They wave and laugh in their cage of cyclone fencing topped with concertina wire.

The dust blows in Juárez, the workers climb aboard white school buses for their one- to two-hour ride down bad roads to their shifts. I'm standing in a barrio searching out the whiff of another recent murder, this time of a former municipal cop. But my attention strays. The roads are dirt here, some of the tracks require punching the truck into four-wheel drive. Everyone here works in a maquiladora. I look to the north and see the blue federal building in downtown El Paso and the sweep of the American city up the slope of the Franklin Mountains. I stand on the slope of the Sierra de Juárez, over the ridge from the giant white horse and the asylum where Miss Sinaloa briefly took shelter. The border is hard-edged, but at times the sweep of the two cities makes them seem like one. But in the end, death can draw the sharpest line.

José Refugio Ruvalcalba was fifty-nine on November 27, 1994, when he turned up exactly on the line—midway on the bridge between the two cities—in his Honda Accord. He'd been a state cop for thirty-two years, and both of his sons were with him that day. All three were in the trunk, beaten, stabbed, and strangled. The father had a yellow ribbon around his head, one that flowered out of his mouth.

He knew where the line was and what happened if that line was crossed.

So do American political leaders, since they never seem to come here.

But everything else does.

The barrio where I look down from Juárez at El Paso is part of the puzzle of the violence in Juárez. These districts are drab, dirty, and largely unvisited by anyone but their inhabitants. Most places are stuffed with people who work in the maquiladoras.

Later, I am with a man wearing black in a barrio across from the asylum that was once home to Miss Sinaloa. The white buses lumber past with the tired faces of the factory workers. The road is ruts. Most of the shacks lack electricity or water. The wind pelts everyone with dust. The houses themselves are a chaos of boards, pallets, beams, rebar, old cable spools, tires, bedsprings, concrete blocks, posts, scrap metal, car bodies, old rusted buses, stone, rotted plywood, tarps, barrels, black water tanks for the periodic deliveries, plastic buckets, old fencing, tires, bottles, stove pipe, aluminum strips, pipe, broken chairs, tables, and sofas—all this the raw material for the construction of the shacks. Like the asylum itself, the place feeds off what the city rejects.

People vanish. They leave a bar with the authorities and are never seen again. They leave their homes on an errand and never return. They go to a meeting and never come back. They are waiting at a bus stop and never arrive at their assumed destination. In the late 1990s, people began keeping lists of the disappeared. One such list hit 914 before the effort was abandoned out of fear. None of these lists covered very many years. Nor did any of the list makers ever think their work was a complete tally. No one really knows how many people vanish. It is not safe to ask, and it is not wise to place a call to the authorities.

Still, we love the hard look of numbers. So murders are tallied, and for fifteen years, until the bloodshed of 2008, Juárez reliably produced two to three hundred official murders a year. Of course, skeletons periodically turn up on the edge of town, and these do not enter the totals. And once in a great while—the FBI announcement of mass graves in Juárez in December 1999, the publicity by the the DEA over a death house in January 2004—homes are found where people are taken, murdered, and buried. Each time such a house of death is revealed, there is a great to-do, a sense of something extraordinary coming into the light of day. People always say they are shocked, the neighbors always say they noticed nothing amiss, the press always says the authorities are digging, digging, digging and will soon get to the bottom of things. Every effort is made to keep this extraordinary moment within the realm of order and to process the corpses so that numbers and structure can be felt and touched.

Forensic experts huddle in these digs at death houses. They have no names, and their bodies appear in the published images, but not their faces. There are few, if any, reports of their findings. They are the costume of order more than the substance of hard facts. For that matter, the various elements of law enforcement at these special charnel houses appear in the newspaper wearing masks. Only the cadaver dogs show up with clear faces.

And then public notices of the death house and its bodies vanish from the papers much as the dead vanished from the city itself. Memory ebbs, and the cavalcade of the vanished and of the dead disappears from sight and becomes some ghost column winding through the city streets that no one professes to see. Or the dead sit in the cafés where they had their last cup of coffee, belly up to the bar where they had that last drink, huddle in the dust and wind at bus stops where they awaited that last ride.

Sometimes, the vanished never reappear. Normally, there are killings because of the drug industry, and these executed souls are found at dawn on city streets like the litter that slaps the eye in the morning light after a boisterous fiesta. But there are periods when no such bodies appear with hands tied with duct tape and a bullet through the skull. There is no way the drug industry with its implicit contractual protocols can take a holiday from death. It is simply impossible in a multibillion-dollar industry that has no standing at law to collect debts or enforce discipline without murder. Sometimes the vanished never even become a name on a list. People fear reporting their missing kin—in one instance, twelve bodies were dug up at a death house and not a single person slumbering in that ground had been reported missing.

So, there are clearly two ghost patrols out and about in the city. Those murdered and secretly disposed of by the drug industry, and those who vanish for whatever reason and are never reported.

During the season of violence that swept through the city and brought me into the circle of Miss Sinaloa, I stopped at a convenience market to buy a bottle of water. Taped below a pay phone was the photograph of a cop with the date he went missing, his name and a phone number where someone waited for a message about his fate. I thought the city's magical powers had reached a new level when even the police must seek anonymous tips to find one of their own. Just down the road was a huge billboard soliciting recruits for the very same police force, an image of a man in a helmet who wore a black mask and carried a machine gun.

Vanishing here is always a possibility and it gives the city a special aura. Kidnappings are frequent, but they at least mean someone wants to return the missing and is acting in a rational manner where a human has a value in money and a feasible transaction is possible. Vanishing means a page left half-written, a tale never fully told. It is more final than execution because it means not simply being murdered but being erased from any real memory or participation in the human community.

Certainly, the city police have become alert to this vanishing thing. Traditionally, they must leave their guns at the station house when they finish their shift. But now they are publicly complaining about this practice that forces them to travel home like any other citizen, without a weapon. They say this policy is now unacceptable.

The avenue curves down by the river and enters the zone in the southeast where Juárez has been migrating to flee its moldering core. The car flows past the giant flagpole erected in the 1990s by then President Ernesto Zedillo so that a gigantic Mexican flag would gently wash across the face of El Paso, but the Mexican park later became a popular dumping ground for bodies.

Finally, the neighborhood looms where the army has detained twenty-one men and seized guns, ammo, and other tools of the trade. It is a "narcolandia," a place where those in the life build their dreams and live out time until their mostly early deaths. The streets have names like Michigan, Alaska, Arizona, Oregon, a roll call of states in the nation just across the river. Mansions rise up—one is three stories of gray concrete with the orange girders still uncovered and is a work in progress, maybe six thousand square feet or more. Next door, workmen install expensive wooden doors on yet another mansion. The men glare. No one is to come here unless they belong here. My friend will not come here alone, and as he drives down the *calles*, he cautions me about taking notes.

Many of the new houses are for sale—perhaps sudden promotions have prompted the owners to new quarters. But there is a second possibility. The killings constantly create vacancies. Just as some architects—and the rising narco-class is a keen market for architects in a city of grinding poverty—have vanished after finishing narco-mansions. No one asks why.

It is a blue-sky day and the sun hits empty streets. No one is out in the yards, no one is walking, no one is visible at all. It looks like a ghost town, but there is a constant feeling of being watched. In the 1990s, a photographer from the local newspaper vanished after taking images in such a district. When he appeared weeks later after his colleagues publicly protested, he had little to say. Except that it was a misunderstanding because he had simply on impulse decided to go to the beach in Sinaloa. A yellow sign tacked to a telephone pole advertises tarot card readings and amulets. This is a world of change and random fates.

We come upon it in a cul-de-sac, two and half stories, gray with dark trim. A black, wrought-iron fence protects the front. The gate and door are padlocked. A colored flyer has been stuffed between the bars touting a furniture sale. This house is empty. Here the military found twenty-one men, a lot of arms, and what they claim was a factory filling little bags with drugs. The supply of drugs was modest. But in Mexico, seized drugs have a way of disappearing once in the custody of the authorities. Sometimes, tons vanish—in the 1990s a full-bodied jet filled with cocaine somehow fell into federal hands, and yet, within a week, by some kind of sorcery, the load was being peddled on the streets of Los Angeles, according to U.S. agents.

The houses are orange, red, green, yellow, blue, and purple, the columns rise at the porticos, the huge windows are tinted and some soar two stories. The garages stare out like blank eyes. Large dogs bark from within. This is "narcotecture," the three-dimensional statement of the dreams of the poor who now prosper. There is no real effort to comprehend the scale of the business here. Officially, the population of Juárez is 1.2 million (or 1.4 million or 1.6 million—even something as simple as a census is hard to pin down here), but all urban populations are pegged by the federal government at a low number so that tax monies that are repatriated to the various cities can be kept low. In the case of Juárez, the population is possibly 2 million, but this is an estimate, just as no accurate map of the sprawling city and its squatter colonias exists. But taking this number of 2 million and making a conservative estimate that 5 percent of the population lives off the drug industry suggests that the minimum number of the people in the life and their dependents is one hundred thousand. By the mid-1990s, conservative students figured 30 to 40 percent of the local economy ran on laundered drug money—others set the figure at more like 60 to 70 percent.

Tijuana, a city officially at around 2 million, is credited with lower drug usage than Juárez. A recent study found over twenty thousand retail drug outlets in Tijuana, mainly cocaine and heroin. In Juárez, there are at least as many such venues. The peddlers earn three hundred dollars a week, there tend to be three shifts, so let's posit for Juárez twenty-five thousand outlets (a conservative estimate) and figure a payroll of seventy-five thousand retailers, each earning three hundred dollars a week. This amounts to a bigger payroll than that earned by the two hundred thousand factory workers earning on average seventy-five dollars a week. And of course, the real money is not in the retail peddlers but in the organizations that control them and import and package their products. This is the economy of the city. This is supply-side economics flooring the killing ground.

The city is studded with narco-McMansions. They have bright colors and often feature domes with brilliant tiles. They are the reward for work.

The work is constant and wearing. The city of Juárez has a monument to fallen officers on a traffic circle, and suddenly that list appeared taped to it, naming cops who would die.

A few days later, four cops on the second list were killed. Forty cops have left the force since the first of the year. In February, a drive-by shooting at the house of a dead cop was accompanied by yet another list taped to the building. This list was not made public. But the police announced they would no longer be answering calls but preferred to stay in their station houses.

All this notice will vanish, that is what happens in this city. When the migration north was just beginning to pick up in 1993, the line between El Paso and Juárez was where the first real effort was made to block Mexicans, an operation that became the source for all the notions of a massively beefed-up Border Patrol. When Amado Carrillo was running a cartel that hauled in $250 million a week in the mid-1990s, Juárez was barely a speck in the mind of the American government or media. When he used the same private banker at Citigroup in New York as the then-president of Mexico, this, too, was of no interest. When the North American Free Trade Agreement (NAFTA) passed and went plowing into the lives of millions like a greed-seeking missile in the early 1990s, this city that pioneered using cheap labor to bust unions and steal American jobs continued to be ignored. Only brief flickers of interest in the dead women of Juárez captures any American audience, and that, too, is a hit-or-miss thing, something that lives in the limbo land of issues rather than of solutions or actions. Only as the killing of 2008 accelerates does Juárez get new press attention and finally draw attention to a simple fact: It is dying.

On February 26, Ricardo Chacon was in Ciudad Chihuahua, the capital of the state. He'd left Juárez even though he was second in command of the unit once headed by Comandante Lozano, the man who survived a fifty-one round barrage and was now hiding in a U.S. hospital. Chacon planned to quit his job. Instead, he was shot in the head and killed. Two days later, Juárez officials decide to address the problem of crime. They launch a campaign against jaywalking in the city.

Murder Artist

He lives in fear. He cannot trust me. Or anyone. We could betray him and then he will die. I hear out these concerns as I sit with my back to the levee. The sun sparkles, the air is brown with dirt. Two big concrete lions guard my flanks, and two blue and white swans cut from truck tires beam plants and flowers into my face. Fluted Greek columns hold up the porch.

It is one of those mornings when the world brushes against me, says nothing, but sits there waiting me out. In Juárez, a gang of killers now operates and calls itself the Murder Artists. There is an abundance of new art. I am far from Juárez. I have come a long way to meet the secret part of Ciudad Juárez. And so I wait in a rough barrio down by the river.

A drunk comes up the lane.

He is asked, "How many times have you been in jail?"

He cannot recall.

"Why do you keep doing dope and booze?"

"I like living this way."

He takes fifty pesos and leaves with his morning thirst.

I return to waiting. I knew he would not be at the café but would send new instructions. I suspect he was watching me in the café parking lot, but I cannot be sure. I suspect he is watching me now. The phone rings about every half hour. He says that he has been delayed but will be there shortly.

Then twenty minutes later it rings again. And so forth.

He is watching me now. And I think he will never arrive until I leave.

This will take time.

Waiting fills my life, a ribbon of motel rooms, cafés, parking lots, bars, and street corners. Time always belongs to someone else and they portion it out in slabs and I simply wait. Two groups in my life have shared my interest in the subject of waiting: drug dealers and narcs. They can never have control and can never be impatient because fast moves lead to nothing at all, the case busted, the deal gone cold. There is an empty book waiting to be written by those who wait listening to the roar of air conditioners in motel rooms and staring at silent phones.

He lives in fear.

He has killed thirty-four people for hire. Or more. Sometimes the number is exact and sometimes the number is a blur because of the nature of the life.

Now fellow professionals are hunting him. They nearly nailed him three months back, it was very close, and so his caution has grown. He was at church when he was spotted. He fled a thousand miles.

So he moves carefully, but he knows that all his caution can only delay the inevitable.

He is a rumor that keeps crossing my mind. He belonged to a crew and they traveled in Mexico killing people for money. They had three sets of uniforms, nicely starched—municipal police, state police, federal police. Also, they would have cars with the proper police insignia on them depending on whatever area they were operating in at the moment. Ambulances also would be mimicked. They would pull you over in their police uniforms and police cars, murder you, and then haul your body away in their faux ambulance.

They traveled constantly, sometimes only being in a city or state for two or three days. The prices varied. For his part, he would earn one grand a killing or five grand or twenty grand. Or more. They had abundant arms.

I walk up to the top of the levee, and a great blue heron lifts off the river and pumps its wings slowly as it courses downstream. The barrio is very poor, the houses often built of scrap materials. The sun feels warm on my face.

I have waited many years for this meeting. Before, I have had glancing blows with contract killers, brief words over beers, they would make vague references to their toils. These were always accidental collisions as we hunted the same ground for our varied prey. They never seemed strange enough. They simply seemed like everyone else, a fact I could not abide.

I am certain he and I agree on some facts. One, if he meets me he is taking a risk because this can only work if he trusts me, and trusting another human being is dangerous. Two, he will be killed, today, tomorrow, the day after tomorrow, no matter, he will be killed. I have come to this place I cannot name to meet a man who will never have a name. We are on the line, but the line is over eighteen hundred miles long.

It must be intriguing for him to be prey after so many years of being the predator. He knows how they will do him. He knows almost certainly it will not be a clean and easy death.

He often has nightmares. Always he is killing someone and they are begging for mercy, for a quick and easy death, and in his dreams, he always hears laughter, his laughter. He calls this "gangster laughter."

He knows fear, and that is why the duct tape is so important. First, you quickly tape their mouths, then put the plastic bag over their heads and bind it tight around the neck. But attention must be paid to the hands and feet. The hands are taped behind the back, the feet cinched together. Because always, once they realize what is happening, they start "jumping around like chickens that have had their heads cut off."

I ask him something: Why is the duct tape sometimes gray and then other times beige? Is this simply a happenstance, or a deliberate decision, a kind of homage to the importance of color in life?

He ignores the question.

There is a thumbnail of his life and I have no idea if it is true. He begins as a gofer for the state police, the little guy who scurries when someone wants coffee or some tacos. He is good at serving people, he seems born to such a role. He comes from poverty but he is quite bright. For example, he knows accounting.

In the state police, he makes a friend among the cops he serves, a man who goes on to be the bodyguard of the governor and then rises and joins the cartel. They drift apart, but this relationship will prove important to him.

For himself, he finds he can kill—I don't yet know the details of how he comes into this knowledge. He joins a crew and operates the uniforms, the cars, the ambulances, the trips. The easy money.

He winds up as the bodyguard for the adolescent son of the boss, and this job is taxing because the boy, seventeen or eighteen, is an asshole. Still, it is a good job—saving the boy from brawls in discos, killing people the boy does not favor, simple chores like that. Also, at times he collects money for the boss, and kills for him. It is a life.

Then he has a problem. He is sent to collect five thousand dollars and he does this. But he spends all the money in one night on a party for himself. This is bad, but he can make up the money. However, the boy he guards has some kind of grudge against him now.

One day, the son tells him to go to the store and get shovels and picks.

He knows what this means.

The other bodyguards take him down to a dry wash and beat him long and hard. But they let him get away—this is simply part of the legend that follows him.

So he gets away. He pays a coyote a thousand dollars to get him into the United States in 2007. He is cheated, of course—the coyote dumps him on the levee. But he crosses, gets works, moves his family north, joins a church. Watches his back.

That is why I wait here in the sun by the levee with a great blue heron wandering the river at my back. He is watching me, I am all but certain of this. I sip ice water out of a clear glass. I am outside in a plastic chair so he can study me. A cat rubs against my leg. I do not blink.

I am fevered and about to pass out. It came to me late yesterday, this fever, but I ignored it and now I sit here wondering if he will show up and wondering if I will be conscious when he shows up. I think he will not show. This is a test, an audition. I sip the ice water, lean down and caress the cat, look out into the glare and feel him watching me.

I must have him. Others question this appetite in me. They say he must be a psychopath. And maybe he is, but how can you know unless you meet him? Or they say he is evil, and then I ask them what evil means and they mutter but never clearly answer me. I think he is essential to understanding. He is my Marco Polo of slaughter.

I have been with mountain lions, twice less than ten feet away, once with the lion standing in the night screaming in my face. I consider them fellow citizens, not predators. The basic American lion kills about once a week—depending on the temperature and how long the meat holds—kills something in the range of seventy-five to one hundred pounds. Their dreams are based on white-tail deer. After the kill, which is quick in order to reduce the chance of injury, they stay on the carcass until it is gone or goes bad. It is not a business. I have no idea how they feel about the killing, but it has to be personal since they kill with their mouths inhaling the scent of the victim, feeling the warm blood flood their tongue as life leaves the body.

I have been with rattlesnakes and often sat a few feet away as they rested in a coil. Their habits vary with the species and the opportunities of the ground, but the ones I spent the most time with only killed about two rats a year. Think of them as armless Buddhas. They are hardly creatures up for duct tape and torture. And they ask for no money for their killings.

The foxes, coyotes, and weasels of my life have been lesser events but all, in balance, quite civil in their behavior and not prone to boasting or excess. I feel no fear, no rancor toward them, not even the coyotes that ripped the throat out of a favored dog.

But the man I am waiting for, he hails from a different country and his tribe is known to me only as rumor and legend and brief flickers out of the corner of my eye. I have sat with the cold men, pistols in their waistbands, and known I was not like them. But I have never known just what they were like.

That is why I have come. That is why I wait. That is why the phone rings, the voice says it will take a little longer. And that is why the man does not come.

It will take time. Days perhaps.

I think it is possible.

And I think it is possible because I have come, and he is not used to that. And because he can see his own death, smell it is near, and he knows he will be soon forgotten because no one really wants to remember him.

My head is nothing but fever. I relax. I could not overpower a fly.

I am ready for the story of all the dead men who last saw his face.

This morning, as I drank coffee and tried to frame questions in my mind, a crime reporter in Juárez was cut down beside his eight-year-old daughter as they both sat in his car letting it warm up. This morning, as I drove down here, a Toyota passed me with a bumper sticker that read with a heart symbol I LOVE LOVE. This morning, I tried to remember how I got to this rendezvous.

I was in a distant city, and a man told me of the killer and how he had hidden him. He said at first he feared him, but he was so useful. He would clean everything and cook all the time and get on his hands and knees and polish his shoes. He took him on as a favor, he explained, to the state police who had used him for their killings.

I said, "I want him. I want to put him on paper."

And so I came.

But my reasons and path are no stranger than those of others. For a while, across the river, there was this man who worked for the cartel. He collected debts. He would fly to Miami and explain that you owed a million and must pay him and no one had to wonder what would happen if the person who owed said no.

Eventually, he found Christ but at that point he owed the cartel one hundred thousand dollars. The story is that men came with guns to collect. But they retreated because they said they found seven guards around the man with AK-47s. The man says this is not accurate. In reality, he was surrounded by seven angels.

So I wait.

The man I wait for insists, "You don't know me. No one can forgive me for what I have done."

He cannot watch the news on television. He says he can see behind the news and hear the screams.

He has pride in his hard work. The good killers make a very tight pattern through the driver's door. They do not spray rounds everywhere in the vehicle, no, they make a tight pattern right through the door and into the driver's chest and head. The reporter who died this morning received just such a pattern, ten rounds from a 9 mm and not a single bullet came near his eight-year-old daughter.

I wait.

I admire craftsmanship.

People talk of those who are innocent and they talk of those who are *sucio*, dirty, people who live and prosper because of illegal lines of work such as the drug industry. This is a comfort, these categories, and of course, these categories are lies. Let us dance through some numbers. In 2004, the budget of the Mexican army was $4 billion. In 1995, by DEA estimates, the Juárez cartel, at that time a wholesale organization moving heroin, marijuana, and principally cocaine from South America and Mexico into the retail markets of the United States, was earning about $12 billion a year. No one on earth thinks its income has declined.

In Juárez, the payroll for the employees in the drug industry exceeds the payroll for all the factories in the city, and Juárez has the most factories and is said to boast the lowest unemployment in Mexico. There is not a family in the city that does not have a family member in the drug industry, nor is there anyone in the city who cannot point out narcos and their fine houses, or who has any difficulty taking you to fine new churches built of narco-dollars. The entire fabric of Juárez society rests on drug money. It is the only possible hope for the poor, the valiant, and the doomed.

As an added factor, the declining cost of drugs has made it possible to create a vast domestic market in Juárez, and this market teems with employees and customers. Who in their right mind would turn down a chance to consume drugs in a city of poverty, filth, violence, and despair?

Look at what people do to survive. Measure their words, and you will find that in Juárez, as in every other place in the world, some people are truthful and some are liars. But don't ask who is innocent and who is dirty, because everyone here tries to eat and drink and we have no pure food or water.

We are the future. We watch governments erode and bluster. We watch cops strut and steal. We watch dealers operate in broad daylight. We work hard and get little.

And we survive.

And don't ask how.

. . .

I watch two guys pretend to work on a car and watch me. I watch a man stand in front of his house and talk on a cell phone and watch me. I notice traffic, and if a car keeps coming by with two men staring out, I think they are also watching me.

I continually search for birds but seem to find few and they are mainly grackles and pigeons. I am in front of a known drug house and it is clear I am not welcome here.

I watch Juárez watch me and wonder if anyone is watching at all.

That is the sense of things: being on camera in a city where no one ever really sees a murder or remembers the faces of the killers.

I am with a man who worked in the business. Years ago, when the *sicario*—the murder artist—was just starting out, he was a mentor to him. That was before he found Christ and found the Bible's hard judgment that must be faced. He says this is the second revolution. The first came in the 1970s, when the government of Mexico started pushing condoms and the birth rate sank from 6.8 children per woman to a little over 2. He feels this was very good. The killings now—these, also, are a great benefit. He speaks from experience.

He is a large man, with fair skin, a moustache and very serious eyes. And a well-thumbed Bible with yellow highlights. He insists I read a passage from Ephesians if I am to understand the killing in Juárez.

I put down my coffee. We are sitting in the sun on a clear day. He does not approve of my cigarette. He lives very cleanly, always has, even those years he spent in the Juárez cartel.

> Finally, my brethren, be strong in the Lord, and in the power of his might.
>
> Put on the whole armour of God, that ye may be able to stand against the wiles of the devil. (Ephesians 6: 10–11)

He says once he thought the power was with the strong, that the power came with the guns.

"I was, you see, a son-of-a-bitch, a real motherfucker."

I nod. He has been told that I do not believe in God and so he is both disturbed by me and yet desirous of finding some common ground so that my soul might be saved.

He lines up two cell phones on his Bible, also a set of keys he keeps fingering. I am to take dictation. He has decided to give me his testimony. For months, he has moved just on the edge of my consciousness, a man of mark with a dark past trailing him, but also a man I am never able to meet until now. He is connected and this makes him seem dangerous in the eyes of others. I can feel caution when others speak of him, because no one can ever be certain who is in the organization and who is out of the organization. And no one can be certain that anyone is ever really able to leave the organization. So he moves with this aura of power and this may be fantasy or fact. There is no number to call where such matters can be verified.

He learned the martial arts in the university in Juárez and became the school champion. When the man was twenty-two, the governor of Chihuahua hired him as a bodyguard. One day, some dumpy-looking guy came to the governor's office and everyone treated him like a God.

Later, the bodyguard asked, "Who was that dumb asshole?"

He was told it was the head of the Juárez cartel.

He thought to himself, I could run that business better than this guy.

So, he joined the game, and soon he was living the life.

He moved marijuana through the U.S. port of entry by using deaf and mute people as mules. When they occasionally got busted, they were released because they were handicapped. Also, they could not reveal anything to anyone. One day, he lost a load to the United States and suddenly owed the supplier twenty-five thousand dollars. That is the rub in the business. The supplier places a high value on the drug even though its cost to him is wholesale. The drug smuggler is making 10 to 20 percent a load—there is an overhead for bribes and muscle. So if you lose a load, you must pay full value, even though you only earn a fraction of that amount if the load goes through. When these economic facts are coupled with whores and cocaine consumption, the drug smuggler winds up working for the company store. Or winds up dead.

He is told he will be killed if he does not come up with the twenty-five thousand. His family also may be killed. It is a business.

For we wrestle not against flesh and blood, but against principalities, against powers, against the rulers of the darkness of this world, against spiritual wickedness in high places.

Wherefore take unto you the whole armour of God, that ye may be able to withstand in the evil day, and having done all, to stand.

Stand therefore, having your loins girt about with truth, and having on the breastplate of righteousness;

And your feet shod with the preparation of the gospel of peace. (Ephesians 6: 12–15)

He drives to Michoacan in central Mexico to face the boss. When he arrives, an AK-47 is pointed at him and he is shoved into a truck. The boss takes him high up into the mountains. Then he is pulled out, and he marches for fifteen minutes with the AK near his head. He expects to have his brains blown out at any second.

They reach a high mesa with twenty hectares of marijuana.

The boss says, "All this is mine."

Then he is marched back to the truck and taken into town. He does not drink or smoke, but when they enter a bar, he begins drinking brandy like water.

The boss says, "I will give you twenty thousand dollars. To come here and tell me you lost my load, you must have big balls. Get a cell phone. You are going to sell a ton of marijuana, and don't steal it."

After bribing U.S. Customs, he moves the ton across the bridge into El Paso in two vans. Then he drives to Miami, and in three weeks, he is back with all the money. After that, he moves five tons a month.

"The game," he admits, "became my life. But I became bored and wanted to retire."

The boss told him he must move one more load.

He said no.

The federal police tortured him for four days and broke some ribs in the process. But finally, they let him go. He was shaking, he says.

"I had been collecting millions in Miami," he continues, "It was an ugly life. You had money but no peace. You love no one. You serve the devil. You don't care about your wife or son. One day I said to the Lord, if you exist, rescue me. But I got no answer."

He starts a real business: He provides security to factories in a city of violence. He makes money hand over fist.

Then, he gets a special job: guarding the brains behind the Juárez cartel, the business genius who disposes of all those billions in investments. The man is a cocaine addict and keeps two kilos of coke on hand for his appetite. His nose constantly bleeds. Part of the guard's job is to clean up the business guy so that he can do fine deals for the cartel.

And he does that and they become friends.

Above all, taking the shield of faith, wherewith ye shall be able to quench all the fiery darts of the wicked.

And take the helmet of salvation, and the sword of the Spirit, which is the word of God:

Praying always with all prayer and supplication in the Spirit, and watching thereunto with all perseverance and supplication for all saints. (Ephesians 6: 16–18)

The business genius becomes a born-again Christian, but his bodyguard does not. One day, he goes for his pay and the guy says he can't pay him, but not to worry, the Lord will.

He becomes furious and is going to beat the business mind when suddenly the guy breaks out in laughter. The bodyguard is confused, he slams the door as he leaves.

That night, he cannot sleep, the laughter of the businessman rings in his mind, as do his words about getting his money from God. Then he finally drifts off, and the Lord comes to him in a dream. He is at a party, and everything and everyone is white. It is very pleasant, there is a lot of laughter, but he is depressed. He feels a hand on his shoulder and turns around, and there is a very large man, but he cannot make out his face. The man takes his hand and they fly through the window and into the sky between the stars. Eventually, they alight on a mountain and sit down. The bodyguard looks like a baby, sitting beside his father.

God tells him people are slaves to consumption. God tells him preachers promise the people wealth and this leads them down a false path. The man is stunned because he has given at least three business speeches in Washington, D.C., to corporate people on how commerce can be done safely in Juárez. God takes him to a fancy hotel, and there is just such a meeting of businessmen going on and he looks up and realizes that he is the speaker.

That, he tells me, is how he came to Christ. Now he sells security in a dangerous world full of demons. He left the cartel and began working with the police since he knew everything they did not know. He cannot be harmed, he tells me, because God protects him.

His only weapon now is the Bible.

And for me, that utterance may be given unto me, that I may open my mouth boldly, to make known the mystery of the gospel,

For which I am an ambassador in bonds: that therein I may speak boldly, as I ought to speak. (Ephesians 6: 19–20)

Now, he leans forward, I must understand that the slaughter in Juárez is necessary. His work with the cartel planted the seeds of violence and corruption, and this is the harvest. All the *sicarios* must die. People must return to decent values and stay home with their families and have good habits. Corruption must be uprooted, the streets made safe. True, the Mexican army is butchering people, raping women and all that. But it is necessary for the cleansing to be accomplished. It is God's will. You see, he tells me, the army is murdering the police so that sound police can be created. They are killing drug merchants so that the drug money can flow to the government and provide decent public services.

Yes, yes, he says, read Ephesians 6:10–20. It is a tale foretold and there is nothing left to do but live out the book. This is the second revolution. First, as he noted, came the reduction of family size. Now, the forces of Satan must be slain, the men, the women, the children, all who are in thrall to evil. His world has perfect order because he knows why people are dying and so the little details hardly matter. For example, he has no idea which cartel now controls Juárez— it is very confusing at the moment, he tells me—but he is certain that the murders are divine justice and so for him, they are nothing to worry about.

He taps his Bible, leans forward, and reads again to me: "For we wrestle not against flesh and blood, but against principalities, against powers, against the rulers of the darkness of this world. . . ."

The present is always acceptable. Period. The city teems with shacks, poor people, dust, violence, and music booming out of open doorways. Women wear lipstick, children scurry past wearing clean clothes, buses rumble down the street spewing black exhaust, and the hours of the day slide by and it is life and it is normal and people cling to it one and all and it is good, good enough to make a life out of and to cherish. The stories float over the city, stories of murders, of executions, of rapes, robberies, stories of men protesting, stories of women holding vigils. At the bridge linking Juárez and El Paso, a memorial stands to murdered and vanished women, pink ribbons fluttering in the breeze, each ribbon bearing the name of a soul lost to life. And yet, each day, men huddle at the base of the memorial hawking newspapers, and cars line up to cross and the little tower of pink ribbons becomes invisible. I stand there, I stare at it, and I still cannot see it. It is not part of the city, it is part of an effort to imagine a different city and this effort is ignored because the present is acceptable. Period.

Everyone knows the facts and yet the facts slip from everyone's hands. Walk a hundred feet from a body on the pavement—the blood puddled around the skull—and it never happened, the young girls smile, the traffic zooms past without slowing, the city beats on and on, and the dead no longer exist and soon the memory of the dead will be a rare bit of fact polished and cherished by the family and ignored or forgotten by everyone else. This is a survival tactic and it crosses all class lines. This is the fruit of living without history. This is the result of amnesia in television, radio, and print. This is the sweet drug that comes from fantasy. The authorities are real. The police enforce the laws. The courts function. The army protects. The streetlights sweep evil from the night. There is a consensus here to believe the unbelievable, to insist that things are normal—the government is in charge, the incidents, should they even come to notice, are accidents, little imperfections in the tapestry that is life and this tapestry is sound and beautiful to both the eye and to the hand as it strokes the elaborate weave of lives that make up the city.

It took me a long time to accept that the present is acceptable. Period. I remember . . . a car pulls over, a man I know tells me with excitement in his voice that the police have arrested a man who has been killing all the women and the guy is convinced, the guy is intelligent—and I think at that moment that what the guy is telling me is nonsense. And then, the killings go on and on, and nothing is ever said of that moment, nothing is recalled of that bubble of excitement, nothing is mentioned of this fantasy that the police here solve crimes rather than commit them.

The bodies are all over the city this spring. People executed who are of the lowest social order, people killed who have never owned an automobile or had a room all to themselves, people slaughtered who stand on street corners peddling this and that, and yet educated people over fine meals tell me the killing is a cartel battle even though not a single fact sustains this argument or satisfies a rational mind. The body is on the sidewalk, the crowd gathers, the police bumble about, then the corpse is put in a van and vanishes, the people disperse, and soon all is normal and there is no taint, not even that drying puddle where blood spurted out of the dead man's head, no, there is not a trace of anything that suggests the world briefly went awry in this place. Just as the crack of the pistol shot vanished into the thin air, so did another life.

I am sitting on the curb outside another death house. Soldiers wear masks to protect themselves from their fellow citizens. The media mill about, chatting, working cell phones, swapping lies and rumors. No one questions that the soldiers must wear masks, that the bodies will come out of the death house and go somewhere that is never revealed, and that the identities of the dead will either never be determined or made public. A woman drives down the lonely street in a fine, large pickup with tinted windows. Her hair is dyed blonde, her face a sea of cosmetics, her lips ruby red. She is stopped by a soldier, says something, and is allowed to continue on to her home, a place now sequestered behind the military barricades that shut off the street. She never even glances over at the death house where the digging goes on day after day. Her face reveals a slight irritation at the hubbub in her neighborhood but not a flicker of curiosity about the television trucks, the cameramen, the talent doing stand-ups as they file breathless reports about another house of death.

Three times I have been blessed to witness the killing moment. I am always standing with a cup of coffee, and suddenly death falls out of the sky in the guise of a falcon. Twice, the killers were peregrines. Once, the blow came as a prairie falcon. Each time, I notice a sequence. The air is fresh, the birds singing, the leaves so very green on the trees, and then suddenly this freeze frame looms before me, a falcon, at the bottom of a dive that can reach speeds up to two hundred miles per hour, stops before me in the air, a dove clutched in its talons, death seeping into the eyes of the prey, and then suddenly both the slayer and slain vanish into the sky. Each time, I notice that a silence descends and continues for about twenty minutes. And then the birds reappear and life goes on as if nothing happened.

The present is acceptable. Period.

. . .

Suddenly, the army wishes to explain how things work. It reveals that it has discovered an account book in the possession of a cartel member and this ledger contains the payouts in Juárez for a ten-day period in March 2006. The tab for those days ran $336,000 and broke down into rivulets of cash. Twelve grand went for "*comp. prensa*," apparently payoffs to the local press. Then came $135,000 for what is termed local troops, and another $80,000 to someone called Juan. Medical expenses ate up $12,000, and another $25,000 vanished in radios for communication. Someone referred to as "R3" is down for $5,473 and also for $320.

"R4" gets $811, then $6,640, and finally, $4,760. The municipal police, according to the army, got $2,000 a week. A person going by the name Markesa got $1,160 and then, a bit later, another $955. Whoever "45" might be got $14,425. "*Comp. Piolo*" required $5,000, "Human 25" needed $10,000, and "*Desp. Ofic. Parve*" $200. Tete got a grand, but it is listed as a loan. On the plus side, "*Cholo abono cab. Pollo*" paid $159,000, and $39,820 flowed in from "R7 *abono*." There is also mention of "*Talon* 452."

The accounting has the careful ring of Benjamin Franklin's early efforts at frugality—a centavo saved is a centavo earned. It is a comfort to discover within the mysteries of the cartel the same attention to small sums that operates in the family budget. At times, the ledger seems like the butler's accounting in some large English manor house. And even some of the unclear things—the listing of people with code names, the assignment of money to unexplained functions—these arcane matters remind one of the techniques of modern corporate accounting, where costs have vague descriptions and where losses spin off into separate funds with baffling names. Of course, there are some puzzles in the tallies released by the army. There seems to be no payment listed for the army, an oversight that staggers belief. Nor is there one for the federal police or for the state police, two outfits no sound drug merchant would leave out of his personnel plan. Then there is the opaque reference to what may be the press. I have a friend in Juárez who refuses to take payments from the cartel and so, even though he spent years working on the city's newspapers, he is now virtually unemployable because, as he explained to me, "Now if you don't take their money, they kill you."

At best, the information released by the army gives one a peek and no more into the money machine of the drug industry. For example, given the murder rate in the city over the past fifteen years, it is eye-opening that the ledger contains no entry for homicide, a basic requirement of the business. Nor is there a bribe schedule for U.S. agents, though it has been proven in U.S. courts time after time that such elements of American law enforcement demand payment for aiding the shipment of drugs into the republic.

Still, it is a help, this partial ledger, like finding some rare manuscript from the ancient world that has survived the hurly-burly of life and speaks, as if from a tomb, of things that normally are beyond our comprehension.

She began to notice little items in the Juárez papers in 1993. Esther Chávez Cano was then a retired corporate accountant who had worked for Kraft in Mexico. The body has been sodomized, strangled, and beaten. The body is half naked, raped, stabbed. The little items kept flowing, dead girls left in the dirt. Nothing much is done.

Besides, women count more in Mexican beer commercials than on Mexican streets. Until 1953, they were not allowed to vote. Until the 1990s, they could not legally hold a job outside the house without their husband's permission. Today, there are thirty-one Mexican states, and in all of them, if, say, a twelve-year-old girl announces that she's been raped, well, she first has to prove she is "chaste and pure." Statutory rape charges are forgiven in twelve states if the man marries the girl—though he then often simply walks out on the obligation. And of course, there is the concept of *rapto*, or bride abduction, which means a man carries a woman off, has sex with her, and then either marries or dumps her, or does both. I once lived in a little place in Mexico where the potato chip salesman carried off a teenager—but then brought her back as unsatisfactory. She was in a state of mild disgrace, and when she walked down the street, I'd hear mothers tell their daughters not to look at her, but to pretend she did not exist.

Esther Chávez waded into this world and by 1999 had founded Casa Amiga, a shelter for abused women in Juárez. That first year, she handled 250 clients. In 2007, the clinic treated 27,400. Of course, since Casa Amiga is the only shelter in the city and in the state, the numbers reflect who can manage the long bus ride to her building more than the actual level of violence against women in the city.

She lives in a cul-de-sac in Juárez in a very nice neighborhood, and now she is seventy-two years old, battling cancer, and still driving each day to the shelter and pursuing the work. The slaughter of women continues, as does the slaughter of men. She is the gatekeeper on the city's savagery against women. And she is very tiny.

Her small house has two bedrooms, a warm kitchen, and a large living room with a fireplace and walls crawling with forty drawings and paintings. Family photographs watch from the coffee table. It is safe here. A raped and murdered woman was found in an abandoned building yesterday. Later, a bank was robbed. Esther has set the table with blue plates, glasses of pink grapefruit juice, and blue and yellow napkins. On the stairway to the upstairs bedroom, a large wooden angel says grace to the home, even though Chávez is not a believer. And her work for women has neither endeared her to the church nor brought the faith alive to her.

We have eggs, chilis, squash, tortillas. And death.

As she speaks, her thin hands with long fingers come together almost in prayer, but her voice, soft and low, has the force of authority. In Mexico, only women with a fierce will accomplish things. The rest go under the wheels of life.

Her white hair is cropped short because of the chemotherapy, and her body has withered and is birdlike.

At first she offers that the growing violence is a battle between cartels— this explanation is always a comfort to the civilized. She tells how the women who come to her shelter now say they are afraid to even go to the market because stray bullets may be flying anywhere. The city is rife with kidnappings, and they seem to observe no rules of class or neighborhood.

But then, she continues, there are always these little gangs besides the major cartels, and these little gangs are everywhere and they are armed and they flourish now because drugs are everywhere and consumption in the city has exploded as people seek syringes and powders as a way to endure the strife of normal life.

"I am trying to get a meeting with the mayor," she explains. "Now things are different. In the nineties, women were being taken off the streets. Now they are killed in their own homes. There have been, as of this moment in February, ten women murdered this year and they were not victims of domestic violence, they were not killed by members of their own families."

The tales tumble out. The young woman from Guerrero who lived with her aunt, a student. She had no life, she studied, she did not go out. And she was killed. That ten-year-old child, her mother was in the hospital, she was left alone in the home—and here Esther clasps her hands together as her eyes burn into me—and the police now say it was men who came to rob the house, found a ten-year-old girl alone, and so raped and killed her. One of the arrested had been detained last year in the case of a raped child, his name is in Esther's files, but of course, nothing had been done then. In both cases, he strangled. In the earlier case, the police said there was not enough evidence, but Esther Chávez knows better. She says that they simply did not believe that the child in the earlier case had been raped. Besides, she notes, the police are afraid to even leave their stations now. There is in Juárez a backlog of twenty-four thousand cases of all kinds, and women are now required to seek counseling with their attackers in order to clean up these files. The man is required to repent of his act and sign some papers and then he is released.

Her eyes stare out from almost square glasses. She is very frail and yet on fire. She explains that her doctor has recommended she avoid movies with violence, lest they upset her.

She laughs at the thought.

"I have ten years in this," she sighs. "The problem is that the violence will only increase because nothing has been done to treat the roots of the problem: corrupt police, the growing population of the city, poverty, drugs, and of course, people get frustrated and they sell drugs, and beat women. The men tell their women that if they go to Casa Amiga, they will kill them. And here the police never catch the murderer."

There is an old wood-cased pendulum clock on the wall in the corner. It has stopped.

She passes a plate of cookies, pours coffee.

"There is now a collective hysteria," she continues. "I am a woman who is never afraid and now I'm afraid. I change my route to work. Two of the police were killed a few blocks from my home. Before, the violence focused on poor women. Now, it can happen to anyone. The gangs fight to control the drug business. Before, it was gangs killing gangs. Now, police chiefs are killed. For fourteen years, the business community here has blamed me for putting a blot on the image of Juárez. Now with this terrible violence, no one is talking about anyone slandering Juárez."

We talk for almost three hours. She says the violence is because of discrimination against women, it is because of the poverty, because of ignorance, because of the culture, because women have so little self-esteem here, because of a lack of faith in the authorities, because of social isolation since so many women come to the city for work without any family around them, because the maquiladoras are about making money, not about the well-being of people.

She calls a cab and then we go outside.

Across the street, a massive new home is going up, and it is topped with a huge dome done up in golden tiles. Two-story windows sketch the face, and big columns frame the portico.

I glance at her and say, "Narco."

She smiles, and then points to the other homes on the cul-de-sac and says, "Narco, narco, narco, narco, narco, five of my neighbors are narcos."

But she contests my statement about the new house going up across the street.

"No," she explains, " he says he is a professor. A very strange professor."

Two years ago, I was at another house a block or so from the home of Esther Chávez. It also was a fine residence. It was a place men in the city came to party and celebrate after performing executions. There would be food and drink, cocaine and women. In that case, they had maintained a death house a few miles away, one in which they committed twelve murders and then buried the bodies in the patio. The state police were paid to be executioners.

I mention this to Esther and she nods without expression.

She says, "I am going to put all the bad stories in my book."

But she is pressed for time, what with the cancer, the chemotherapy, the work at Casa Amiga. She is seventy-two, she notes, and is running out of time.

But her book will be the real history of the city because the real history of the city is violence against the people of the city and the most powerless people in the city are the women. The real history of the city is written on the bodies of women, and this is not a history men are likely to sanction, even as they record it in the day and the night on bleeding flesh.

Sometimes the bodies have tattoos that say Juárez. Or sometimes there is a marijuana leaf etched into the brown skin and the message: I Always Consume.

. . .

The army's work in Juárez is barely reported because writing or saying what the military is up to could result in serious injury or death. So, at best, the newspapers will report some execution and say that the neighbors described the killers as dressed like commandos. The exact meaning lurking in the word *commando* is never spelled out. On other parts of the border, where the army has descended in order to reinstall peace and tranquility, locals mention a sudden bloom of robberies by men wearing military-type clothing and masks. But this also is never elaborated upon. When, in a few instances, there have been demonstrations protesting the violence and heavy-handedness of the army, this has been dismissed by both the generals and the federal government because they insist these demonstrations are really shams sponsored by various drug cartels.

The army has been operating in the Mexican state of Michoacan for at least a year before it arrives in force in Juárez. Norberto Ramírez says that in his village in Michoacan, the soldiers seized him, put a plastic bag over his head, cinched it tight, and spent all night taking turns suffocating him to the edge of death. They also beat him with rifle butts and shocked him with electric cattle prods. Of course, he did better than the seventeen-year-old boy shot dead. Ramírez, though lucky, can no longer work, because his frolic that night with the military damaged his liver and intestines beyond surgical repair. Also, he had a green card for working in the United States, but the soldiers took this away with his health. So far, over 421 human rights complaints have been lodged against the army since it began its war on drugs in December 2006. No soldier has been charged with any offense. Including the ones who gunned down two women and three children at a highway checkpoint in Sinaloa.

The U.S. State Department has issued a travel alert for Americans visiting Mexico, especially Juárez. The federal diplomats advise that if an American feels he or she is being followed, then the prudent thing to do is immediately contact Mexican authorities. Also, it is advised that American visitors stay out of areas where prostitution and drug dealing take place.

The alert states: "Violent criminal activity fueled by a war between criminal organizations struggling for control of the lucrative narcotics trade continues along the U.S.-Mexico border. Attacks are aimed primarily at members of drug trafficking organizations, Mexican police forces, criminal justice officials, and journalists. However, foreign visitors and residents, including Americans, have been among the victims of homicides and kidnappings in the border region."

Miss Sinaloa

I am looking in at her cell in the asylum. A small mattress fills it, and at the foot of the mattress is a yellow five-gallon bucket for defecation and urination. The walls are white tile because patients such as Miss Sinaloa tend to smear their feces on surfaces. The door is solid metal with a tiny slot because the Miss Sinaloas of the world tend to throw their feces at the staff. Plaid blankets cover the mattress.

This was her home for at least two months. No one could reach her. She raved, she was very angry. In part, she was locked up to protect her from the other patients who craved her fair skin and beauty. And in part, she was locked up because she would go berserk without warning.

And she was bald. The staff had to cut off her long, beautiful hair because it is an occupational risk here. Other patients have a tendency to take long hair and strangle the person with it.

At first, Miss Sinaloa is very violent. She cries constantly and throws things. So the staff gives her pills and she sleeps for two or three days. Then she awakens and is more calm. She tells everyone in the crazy place that she won a contest, she is a beauty queen and also a model. She says that she has known oh so many men who wanted to fuck her, but she had known no one like Ramon, who truly loves her for herself.

Her beauty becomes a problem. When she is let out of her cell into the yard in the crazy place, she stands out in her glory. El Pastor says, "She was like the last Coca Cola in the desert and so proud and the other ladies were jealous."

She would spend all day doing her makeup, doing it over and over and over. She was very clean. Each morning, she made the bed in her tiny cell and washed all the walls, scrubbing endlessly.

Ramon is a twenty-five-year-old drunk who has wandered into the crazy place and earns his keep serving meals. He is a homely man—El Pastor thinks he may be the ugliest man in the world. He takes plates of beans to Miss Sinaloa in her cell. She falls in love with him and he falls in love with her. Ramon has never had a girlfriend before—he is dazzled by even this ghost of the Miss Sinaloa who arrived in Juárez to party at the Casablanca.

She says, "How wonderful that this happened to me. Because of it I was able to find you, the most beautiful creature ever created by God."

El Pastor overhears Miss Sinaloa whispering her love to Ramon and is alarmed. Then he notices love marks on Ramon's neck and dismisses him.

Miss Sinaloa regresses and soon returns to her deep madness. She denounces El Pastor for ruining the great love of her life.

El Pastor stares with me into the cell—maybe nine feet by five feet.

Originally, he came out here and lived in a hut with his wife. He had two donkeys for gathering wood. He started stacking up blocks and bricks. This went on for three years. The police would bring the rejects of our world— whores burned out by lust and drugs, illegal immigrants kicked back by the United States because it did not want to tend to their damaged minds, topless dancers who had lost that half-step, street people who had sniffed so much glue and paint that they were now residents of oblivion, all the damned of our world.

El Pastor now houses and feeds one hundred. He walks me around and shows his expansion dream that will give him the capacity for two hundred fifty souls. He will have the patients making bricks—those who can still function well enough to mix up mud. He will sell these blocks and so give people a kind of dignity and himself some cash flow for the medicines they require in order to bottle up their rages.

A small, retarded man stands next to me clutching a children's book. It is in English, but then, he can't read any language. On October 11, he murdered another patient.

"You can't do anything to be safe here," El Pastor explains as we stand in the yard with eighty of the maimed milling about us.

"Heroin in the city," he explains, "is twenty-five pesos."

This means less than $2.50 a hit.

"Cocaine," El Pastor continues, "is everywhere here and cheaper than marijuana. And now they smoke cocaine with marijuana. We're talking about people eighteen to twenty-five now, the people who get executed. They are ghosts, human trash walking naked in the city."

In Nuevo Laredo, the sister city to Laredo, Texas, people notice a huge banner floating over one of the major thoroughfares. The message is simple: "Operative group 'The Zetas' wants you, soldier or ex-soldier. We offer a good salary, food and benefits for your family. Don't suffer any more mistreatment and don't go hungry." The banner also advises, "We don't feed you Maruchan soups [a brand of ramen noodles]." It lists a cell phone number. In Tampico, another banner appears that says, "Join the ranks of the Gulf Cartel. We offer benefits, life insurance, a house for your family and children. Stop living in the slums and riding the bus. A new car or truck, your choice. What more could you ask for? Tamaulipas, Mexico, the USA and the entire world is Gulf Cartel territory." The authorities in Mexico City say they think the advertisement is authentic.

The Zetas, besides maintaining training camps for new employees, also equip their people with automatic weapons, grenades, dynamite, and rocket launchers. Presumably they also get machetes since the group sometimes decapitates its adversaries. One of the Zetas' leaders is said to have elite Guatemalan soldiers as bodyguards. On March 17, Mexican authorities in the state of Tamaulipas seize a Jeep Cherokee with special features: a smoke-screen generator, bulletproofing, and, attached in the rear, a device to throw spikes on the road.

The Mexicans slaughtered in this killing season get to die twice. First, at the hands of their murderers, and then later, they are killed again by the explanations of their deaths. They are said to die from a cartel war, or from a war between the president of Mexico and the cartels, or a war between the Mexican army and the cartels or possibly as a result of drug consumers in the United States financing evil people with their habits and thus creating the slaughter every time they roll a joint.

These explanations are efforts to streamline a messy torrent of events. But what is happening in Juárez and increasingly throughout Mexico is the breakdown of a system. There are no jobs, the young face blank futures, the poor are crushed by sinking fortunes. The state has always violated human rights, and now, in the general mayhem, this fact becomes more and more obvious.

Killing is not deviance, it is a logical career decision for thousands floundering in a failing economy and a failing state.

There are certain economic incentives in becoming a murderer. Not only is the pay good, but it is an actual job with actual skills. The other choice of decent wages entails illegally migrating to the United States. Thirty years ago, about 10 percent of the Mexicans coming north were women—now females are at least half the migration.

Zacatecas, an old Mexican state initially settled because of a silver strike, testifies to the job opportunities in Mexico. Over half its population is now in the United States, and more Zacatecans live in Los Angeles than in their home state's biggest city. As one longtime resident of a Zacatecan town put it, "There is nothing here."

Or as a professor at the University of Zacatecas in the Department of Economics explains, "Work opportunities here are nonexistent, so this is going to cause more migration to the United States, even though it is getting harder to find work over there."

There are some openings in journalism. In Ciudad Victoria in the Gulf state of Tamaulipas, members of the local police kidnapped the pressmen of the daily paper to end its irksome publication. Some radio reporters were mowed down in Oaxaca. In Agua Prieta, Sonora, a border town facing Douglas, Arizona, a protest march marks the first anniversary of the killing of newspaper editor Saul Noe Martinez. He was kidnapped from the town jail by gunmen, and his body was later found in Chihuahua.

Underneath the headlines and the news bulletins, these hard facts grind people up and remold them into new destinies and sometimes monstrous decisions.

"It's beautiful," she begins, "I've been a policewoman for years. It's something I have inherited. My father was a police officer. I can serve my country. But it is dangerous, our society, our times, well, values have changed. People don't respect police officers now. And the violence—families are falling apart."

She stands in the bright sunlight on the edge of a mall parking lot, one with a police tower in the center to guard the shoppers and their cars. Her uniform has no name, her badge has no number. She is fat, and carries a .40-caliber semiautomatic. She belongs to the municipal police, the same force that has been losing comandantes to executions.

Her post is across the street from the monument to fallen officers.

There are thirty-five names on brass plaques on the monument. The first dead cop came in 1969, but things sort of ambled for almost twenty years, and then around 1990, business picked up, with thirty-five of the dead coming since then. And the most recent dead cop memorialized is September 2007—none of the recent corpses have been recorded. Nor does the monument pay any heed to missing cops. The monument is painted a faint green.

The statue of a giant cop stands before it and stares down at the hat of a fallen officer.

Twice, she refuses to speak of drugs in the city.

And when asked if she had heard about fellow officers picking up a raped beauty queen on the streets of the city, a woman called Miss Sinaloa, she snaps, no.

She answers this question very fast and her face does not smile at all.

Fear has been my pale rider. I have never faced an audience without fear, nor gotten out of the car to do that first interview on a story in some strange city without fear. Sentences also cause fear, as does that blank page waiting for words to fall on its white expanse and clot it with stabs at meaning. Violence rocks my body with fear, as does great sorrow in others since I fear my inability to stop the tears.

When I was in high school, in freshman English one of my fellow students read a paper on fear, and it was about chemical changes in our bodies and how these various juices both signaled our fear and created the state of being we call fear. I was struck at that moment and rather disappointed. I wanted fear to be something exalting, like courage, not compounds that could be written on a chalkboard like a recipe. And I was suspicious of the argument because it seemed to reduce something out of control to order. Fear is not only paralyzing, but also explosive. I have learned in life to never trust people who are afraid, because their behavior cannot be predicted. The killer facing me over a plate of food is rational. He kills and sometimes he feels nothing. There are such people, those who are calm while taking a life. They do not induce the fear in me that I feel when around the fearful.

But for me, fear is a sometime thing, almost a special event. But what if it is like oxygen, part of the very air one breathes, and so is not noticed and yet is not ignored? To notice it would require concentration, to ignore it would be an invitation to death. Imagine living a life of constant caution, of fearing police, of avoiding the authorities, and yet this blanket of fear is so steady and pervasive that awareness of the sensation ebbs because fear becomes the fabric of life. All doors must be locked, the windows barred, the drapes—should one have the money for such things—be pulled tightly shut, the stranger knocking at the door suspect and possibly dangerous, the traffic cop on the corner a predator, the sirens in the night promising no succor to a single soul but simply blaring the obvious danger that rises like a vapor from the very ground under one's feet.

There is recourse to magic. If things are not said, then these things do not exist. Just as some people cleanse their vocabularies of racial slurs or sexist terms and, by that act, convince themselves they are altering reality and ending tribal or religious or racial strife and bringing men and women into some kind of parity and joy, so there is a magical belief that to ignore the killings, to deny the violence, to refuse to admit to fear, these decisions lower the temperature of human rage or human mayhem and erase fear or the things to fear. It is a form of prayer practiced without a church or priest. And it is a return to childhood when we all had secret ways—don't step on the crack of the sidewalk, carry that lucky stone—to slay the sensation of dread.

So it is quite possible to live in a violent place and not speak of fear and for days at a time not to truly feel fear. Just move and act in a fog of fear. If you are a success in the drug industry, you will have police credentials, most likely federal or state, and these credentials will identify you as an officer. If rich, you move with bodyguards in a car with bulletproof glass and slabs of armor—and if you are a significant person in the drug industry, your body-guards will be federal police officers, your own private posse. If not so rich, you live in a gated community. If not rich at all, you lock things up, try to arrange a life where someone is always home. And get robbed now and again.

Regardless of your station in life, you may vanish or be murdered. There is this fatalism in Mexican life, and it is based on fatalities.

You try to recall incidents, but this is difficult, because all the moments when someone brought out a gun or when the police swarm you and demand papers and there is no one else around, or when the gang kids eye you, and you stare into the emptiness that seems to take up all the space in their skulls—all those events have ceased to be events and have been sanded smooth by time. And by fear. The fear especially grinds away at them until they can no longer be glimpsed and never really happened. The only incident you will ever truly remember clearly and vividly is when you are taken, perhaps tortured and raped, and then killed. And you will not remember that one very long.

I have a friend who tries to explain this way of living. His small pickup is his joy, and he keeps it secure at night behind a heavy metal gate. But when he drives, there is always the risk of someone swerving ahead of him, pushing him to the curb, and coming to his truck window with a pistol in his hand. Auto theft is almost a white noise here, the random buzz of small violence below the larger barrages from machine guns. In the past, he notes, there was always some name, some number you can imagine calling and at the other end of the call would be someone with power who could speak for you or speak to someone yet more powerful, and so there was a way to feel safe.

Now, he tells me sadly, there is no one to call. No one at all.

So you are left with the fear, a fear you no longer recognize and yet never seem to escape.

Since the time of troubles began, the police of Juárez have responded in kind. Many have fled, and so now at any given shift there are, at most, two hundred cops looking over the city. Also, if they leave the station, they are careful about getting out of their patrol cars. Residents complain they no longer see them out and about. Then, there is the fear the cops now have of the army since fellow officers are periodically snatched by the military and return with tales of woe. People have discovered that if they call the police, no one comes.

Bank robberies, store robberies, and car theft have boomed. Increasingly, guys are robbing stores armed with nothing but toy pistols.

Mexico itself is exploring a new kind of installation art, beheadings. In the first four months of 2008, there had been at least forty decapitations. Some are left on fence posts.

On the U.S. side, Margarita Crispin, a thirty-two-year-old U.S. Customs and Border Protection agent, gets twenty years in prison. For four years, she'd worked at the bridge separating Juárez and El Paso, and for four years, she'd waved drug shipments through. One load, the one that did her in when the van broke down, held almost three tons of marijuana. The federal government seized $5 million she had stashed and a lot of jewelry.

It is hard to stay clean when such possibilities dance before one's eyes.

We put too much emphasis on who is clean and who is not clean. There are places where being clean is meaningless and Juárez is one such place, and the entire border is like Juárez when this issue of being clean comes up. There is too much money made both in the drug industry and in the people-smuggling industry for this wealth not to flow across everybody's life. If you refuse to be in the business, someone in your family is in the business, and someone in your family who is totally clean is bankrolling little business ideas off drug money or people-smuggling money. You might be a DEA agent, but you'll have a brother who has a nightclub bankrolled by people from this other world or you'll have a sister who marries a guy who works for a cartel. And you'll spend your own free time running a "Just Say No to Drugs" basketball league to keep kids clean, but these facts will just be facts. And this sketch I've just laid down is not a hypothetical, it is the human architecture of a friend of mine. And he is hardly unique.

I've never done any kind of drug deal in my life. But I've loaned out scales to friends who felt differently.

So drop the notions you carry about who is clean and not clean. Who is honest or dishonest will get you closer to reality.

Her husband is driving in Juárez, she sits beside him, the three-year-old is in the backseat. It is Sunday, April 20, 2008, and Algae Amaya Nuñez is twenty-nine years old at this moment and the moment is 10 P.M. Her brother, mayor of a community in Chihuahua, was assassinated on September 24, 2006. Her father, a former mayor, was assassinated in February 2007. Algae rides in a red 2007 Fusion with Texas license plates. The family straddles both sides of the line. One bullet goes through her neck, the other her belly. Five spent 9 mm casings are found by the vehicle. The husband pulls over to help his wounded wife. He vanishes—witnesses saw commandos in two pickups take him away. But they leave the three-year-old. Kin come over from the Texas side for the child. They are pursued along the road that leads to the bridge by the hit men who shoot at them. They make it back alive to the United States.

Algae helped found the school where she taught history and sociology.

Now she is a corpse and joins her executed brother and father.

So tell me, what does clean mean?

The lunch is very long—a feast of carnitas, pork chunks fried in a big vat of oil. The man wolfs down his food. He was a *sicario*, an assassin. His work was for Barrio Azteca, the key Juárez gang, which has at least three thousand members. The other five hundred or so gangs work for Barrio Azteca and dream of making the grade and joining the big shots. Once, when he was arrested by the police, it took ten cops to beat him down. He did enough killings to join the leadership under the late legend El Diablo. I do not ask him how many he has killed. Surely over twenty if he was in a council with El Diablo.

"When you are an Azteca, the police protect you. And you kill for the police."

He explains a thing called La Linea, a consortium of the Mexican army, the mayor, gangs, the federal police, the state police, and the city police.

I ask how Aztecas move drugs into the United States.

He looks at me with mild surprise and says, "We bribe the Border Patrol and the U.S. Army."

Who is killing all these people in Juárez?

He says, "Now the military is killing people who are no longer useful. If there is any dispute over drug money, they kill."

He has no idea what the Juárez cartel is up to. "Such information is only available to the highest-ranking police officers."

The meal is over.

He has one more thing to say when I ask him about the late Amado Carrillo, the fabled head of the Juárez cartel.

"He is a god."

Daniel Escobedo, twenty-one, is driving to school in Juárez. He stops at a roadblock and hands over his ID to uniformed men. Then, he is taken away by a team in two SUVs, and for six weeks, he is blindfolded as the men deal with his lawyer father over a ransom. Eventually, he is rescued by the military during one of its sweeps on April 1. Some U.S. security firms figure Mexico is experiencing thirty to fifty kidnappings a day—of course, they only count ones where real ransom money is involved. As a rule of thumb, maybe one out of ten kidnappings is reported to the police. A study found that only 52 percent of the Mexicans surveyed thought they would "very probably" report being the victim of a crime. For example, Daniel Escobedo's father never reported his son's kidnapping.

Dead Reporter Driving

The priest goes to the fiesta to christen a child. The food is lavish, as is the rancho. There are many men of power there, men who have survived the life and now live large and feast on danger. One old man there is the boss and he wears a very large crucifix of gold. This gleaming treasure catches the priest's eye. Later, when the padre has left the fiesta, he goes to the federal police and tells them of this convocation of *narco-trafi-cantes*. He is a very good source for the police because he takes confessions from the men in the life and then sells this information. The police hit the fiesta and they find a lot of cocaine, which, of course, they seize for resale. And they take a million in cash from the partygoers. The priest gets the gold crucifix as his reward. He blesses it and now it links him to his God.

Emilio Gutiérrez sits and watches the video captured by the security camera. A long caravan of fine pickup trucks with darkly tinted windows takes up both lanes of the highway leading into Ascensión. There must be twenty or thirty vehicles rumbling into the isolated community of eighteen thousand in the Chihuahuan desert. The town is surrounded by dying farms, many of them abandoned because of low prices for what they produce. Now the army has seized some of these farms and squats on them. People live off a few bars, some small stores, and the drug industry. Right now, at the moment the caravan arrives, the streets are empty and no one looks out a single window. The man cannot make out any faces in the video of the big, fine trucks with dark glass. He will never know who this convoy is guarding. He will never ask. Just as the Mexican army stationed in the town will never record the arrival of this force bristling with machine guns. Rumors say it is Chapo Guzman, a leader of the Sinaloa cartel, but it could be the ghost of Jesus Christ or the ancient frame of Adolf Hitler. To investigate such matters is a fatal decision.

There is a curious disconnect between the Mexican press and the U.S. press, one where the U.S. press pretends that reporting in Mexico is pretty much the way it is in the North, where the Mexican press considers American reporters to be fools. Sometimes, Gutiérrez deals with American reporters who are fluent in Spanish, but that is not enough because "they imagine things but they don't know, and so the U.S. reporters are marginalized by the Mexican reporters because they figure they are hopeless."

We are sitting in the sun somewhere in the United States of America as he tosses out the tale of the priest and the story of the strange caravan of fine pickup trucks. He is hiding now with the family of a man who has connections in northern Chihuahua. But if this fact were known, the man's relatives in Chihuahua would be kidnapped and possibly killed, his businesses seized. As we soak up the sun at this fine moment, Ascensión is in a state of siege. Four women have vanished and are probably murdered. The head of the bank there and his wife have been kidnapped and then returned in bad shape. Also, the bank has just been strafed by machine gun fire. In Palomas, a border town in the same county as Ascensión, two dead women have just been found in the dump—one of them pregnant.

The Mexican army is everywhere and can be ill tempered. Six months ago, I was with a friend who took a photograph of them in downtown Palomas, a block from the port of entry, and they came racing at us with machine guns. The town is dying. Few people cross from the United States to shop because of the violence. In the streets, children beg, their skin a gray cast that suggests malnutrition. Work has fled—the people-smuggling business has moved because of U.S. pressure in the sector, and so the town is studded with half-built or abandoned cheap lodgings for migrants heading north. Also there is an array of narco-mansions whose occupants have moved on to duck the current violence. And there are eyes everywhere. I walk down the dirt streets tailed by pickups with very darkly tinted windows. The biggest restaurant in town for tourists closes every day at 6 P.M.—get home before dark. Last year, the U.S. port of entry was accidentally strafed during a shoot-out in Palomas. There is more dust than life in the air of the town.

The Mexican army arrived in new numbers in April 2008 in northern Chihuahua, and the general in command held a meeting with the press to lay down some ground rules. He said there would almost certainly be a spate of robberies and rapes, but these were to be explained by the press as the evil deeds of poor Mexicans who came from the far south and who were migrating through the zone to reach the United States. Any questions?

As I sit in the sun with Emilio he tells of the current violence in the towns he once covered, and none of these incidents have been reported in the U.S. press or the Mexican press. Nor will they be.

He knows what is happening because he has retained his sources. And he knows that it will not be reported because to publish is to invite death.

He is one of eight children and was raised in Nuevo Casas Grandes, a small Chihuahuan town against the Sierra Madre. His father was a master bricklayer, his mother a housewife. His childhood was poverty. He always wanted to be a writer and worked on the high school paper, a weekly printed on a mimeograph machine.

The army has a post in his town. One day, a very pretty classmate named Rosa Saenz shows up, her hair and skin coated with mud. Her breasts have been sliced with blades and she has been stabbed fifty times. She has been raped. Her body is found in an abandoned chicken farm on the edge of town. Emilio sees her body in the back of a car in front of the police station, a vehicle dragged in as a monument to a quest for evidence. Two of her classmates are blamed for the murder. The police smash the testicles of one. The other flees, and when he returns much later, he is kind of crazy and never recovers. In the end, no one is charged with the crime. But everyone in the town knows the girl was raped and murdered by the army. And no one in the town says anything about it.

Emilio is thirteen years old.

This is part of basic Mexican schooling: submission. I remember once being in a small town when the then-president of Mexico descended like a god with an entourage and massive security. The poor fled into their huts until it was over. The streets emptied, and when the president did a staged stroll to greet his subjects, no one stood on the sidewalks except party hacks. Just as when I attended the fiesta for the official candidate for the state governorship (a man who had spent most of his years in Mexico City and far from his claimed home), the campesinos had to be bused in by the government and given free food and, even with that, proved so listless the crowd seemed to be on sedatives. Every Mexican learns early on, by watching the elders, to retreat or cower before authority and to lead very private and quiet lives. Mexican literature is rich with recording this obliteration of public self and sequestering of private self amid the illusion that family provides security. Mexico's Nobel laureate poet, Octavio Paz, etched this trait indelibly in *The Labyrinth of Solitude*: "Modern man likes to pretend that his thinking is wide-awake. But this wide-awake thinking has led us into the mazes of a nightmare in which the torture chambers are endlessly repeated in the mirrors of reason."

Of course, there are releases from this in fiestas, drinking into the night with friends, and jokes. I have almost never had an intelligent conversation in the United States about what life means. But I have had many after midnight, sitting outside under a tree with a bottle in Mexico. Emilio emerges as a young man in high school with a first-rate mind in a country where intelligence can be a fatal trait.

He learns photography, and when he graduates at eighteen, a new daily is starting in Ciudad Juárez, *El Diario*, and he gets hired to take pictures. Soon he is a reporter.

He learns corruption almost instantly. He is paid very little, and payday is every Friday. He explains the system in simple terms. Let's say, he offers, that a reporter earns a hundred dollars a week. Every Monday, a man comes who represents the police, the government, the political parties, and the drug leaders. He gives each reporter a sum that is three or four times his actual wage. This is called the *sobre*, the envelope.

"Every since I was a little kid," he continues, "I listened to my parents criticize bad government. We knew it was corrupt."

Now he is part of a corrupt system.

"Corruption at the paper," he explains, "was subtle. The politicians would win over my boss with dinners and bags of money. The reporter on the beat would get pressure sometimes from the boss not to report certain things like the bad habits of politicians, the houses they own, the girlfriends. And it was understood that you never asked hard questions. The narcos also gave out money but I was always afraid of them. They own businesses, buy ads, have parties and celebrities and horses and you cover that, they would pay you to cover that, but you never mentioned their real business."

He sees his Mexico as genetically corrupt. A corrupt Aztec ruling class fused with the trash of Spain—the conquistadors—and produced through this marriage a completely corrupt Mexico. This thesis helps him face the reality around him.

"In Mexico," he says, "we operate in disguise. There is one face and under that is another mask. Nothing is upfront. The publisher wishes to perpetuate the system. But if it is clear you are taking bribes, you will be fired. You must take it under the table because if you talked about it openly, that would affect the image."

He is entering a bar one night, when he sees the mayor of Juárez leaving with some *narco-traficantes*. The mayor pauses by the street, drops his pants and pisses into the gutter. Emilio writes up a little note and puts it in the paper. He is nineteen and he does not understand.

The next day he is called to the mayor's office.

The man is at a big desk with a check register.

He says, "How much?"

He wants Emilio to publish a story saying his earlier story was a lie.

Gutiérrez does not take any money. He realizes later this is a serious error because he learns the mayor and the publisher are very close.

"I quit and take a job in radio before something bad can happen."

Later, when things calm down, he returns to *Diario* a wiser man.

Here is what a wise man knows: that certain people—drug leaders, the corrupt police, the corrupt military—these things cannot be written about at all. That other people should be mentioned favorably unless they are caught in circumstances so extreme that the news cannot be suppressed. Then, they appear in the paper, but the blow is softened as much as possible. Nor are investigations favored. If someone is murdered, you call the proper authorities and you print exactly what they tell you. But you don't poke around in such matters.

Emilio loves politics and develops page-one stories by dutifully interviewing politicians and then nakedly publishing their inane answers. Sometimes, when a leading drug figure is arrested, usually as a show to placate the U.S. agencies, he interviews this person, also. He is hard-driving, at least until his son is born. After that, he becomes cautious because he must think of his son and not give in to the dangers of ambition.

For a while, he works for a small radio station and he makes one report on how a mayor in a neighboring town has fired the local drug counselor for the schools. He wonders on the air if the officials themselves are actually clean.

He soon finds out because a mayor of another town is listening. This mayor has just gotten out of a treatment center in El Paso for cocaine addiction. He storms down to the radio station and offers the owner ten thousand pesos to fire Emilio. The owner obliges him.

He moves from paper to paper and eventually winds up at the paper in Ascensión, the region of Chihuahua where he was raised. He has mastered, he thinks, the rules of the game. He writes down answers and publishes them. He avoids drug dealers. He is careful about offending politicians. He does not look into the lives of the rich, nor does he explore how they make their money. He is clean, he avoids taking bribes. But he also ignores the fact that other reporters are taking bribes. He is not looking for trouble.

This is the reality of Mexican reporting, where a person is inside but outside, where a person knows more than the public but can only say what is known in a code and this code had better not be too clear. A world where submission is essential and independence is eventually fatal.

He is stressed because, even though he plays by the rules, he cannot know all the rules and he cannot be certain when the rules change. He can understand certain things. When a general comes to Chihuahua in April 2008 with an army and says if there are any rapes and robberies, they are to be assigned to Mexican migrants, well, that is the way it will be reported.

He will obey his instructions for a very simple reason.

For three years, he has been afraid he will be murdered by the Mexican army. He has, to his horror, committed an error. And nothing he has done in the past three years has made up for this mistake. He has ceased reporting on the army completely. He has focused on safe things such as fighting the creation of a toxic waste facility in the town. He has apologized to various military officers and endured their tongue lashings. Still, this cloud hangs over him.

He can remember the day he blundered into this dangerous country.

Miss Sinaloa

After two months or more, Miss Sinaloa seems to recover some of her mind. El Pastor estimates that she eventually regained 90 percent of her sanity. He locates her relatives, and her family comes up from Sinaloa. They must be surprised that she is alive. I am. After such a frolic, death would not be unusual, and Miss Sinaloa would be just one more mysterious dead woman in the desert on the outskirts of Juárez.

But something saved her—perhaps her madness set her apart.

And so she came here and lived with people considered beneath even the dirt flooring the city of Juárez, people from the streets, people rejected by the mental institutions of the state, people beyond the help of families, people who slept on sidewalks and ate out of garbage cans.

She said she knew many languages, but she never spoke them. She would sing all the time, but she sang badly. Her favorite songs were very romantic. She moved around the crazy place like a queen. She read the Bible a lot. She remains a myth even standing in the yard at the crazy place. El

Pastor decided that 5 percent of what she says is true and the other 95 percent is her imagination.

That is the world of Miss Sinaloa, a place of dreams and songs, a place for a beauty queen to rule. She sits and draws, mainly lines and spirals. And lips, lots of kissing lips.

She dresses well, always a blue dress that shows her legs to advantage. Also, high heels—she navigates the asylum in stilettos.

To El Pastor's horror, she says a lot of bad words. He thinks maybe the rapes made her talk this way.

He prays with her and she closes her beautiful brown eyes.

She never mentions her family.

She only talks about her beauty. Nothing else really, just her beauty.

She is Miss Sinaloa, after all.

So when the family comes to retrieve their daughter, the father draws an obvious conclusion—that El Pastor and his patients have been having their way with her.

El Pastor is horrified and there is a terrible argument and then, Miss Sinaloa leaves for home with her family.

But as we stand in the dust and wind outside the asylum walls and he recounts that moment—"I am a family man!"—we both understand the reaction of the family. They are middle-class people, El Pastor notes. They had a nice car and they paid for all the medical bills Miss Sinaloa had run up. But in a country where the weak are always prey, where the favorite verb is *chingar*, to fuck over, such a conclusion is inevitable. Just as the gang rape for days of Miss Sinaloa in the Casablanca is the normal course of business.

The warehouse waits on the side street off a fashionable avenue in a middle-class neighborhood. The army has blocked the streets, and the men wear black uniforms, flack jackets, and blue trousers and clutch automatic rifles. Their faces are covered with black masks lest someone make their identity. A few weeks ago, they hit this very warehouse and found 1.8 tons of marijuana and two men. The two men were taken away.

And now the military is back at the warehouse in an operation sponsored out of Mexico City. Inside, a backhoe digs and two cadaver dogs help in the work. The story floating among the Mexican television, radio, and print people outside is that the informants said there were twelve bodies buried in the warehouse. The work began at 8 A.M., and now it is almost noon and nothing has been found.

Pigeons coo on the roof of the three-story concrete block and windowless building. The street is lined with two-story houses, trees, big iron walls, and gates to protect cars, people, and appliances. Here and there, large dogs stare out through bars. A cluster of cops stands around down the street, but mainly nothing goes on but the slow rhythm of life in a middle-class neighborhood. The press tries to snare the locals in a conversation, but they are not anxious to speak. This is the normal neighborhood with the normal death house—no one saw anything, no one heard anything. And of course, no one smelled anything. A slight woman of about twenty with light skin, tight jeans, and maybe ninety pounds of flesh does a standup for television. Then the torpor returns as everyone waits for the shot they want—bodies coming out.

There is a sound that is everywhere in Juárez, and it is not of sirens or gunshots or the cries of the dead and dying. It is the skittering of litter down a street by a warehouse of death, the flapping of plastic bags caught on the barbed wire, on fence posts, on iron bars. The city has this skittering and flapping, and all is wrapped in endless waves of dust and plumes of exhaust pouring out the tailpipes of dying buses carrying workers to endless toil. Also, the scraping of shoes on the ground as tired people, usually very dark and dressed in cheap clothing and big shoes that do not really fit their feet, trudge by carrying plastic bags of groceries as they go to their shacks and think of preparing something to eat. The other sound is of the better-off, the young women in tight jeans who clatter past on high heels with the confidence of mountain goats scampering up a cliff, the young women who wear the faces of femme fatales as they navigate a city that eventually consumes them.

A car rolls past with the heavy boom coming off the speakers.

A black column of smoke rises off some burning shack in the barrio and the fire engine screams past.

Here and there around the city, pink bands with black crosses are painted on the utility polls to memorialize the dead and missing girls—a row of such poles lines the highway near the crazy place where Miss Sinaloa healed her wounds.

But nothing really registers in this place, the city erases not simply lives, but also memory. And those who remember are the most likely of all to be erased.

Back in May 1993, back when violence was more focused in the city and everyone sensed a gray sky of power hanging over their lives and directing their fates, Javier Lardizabal was thirty-three years old. He worked as an investigator for the attorney general's office of Chihuahua. He noticed things and turned in a report of links between the police and the drug dealers, even noticing that one major capo moved around Juárez with police bodyguards. Then, he disappeared—until November 16, 1994, when a bulldozer loading sand in the nearby dunes dug up his body. The driver was hardly surprised—already in his sand-loading toils, he'd discovered the former head of the national security office in Juárez.

Of course, that was then and now it is not even a memory as I sit on the curb by the warehouse of death, listening to dry leaves flutter down the pavement, and waiting for a new crop of corpses to come back into the light.

It goes like this at the new death house. On the first day, they announce one body. On the second day, three bodies. On the third day, one more body. Now it is a week in, the digging continues, and the tally seems to be nine bodies. But since heads are severed from bodies, the exact count may take a while. Besides, there is more of the patio to dig up.

No one really knows what is going on. The editor of one local daily estimates that his publication reports maybe 15 percent of the action. For example, fake cops have been setting up checkpoints in the city and seizing guns. In a forty-eight-hour period toward the end of February, a top cop is mowed down, four other residents are murdered, three banks are robbed, and, by a fluke, $1.8 million is seized by U.S. Customs because a driver from Kansas got turned back by Mexican Customs and reentered the United States. Also, the Mexican army bagged 4.5 tons of marijuana. All this is in the 15 percent that gets reported.

The street is always rutted and claws up the hillside. The girls are always clean, their hair shines, their clothes shout colors. And they walk with little plastic bags in their hands, small items bought at the local *tienda*. Their eyes stare straight ahead, and so the fourteen- or fifteen-year-old goddesses state their indifference to the world that chokes in the dust around them.

There is a way out, and to those who do not understand the world, this way seems like an appetite for fantasy. The *cholos* on the corner with their hard, empty eyes, close-cropped hair, baggy pants, and sullen faces have a dream. It is of exercising power through killing, having women because of money, wearing tattoos as billboards of their ambitions. And of dying, and dying young and without warning, and for reasons they can barely say or comprehend, something about honor, or turf, or something, just something that they really can't say. There is no point is discussing an alternative future because this is a thing they cannot dream or feel or crave, so an alternative future is beyond words or meaning. All the nostrums of our governments—education, jobs, and sound diet—mean little here because they never happen to anyone. At best, the way out is a lottery ticket. Or the fame and savor of a violent death.

I am sitting with a gang member—one in his dotage now, his late thirties. He straightened up for a spell, became a trucker in the United States, married, had children. To keep his long-haul schedule, he started using amphetamines, and then the pills took over, he became surly, beat the wife, went to jail, got out and beat the wife again, was back in court. And leapt up at his hearing and attacked the judge. After prison, he was still angry and still busy with the pills. The United States shipped him to Juárez, and there he tried to kill his mother and father and siblings. And so they cast him out.

Now he has been clean for nine months and still he is not really anywhere. He is not in the present, except in a blank way, and living on thirty dollars a week. He cannot see the future. He can remember being a leader and killing, and this is as close to a dream as he is likely to get. His eyes glimmer with intelligence and yet look as empty as a tomb. This is the place those with safe, fat lives call a fantasy. But here, fantasy seems like a sound decision because what people like myself call fantasy throbs with reality.

I meet these people with dreams who paint rocks outside towns, who take old cars and make them mosaics with steer horns sprouting off the hood, and that *wa-wa* horn shouting out, the driver with glazed eyes and a leather hat roaring with laughter as he cuts through the fiesta. Sometimes they create sculptures, sometimes drunken poems in the cantina, sometimes murals of cheap pigments and distorted beings, but always they dream and drift into a place called fantasy.

Listen to the sensible people, the governments that have told you since before you were born that everything is getting better. Skip those failures— they are bumps on the road, and the road leads to Shangri-la, to the bright, light-skinned children, good jobs, fine schools, public health, and women who lick your toes and men who respect your body and safe streets and nights where the darkness holds no dread.

Or consider the market forces, the magical pulse of an economy now global, and hitch a ride on an information highway or bask in the glow of market forces, become part of a giant apparatus that is towing us all toward the golden shore. And you'll have a bathroom and the toilet will flush every single time. Lady, you will be beautiful and your hands will be smooth and soft and never will a single wrinkle touch your face, nor will your breasts drop a single degree. And they will be full—we have our ways.

So I am sitting with the gang guy who is violent and will die, or I am sitting with the man full of art dreams who has no schooling but explodes with paint on cliff sides, or I am sitting with the young woman who banks it all on cosmetics, thong panties, and a sullen face protecting a heart full of hopes.

Here's the deal: Given the choices, what would you do? I'd kill to get in the gang, I'd put on the high heels and the perfume, I'd pick up the guitar, I'd go through the wire, I'd open the bottle, I'd sniff the glue, I'd say tell me the lovers are losers and I'd certainly piss on the winners anointed by the authorities. And I'd maybe kill in Juárez, but far more certainly, I would die in Juárez. With a shout and a scream and a head full of dreams.

And I imagine sitting with Miss Sinaloa, who should have known better. I can hear the voices of reprimand in my ears that announce with certainty that sensible women of good features do not go to private parties in Juárez, where many men will gather whom they do not know—yes, I can hear these wise voices telling me the facts of life. I say dream, I say fantasize, I say escape, I say kill, I say do not accept the offerings of the cops and the government and the guns that have slaughtered hopes for generations and generations.

I say fantasy.

I say go to Juárez.

I say, Miss Sinaloa, will you take my hand?

The nights grow more difficult. The Mexican newspaper photographers learn to avoid the military roadblocks, to swing down side streets and chart a new city of alleys and detours. This is the only sensible thing to do.

One night in early April, just days after the full military presence swarmed into the streets of the city, two photographers respond to a police call and find two municipal squad cars. One of the cops is a woman. They are to transport a sick man, but when the squad tries to leave, the army blocks them. They let one squad car go on, but keep the other vehicle carrying the policewoman. When finally rescued from the custody of the army, she is not in good shape and so her fellow cops take her to the police station. Her panties and bra are torn and she goes into shock, her face paralyzed. She cannot speak of what happened, because she says they would kill her if she talked. Three policewomen have been raped in recent days, but the department will not say if she is one of them.

Her adventure occurs on a city street at night and takes up a lot of time— and during her adventure, no one comes out of a house to see what is going on. When a photographer for the paper raises his camera to photograph her, she covers her face.

Later, he tells me that if he had not happened on the scene, he is not sure she would have come back from the embrace of the Mexican army.

Jaime Murrieta always has a smile and, with luck, a bottle of beer. When I first met him in 1995, he had already photographed hundreds of murders for the Juárez newspapers. On September 9, 2006, he was out cruising in the night, looking for his dream photograph. In this ultimate image, he will be holding his camera, the killer will come toward his lens, and Jaime Murrieta will faithfully record his own murder. I remember him telling me in the 1990s of this dream shot with a smile on his face and passion in his eyes.

But on that September night in 2006, he comes very close to his dream. He and two other members of the press stumble upon a street party of Aztecas and a herd of Chihuahuan state police, including three comandantes. They are drinking and having an impromptu fiesta. He raises his camera.

They beat him close to death. He winds up in a hospital with a police guard—and of course, given the circumstances, such a guard is hardly reassuring. He loses the sight in one eye—but luckily, not his shooting eye. He refuses to leave town even when I send him money for such a flight.

After all, he did not get the photograph of his dreams, although he came close to that ultimate image.

Of course, none of this can be really happening. Mexico was to become a modern nation, and then when Mexico did not become a modern state but lingered in the shadow of tyranny and poverty, this was papered over by successive American governments since a quiet neighbor was, and is, the best neighbor for a global empire. When Mexico became a trampoline for drugs to bounce from the cocaine belt of South America into the United States, then it was the fault of American habits and addicts. Finally, when even this rhetoric of deceit failed to paper the wounds, NAFTA was ballyhooed by the administration of President Bill Clinton and President Carlos Salinas (a man reputed to have stolen ten to twenty billion dollars for six years of service) as the answer that would bring prosperity and end illegal immigration.

The trade agreement crushed peasant agriculture in Mexico and sent millions of campesinos fleeing north into the United States in an effort to survive. The treaty failed to increase Mexican wages—the average wage in Juárez, for example, went from $4.50 a day to $3.70. The increased shipment of goods from Mexico to the United States created a perfect cover for the movement of drugs in the endless stream of semi trucks heading north.

American factories went to Mexico (and Asia) because they could pay slave wages, ignore environmental regulations, and say fuck you to unions. What Americans got in return were cheap prices at Wal-Mart, lower wages at home, and an explosion of illegal immigration into the United States. This result is global, but its most obvious consequence is the destruction of a nation with which we share a long border.

The main reason a U.S. company moves to Juárez is to pay lower wages. The only reason people sell drugs and die is to earn higher wages. The only reason people go north, aside from the legendary beaches of Kansas, Chicago, and other illegal destinations, is to survive. This is not simply an economic exchange. Unless you are one of those people who own a factory, this is a deal with death and money. Juárez, the pioneer city of Mexico in foreign factories, is full of death, poverty, and violence after decades of this busy notion of the future.

Let me ask you one question: Just what is it you don't understand that every dead girl here understands, that every dead *cholo* understands, that everyone ending a shift at the plant understands, and that every corpse coming out of the death warehouse understands?

To sit on the curb by a death house in Juárez is to smell all things that cannot be said out loud in American political life.

And as El Pastor said, "Dementia smells."

. . .

The clothes hang on barbed wire, on old loading-dock pallets that now serve as fences, on bushes and shrubs. Water in many of the new colonias comes by truck and is stored in containers also pilfered from the factories and still rich with toxic chemical residues. The street will be dirt or sand, the electricity stolen off power lines, the wires snake on the ground to the individual shacks. The air feels like a solid because dust and fumes wrap Juárez in an atmosphere that can be chewed.

The city trails along an ebbing river and is cradled by dunes, and when the wind rises, the air goes brown and the dirt is everywhere. This is where the women come into a miracle: Almost every morning, Juárez teems with poor people in clean clothes, and these clean clothes come from the labor of women who lack running water or even conventional clotheslines. They are the secret engine of the city, the cooks and bottle washers, the laborers in the factories where women have been supplanting males for decades, the beasts of burden carrying groceries, the mothers of children, and always the dirt police who turn out family members each and every morning in clean clothes. Their hair pulled back, their lips red, their eyes weary, the women are the washing machines in a city of dust.

Every time I come to Juárez, I swear it is for the last time. And then, I come again and again. I seldom write about these visits, so that is not why I come. I seldom enjoy these visits, so that also fails to explain my returns.

I think it is about tasting the future. Juárez is the page where all the proposed solutions to poverty and migration and crime are erased by waves of blood.

I feel at one with El Pastor.

He keeps telling me of his mission, how back in 1998, when the bad snow came, and "I was driving that day and singing to the Lord and it was snowing. I said, 'Lord I'm working with you,' and the Lord pulled my hair."

That is the moment when he began scooping the crazy people off the streets and creating his asylum in the desert.

Now El Pastor is jubilant because he is talking about Juárez.

"I love Juárez," he says, "I know it is dirty and very violent but I love it! I grew up in Juárez. I love it. It is a needy city and I can help my city. I can make a little difference."

As he blurts out his love, we are at a red light. A boy with needle marks racing up and down his arms fills his mouth with gasoline, raises a torch, and then spits fire into the air.

I tell people I hate Juárez. I tell people I am mesmerized by Juárez. I tell myself Juárez is a duty. And I keep going back, month after month, year after year. I tell people I go to Juárez for the beaches. Or I tell people I go to Juárez for the waters.

Often, people tell me I don't know the real Juárez, a place of discos, party-hearty souls, laughter, and good times. I do not argue.

I go for what I do not know. I go in the vain hope of understanding how a city evolves into a death machine. I watch modern factories rise, I see American franchises pop up along the avenues. Golden arches peddle burgers, but old MacDonald no longer has a farm. He lives in a shack in an outlaw colonia, there is no water, the electricity is pirated, and dust fills his lungs.

Everyone has a job, according to the authorities.

Every year, some mysterious form of accounting belches forth new economic statistics, and these numbers get bigger and bigger.

The city slowly crumbles, the dead clutter the *calles*.

And I keep going back and I have given up explaining my task to others. Or to myself.

Like so many people in the city, I am a slave to it and no longer question my bondage.

. . .

The new death house is about a mile from the old death house, the one uncovered in January 2004 that had twelve bodies buried in the patio. And about halfway between the two death houses is another house where the Mexican authorities staged a raid and found a lot of guns and bullets. It is a lovely two-story building with nice tile forming a frieze just under the roofline. The front door is open—it's been smashed by a battering ram, but no one is at home at the moment. They've been taken to a frisky interrogation by the authorities. Two cameras stare at me—and I know they are operating because the wheel on the electric meter is spinning.

I reach down and pick up a big key made out of wood with little hooks for all those household keys. It has the name of a man and a woman burned into it, plus the phrase, "Remember Durango," and two scorpions, the famous symbol of that Mexican state.

But the wooden key is not what catches my real notice, nor do the surveillance cameras matter much. It is the red Jeep Cherokee with dark, tinted windows and two burly men that suddenly shows up, slows, and rolls on. Then it comes by again, and the men do not smile. Across the street, I see a man standing next to a fine black Audi. He is on his cell phone, staring at me. In traffic, a few moments later, the red Cherokee again appears by my side. I peel off and return to the newly discovered death house.

I have been given notice, and now I feel at home.

Eventually, thirty-six bodies come out of the second death house. The Mexican forensic pathologist at the dig begs the newspapers not to publish her name or face, though the story reveals the name of the cadaver dog, "Rocco." The neighbors say they noticed nothing and thought the occasional gatherings at the walled compound must be for fiestas of some sort. The bodies have a curious fate. The government will not reveal where they are, or permit families with missing relatives to view them.

In late February 2008, ten or twenty men with automatic rifles and black masks descended on a poor barrio of shacks in the hills above Juárez. The area is home to men and women who work in the maquiladoras. One man, a former municipal cop in his early thirties, runs a little store that sells beans, bread, and milk. That day, the armed men tortured him until he revealed who supplied him with the drugs he also sold out of his little store. He could not have been really surprised by the visit—after all, he'd been warned in two phone calls to stop selling drugs. The armed men took him to where his supplier made concrete blocks. There they beat up some workers until finally, one man came out of a building and said, "I am the man you are looking for." The armed men then took the two captives off a short ways and executed them—everyone in the barrio heard the shots. All this action was hard to miss since it happened around noon on a sunny day.

Now I am here at the kill site. A woman stares at me and shouts, "Who are you looking for?" and from her tone, I don't think she is trying to be helpful. As I rolled in, I could feel the eyes of loitering *cholos* burn into my hide.

So I leave.

But I have a question. If the violence in Juárez is simply a battle between big cartels to control this crossing into the United States, then why are murders happening all over the city to small-time drug sellers like the man who ran the little grocery in this poverty-stricken neighborhood?

After the killing, the armed men took the bodies away and dumped them down by the river, where the huge Mexican flag lords over El Paso.

The giant flagpole was the creation of a Mexican president in the 1990s, a matter of national pride in the spot where his nation confronts its rich and powerful neighbor. This moment of patriotism has now been turned to other uses.

Killers seem to like this place, the linear park around the giant flagpole down by the river. Since 1997, at least fourteen bodies have been dumped here, including the former cop who ran the small store and sold drugs, and his friend who made concrete blocks and supplied him with drugs. The neighborhood facing the park is middle class, and signs ask residents to keep the park clean. At one point, a prominent lawyer who lived there posted his own sign asking people not to dump bodies or garbage. In October, he was executed in his home. A month later, one daughter was killed, and then, in the funeral procession for her, another daughter, a nurse from El Paso, was killed. The authorities blamed the murders on domestic problems.

For me, it is a piece of memory, as are other spots in the city. In the summer of 1997, when Amado Carrillo died, there was a spate of murders in Juárez as a new arrangement of power evolved. On August 3 of that year, two well-dressed men entered the Max Fim restaurant. When they left, six men were dead. Another killing happened nearby at Jeronimo's, a popular bar and restaurant. Dozens died that month, and then the city calmed and everyone tried to return to business as usual.

I sit in a sushi parlor, the one whose owner was the former head of police and now faces serious charges in El Paso for running drugs. In 1997, another player in the drug world died two tables away from me. The restaurant is upscale, something that seems airlifted out of midtown Manhattan. The blank faces of the diners betray no awareness of the past. In a sense, it never happened.

History erases itself in Juárez. The newspapers cast out their photographs of murders, and the clippings vanish, also. Police records disappear. In the end, there is a spicy tuna roll on a small plate, some soy sauce, and the wind moving dust down the streets.

For years, people have sought a single explanation of violence in Juárez. The cartels are handy as an explanation. Serial killers also help in explaining dead women. The hundreds of street gangs also can be pulled off the shelf to retire any question. As can mass poverty, uprooted families that migrate here from the interior, corrupt cops, corrupt government, and on and on.

We insist that power must replace power, that structure replaces an earlier structure. And we insist that power exists as a hierarchy, that there is a top where the boss lives and a bottom where the prey scurry about in fear of the boss. Also, we believe the state truly owns power and violence, and that is why any nonstate violence by people earns them the name of outlaws.

Try for a moment to imagine something else, not a new structure but rather a pattern, and this pattern functionally has no top or bottom, no center or edge, no boss or obedient servant. Think of something like the ocean, a fluid thing without king and court, boss and cartel. Give up all normal ways of thinking. We live in a time where fantasies focus on omnipotent authorities. We think someone reads our mail, listens in on our conversations, watches us from spy satellites, stalks us with computers. As a mirror image of this, we imagine underground networks of power—cartels, terrorist organizations, mafias, rogue intelligence agencies, and the like. These illusions are teddy bears we clutch in the dark hours, comforts that enable us to sleep.

Two towers fall.

Fifteen to twenty million people enter the country illegally.

The drugs reach Main Street on schedule.

The largest war machine in the history of the world grinds to a halt in the sands of Mesopotamia.

Violence courses through Juárez like a ceaseless wind, and we insist it is a battle between cartels, or between the state and the drug world, or between the army and the forces of darkness.

But consider this possibility: Violence is now woven into the very fabric of the community and has no single cause and no single motive and no on-off button.

Violence is not a part of life, now it is life.

Just ask Miss Sinaloa.

I sit on the mezzanine in the fine shopping mall and have a pastry with a cup of espresso. The air is cool and clean. Outside, men guide cars into parking spaces. This big chamber of business is an escape from the noise of Juárez. I buy ten kilos of beans for the people out in El Pastor's crazy place.

A week or so later, there is a shooting in the parking lot. One of the old men who guides cars into the slots goes down, a sidebar to a barrage of automatic gunfire.

The city protects itself by telling stories about itself. The police captain who was machine-gunned with his eight-year-old son is now explained by the city in this fashion. He was a dirty cop, kidnapping rich people for ransom. But then the families of the kidnap victims grew angry about him. So, in order to stay safe, he always traveled with his child, since he believed no one would kill an innocent child in order to kill him. But, the city tells itself, he was wrong. A family member of a kidnap victim did kill the captain and in that act also murdered his eight-year-old boy. But this was excusable because the killings were an act of retribution.

And so in this story swirling around Juárez, the murder of a child is made sense of and thus made safe for everyone. The story is not based on facts. No one requires facts. The story is based on need.

And the need for explanation is great.

Good Friday brings eleven executions, La Gloria brings six, and on Easter Sunday, another eleven die. I float in a dreamtime of death.

It is 1 P.M. on Easter Sunday, and in a street of maquila workers, a crowd gathers to look at a corpse. The guy is nineteen and belongs to a gang. A hole in his head has blown out one eye. Members of the opposing gang sit in the bed of a police pickup truck while one cop fills out a form. I stare at a young gang kid. As a photographer raises his camera, he pulls his sweatshirt up to cover his face. His eyes are dead and empty, maybe the gaze left by too much glue and paint sniffing. But his middle fingers flash a gang sign and they are covered with blood.

A car stops, three young girls—twelve or thirteen years old—race across the street as the father keeps the motor idling. They hold hands as they skip into the crowd and form a smiling chorus line of Capri pants and tube tops. This has become the norm—kids, parents, babes in arms, all show up on the killing grounds. Some people bring their dogs, children make videos, snap photographs. Sometimes the kids get a bonus, since the bodies now and then are of children.

It is now 1:30 P.M. and suddenly the police race away with the body. Another killing has been called in. The city morgue is overwhelmed—by midnight there will have been 103 murders in Juárez in March. Forty bodies are tossed into a common grave due to lack of space and because the families either do not claim the corpses or cannot afford a funeral.

President Calderón's war against drugs has been officially rolling since December 1, 2006, and so far, according to the government tally, 3,800 Mexicans have gone down in drug killings, 334 cops have been murdered, and 39 soldiers have perished. Since January 2008, the number of drug killings is officially up 30 percent nationwide, but in Juárez, it is more like 60 to 70 percent and rising.

The hillside is rock, soil, yuccas, and creosote. This is Granjas Unidas (United Farms), a sweep by the poor into the hillside just above Juárez. It is nearing 3 P.M. and the ambulance rolls down the dirt track with the body. Off the road, a valley fills with tires and other garbage, and around this dump, people live in shacks and raise a few pigs, chickens, turkeys, and goats. The tiny grocery store is called Illusion. Just off the track is a fading carton of Mr.

Clean. A generous splotch of red blood gleams, and flies buzz around it. This is where the executed man fell. Broken glass glitters on the ground. The wind is about thirty miles per hour, and Juárez chokes on dust. A man walks his dog, mainly pit bull from its look, and he uses a tire chain as the leash. A woman comes by with three children. No one looks over at the flies buzzing above the fresh blood. The dead man has already been erased from memory.

At 5:21 P.M., the comandante of Grupo Delta dies in front of his home. His task force focuses on drug dealers and gangs. He is new to the job—the previous comandante of the unit was executed in January. A group of armed men machine-guns him. Then they leave, but soon return to *rematar*, to re-kill. Maybe they were worried their initial barrage was insufficient. Besides, they are in no hurry. It is broad daylight in the neighborhood, but the killers linger over the body for thirty minutes. An ambulance arrives, sees the killers, and is ordered over the radio to back off. The press arrives and also retreats. Finally, when it is safe and the assassins have left, the police arrive. That is the way it goes now in Juárez.

The day moves into night. In the dark hours near the Zaragoza Bridge, a major crossing point for trucks into the United States, five bodies are dumped. They have been tortured and strangled.

And then at the end of March 2008, the governor of Chihuahua suddenly emerges from his seclusion, thanks to some sessions with acupuncture that have unfrozen his face. He announces that every police element in the state has been infiltrated by drug people. He also says that federal experts are coming to cleanse the forces. A state legislator goes the governor one better. He says the economy of the state is completely overrun by narco-trafficking. But no matter, the governor promises that the violence will soon lessen.

The Mexican army arrives with yet more force on March 30–31, an additional two thousand men are added to those already patrolling the city. Before, the troops appeared unannounced. Now there is fanfare as the military begins the Joint Chihuahua Operation. For days, they have been noticed trickling into the city, and for days, the army has denied the presence of any new units. In addition, five or six hundred federal police agents descend.

Juárez is now secure, that is the official word. The newspapers are suddenly empty of murders. The American press says order has been restored, which is odd in one way, since the slaughter in Juárez over the past three months has barely merited mention in the U.S. press. But of course, there have been quiet moments before, times when it seems Juárez wallows in a Quaker calm, and then, someone finds a death house and bodies come spewing out to make a lie of those moments of peace. Now, death goes underground in Juárez and citizens celebrate the return of normal times.

Six city cops are grabbed by the army when it discovers that the cops are broadcasting army movements. This last act is hardly strange since many cops feel the army is hunting and killing them. The six cops are tortured, pissed on, and eventually released by the army so that they can tell other officers of their lesson.

"If there are bad elements," one cop with seventeen years on the streets tells the press, "then they should go after them, but those of us who are doing our jobs well and trying to do the best for the citizens, we do not deserve to be detained, nor arrested and accused of crimes. It is an injustice to us and our families who are filled with anxiety that they will arrest us or kill us."

The vague "they" refers to the Mexican army sent to give Juárez peace and security. During March, forty-seven Juárez cops resign or request reassignment.

For over fifty years, Mexico has been reinventing law enforcement to pretend to fight drugs and placate the United States. Sinaloa in the 1940s was drug central and run by a former Mexican secretary of war and defense. In 1953, a flying school in Culiacan was closed to placate the United States, and yet by the late 1960s at least six hundred secret airfields flourished in northern Mexico (the beat goes on—in 2007, the Mexican army claimed to close two secret narco-airports a day).

More recently, a series of agencies have tackled drugs. Dirección Federal de Seguridad (DFS), trained by the CIA, was supposed to eliminate drug merchants and radicals in the early 1970s. By the 1980s, its staff either worked for or led cartels, including the one in Juárez. In the mid-1990s, a new force under a Mexican drug czar flourished, until it was discovered that the czar worked for the Juárez cartel and so did many of his agents. It was dissolved.

Under President Ernesto Zedillo (1994–2000), a new incorruptible force, Fiscalía Especializada en Atención de Delitos contra la Salud (FEADS), was created. One part deserted, became the Zetas, and functionally took over the Gulf cartel in the early days of the new century. In 1997, an organized crime unit was formed to tackle the cartels, and at the same moment in Mexico City, the agents of yet an earlier squad assigned to fight drugs were found dead in a car trunk. FEADS was finally dissolved in 2003 when it was found to be hopelessly corrupt. Under President Felipe Calderón, yet a new federal mutation emerged—AFI (Agencia Federal de Investigación). Its head was murdered in the spring of 2008. His dying words to his killer were, "Who sent you?" The government later determined the hit was done by the Sinaloa cartel, with the killers led by a former officer in the agency.

Now all hopes rest in the Mexican army. In over a half century of fighting drugs, Mexico has never created a police unit that did not join the traffickers. Or die.

A teenage girl from Juárez crosses into El Paso with six large cans of hominy and jalapeño peppers. U.S. Customs finds that the containers hold twenty-five pounds of marijuana.

Jonathan Lopez Gutierrez heads a forty-year-old charity, Emmanuel Ministries, that runs a shelter for one hundred children in Juárez. He crosses from El Paso on March 19 with a van full of roofing shingles. U.S. Customs finds six .223-caliber high-powered rifles and a .50-caliber semiautomatic under the roofing material. He confesses that since June 2007, he's brought at least fifty weapons into Mexico.

There is punishment for police failure in Juárez. The cop assigned to guarding the monument of fallen officers, the man on duty when hooded men came in a pickup truck and left a funeral wreath with the names of recently murdered cops and of the seventeen cops they planned to murder, well, he is arrested for thirty-six hours. And then charged with negligence. Of course, he is probably simply grateful to be alive. Also, the city police go before a local judge and ask him to stop the army from torturing them. The final kill tally for March hits 117, with the government figuring 60 percent of killings as gang violence over retail drugs.

The government offers up a scorecard on murder so the hometown fans can keep track. It goes like this and insists on a drumbeat: For the year 2008, there are 211 killings through March 31, for all of 2007 there were 301 killings, 2006 had 253, 2005 had 227, 2004 had 204, 2003 had 186, 1995 had 294, the year I first find my Juárez, as everyone will in good time, and baby won't ya follow me down?

The forty-five bodies found in the two death houses are difficult to assign since no one knows the exact year of their murders. So are the twenty people, according to official reports, who have been snatched from the streets and who have not returned. The dead and missing linger like bitter wine on the tongue of the city. Besides, no one knows where these remains have been moved—the authorities remain silent about the secret new bone yard—so fuck 'em, the dead, and the officials that won't let us embrace our dead.

But now that the military patrols the city, all is well. On March 31, the Juárez paper captures the new calm: The police fear the army, two dead bodies are found, tortured, strangled, with bags covering their heads, the military arrests five and confiscates drugs, there is an assault on a perfume store, a man is severely beaten in an attack, a man and woman are beaten to death in houses next door to each other, a municipal employee tries to hang himself in a shopping mall, the secretary of public security pleads with the public to care for their children after four cases of child rape in the city, and a drunk is run over in the street yesterday before dawn. Within ten days of the army patrols of the city, forty-seven cops have officially fled the force, thirty-seven cops have been busted by the army, three female police officers are rumored to have been raped, and a silence descends on the community.

The town feels emptied out even though the church is full of flowers from a big, expensive wedding. Padre José Abel Retana stands in his vestments as the bride and groom beam on the church steps, a mariachi band playing them into their new lives. The padre is a short, solid man who looks a lot like El Chapo Guzman, leader of the Sinaloa cartel that is credited with many of the murders going on in the area of Palomas, a dwindling community on the border just below Columbus, New Mexico.

"Yes," he softly smiles, "many people tell me that. Let me change into my jeans, so I look *guapo*, handsome."

And then he disappears to change. His flock is now a bloody mess. In May, Padre Abel held funeral masses for nine murdered men in one week—two for a father and son slaughtered on the main street of town on a Friday, five more for men leaving their wake on a Sunday. At the burial, soldiers stood at arms since more killings at the cemetery are a real possibility in the current climate of Mexico.

For decades, the town fed off tourists who came for cheap dentistry, medicine, glasses, and the drug trade—when Padre Abel arrived five years ago, he remembers how each week, a shipment of three to five tons of marijuana would roll through and pass, without a problem, right into the United States. In the late 1990s, people smuggling boomed, and today, the town is rimmed with ghost motels, big units thrown up for storing people for shipment and now empty. Also, on every street there are houses for sale, and big houses on dirt lanes stand abandoned. As the border tightened, people smuggling moved away and Palomas starved.

But the killing boomed. By late May 2008, this small, broken community had witnessed thirty-seven murders, mainly drug executions, that year, and seventeen more locals had been snatched and disappeared. Now the Mexican army is here, camped on the edge of town.

In a town this small, the killers and the slain know each other. And Padre Abel tends to all of them. He has two churches: an old, small stone one facing the plaza built in 1948, when work meant ranching, and a new, large one with many big stained-glass windows built a half dozen years ago, when work meant drugs, people smuggling, and slaughter.

Padre Abel's office is in this new church, and that is where we sit.

He is a very serious man. He comes from Jalisco, a drug center in Mexico, and has been a priest for twenty-two years. Before Palomas, he served the migrant community for years in Chicago, a city he loved. The padre out of his clerical clothing looks like the guy you meet in the store on Saturday toting a twelve-pack, after a week of toil, but in his case, the toil is too bitter and harsh for a good Saturday night.

I'm here because on May 11, 2008, he gave a sermon against the killings, naming names in the drug industry and saying this must stop. The newspaper account notes everything in the sermon, but does not print the names. Such announcements are generally fatal for reporters and priests. Padre Abel says that no one will kill a priest and insists the naming thing was overblown, that he mentioned only a few, and that everyone knew who they were and so forth. I can hear the door closing as it often does in Mexico—there is a brief moment of truth, then this is followed by a growing silence, and then the memory of the truth vanishes and is no more.

"It started last year in April," the padre says softly. In one case, a car with four men drove up to U.S. Customs full of bullet holes. Three of the men were dead, including the driver—"And then it got calm and it came back in January and we are not just talking about dead people, but the disappeared, a lot of people, they just take them away."

He seems to sink into himself as he rolls through the history and nature of the business, how each place has a man in charge, and how this person controls all the smuggling and killing and it has always been that way, and yet this tidal wave of blood is without any precedent and so something is new.

"The plaza," he offers, "belongs to the Juárez cartel, and it seems like Chapo Guzman wants this area. The army drives around, but they don't do anything. There are a few cops here, but when the hit men come, it is like a thousand against ten." He suddenly becomes animated and imitates the burst of an AK-47. He is fumbling now, reaching out for conventional explanations—a cartel war, the army, hit men—things that worked in the past, but this is not the past.

He almost sighs and he says, "I think the government is causing more insecurity . . . because the army does nothing. There is a shoot-out and the army does not come because they say they don't have orders to get close. I don't know if the army is killing or the hit men, but whoever it is, we think the government is behind it."

I leave the office and now I stand three blocks from the church in front of a big disco named Los Tres Amigos. The padre's words ring in my head—"There was a person taken from here and he saw the faces of his kidnappers and they said, 'We don't care, we're going to kill you, anyway,' but he escaped and he knows that some of them are from here." The Tres Amigos features a logo with a frog, crocodile, and parrot—all three animals slang terms for cocaine. The man who saw the faces and escaped owned this place, and he vanished during Carnival in early March. The doors of the business still tout a big party on the lip of Lent.

The man is okay. He was left alone for a spell, broke a glass, cut his plastic handcuffs, and fled. He now lives in Phoenix. The padre is okay for the moment. He believes no one will kill a priest.

A week after our conversation, a man crawls into the U.S. port of entry at Columbus. His body is burns. Someone had spent a week pouring acid on his skin and applying hot irons, all this while the padre and I talked about the slaughter.

The army claims it has killed fourteen in a shoot-out in early April in Parral in southern Chihuahua and one of the dead is from a town, Villa Ahumada, a little south of Juárez. At the funeral, two hundred people gather. And then the military blocks off the burying ground and helicopters hover overhead and command the mourners to hit the ground. Soldiers search the cars of the grieving; they also open the casket and search it. This goes on for three hours. Children are allowed to leave, and they stand outside the cemetery crying for their parents. The body is finally buried at 7:30 P.M. They are searching for nothing. They are delivering terror.

The mother of the dead boy cannot be found. Her house is empty, the lights are on, and the doors are open, the contents are in disarray. She is somewhere out there under the protection of the Mexican army, or at least the last time she was seen she was with them.

A block from a death house, and the city hums with its little bits of business. The faces of the people are about work and bills and Friday night and that first cup of coffee in the morning. It is the same a block from a murder. The killings are tiny tears in a huge tapestry called Juárez. When I walk across the bridge into El Paso, there are no murders and Juárez becomes a mural covered with dust that lacks events.

Success has come to Juárez. Thanks to the army's vigilance, there are only 52 murders in the month of April, a 55 percent drop from March. Officially. Of these murders, there are zero arrests. This brings the score for the first four months of 2008 to 262 dead and compares with 101 for the same period in 2007, 70 in 2006, 71 in 2005, and 64 in 2004. If this success rate holds— the army has announced it plans to be around indefinitely—that would produce a slaughter in Juárez of 600 souls every twelve months, double its recent kill rate.

A drink in hand is necessary for thinking about this military achievement. First, no one knows who is doing the killing, but two thousand soldiers and six hundred federal police have managed to bring Juárez to its highest annual murder rate in history. Second, there are no arrests, and it seems strange that such a massive force with roadblocks all over the city cannot, even by accident, bag one single killer. Third, there is the matter of the army torturing cops, raping female cops, and answering to no one. And finally, there is the thing whispered in the city, the thing no media on either side of the line will publish: that the army is doing the killing and, hence, sees little need for arrests since the cases are not mysteries to it.

Violence in Juárez always has an ability to become invisible. Since no one trusts the police, crime statistics are often guesswork because citizens of the city do not report what has happened to them. Since the police are often criminals, there is little incentive for them to fight crime. Since torture is the basic forensic tool of law enforcement, the elements of law and order have developed few, if any, skills in solving crimes. Since virtually everyone arrested confesses after enough beatings, there is a patina of crime fighting to disguise the actual business of a gangster state. Since all of this is obvious, it is almost never said and very often not even consciously believed. In most instances, the criminal police and the citizens both share in a fantasy that the crimes are being investigated, the criminals being tamed, and the person standing before them in a uniform and carrying a badge is part of the solution rather than part of the problem.

In the past, violence has flowed through the city like a river of blood, and sometimes the river ran on the surface and at other times, in order to make a political point or calm public apprehensions, the river went underground—literally—with the dead tossed into holes in the desert or buried in town in the backyards of death houses. But given the poverty, the corruption of the police, and the needs of the drug industry to enforce deals, the killing was fairly constant. No one wished to believe this fact. When murders declined, especially drug executions, there was a feeling something had passed by and now that it was behind everyone, a new kind of Juárez had evolved. When the killings got bad and the bodies were left in the streets like ornaments decorating the city's secret way of life, then everyone said that it hardly mattered because only those in the life died and they were only killing each other. Few wished to consider what the expression "in the life" meant and how much of the city was either given over to the drug industry or fed off it.

Now the killing is more public than ever and the numbers keep climbing, and no one can explain why, except by claiming the tools of the past—the cartels are responsible and they have suddenly gone crazy.

Everything is supposed to get better. This conclusion is never explained, it is simply asserted. The economy will always get better, and this will make every single human being better. The drug consumption will go away, and all the bodies will glow with new health. The energy systems that drive human communities will morph from one form to another form, but they will always deliver the amount of energy desired at the price that is bearable. Eventually, with some more work in the laboratories, we will live a hundred, maybe two hundred years, maybe forever. We must be patient, but this future is certain. Places without factories will get factories, places that have seen factories close will get something even better for employment. No one will be hungry, no one will be fat, no one will be ugly, and no one will be without love. Education will spread like a plague, and everyone will know more because information is the future—not fabricating metals, or digging in the earth, or plowing fields, or sewing clothes. The distinctions between the sexes will erode, and rights will be equal for both man and woman. Tribes will melt away. So, too, will nations. Wars will cease, and peace will come. Democracy will win. There is no other choice: It is written. Tragedies will not be performed, because they will have no meaning. There will be no sacrifices; such acts will be unnecessary and unintelligible.

Miss Sinaloa knows a different future. There will be cocaine and whiskey and it will help, but it will never prove sufficient to the need. And the need will not be denied. She knows these things but will not tell me the answers. What is violence? What does it mean for violence to be out of control? And where, within this thing called violence, do we fit this thing called murder? Maybe it is the coke, she loves that coke. Or the whiskey. And maybe it is neither. Maybe the problem with my understanding her is that I already know and refuse to see what is before me and to face what is in me.

I want to explain the violence as if it were a flat tire and I am searching the surface for a nail. But what if the violence is not a kind of breakdown, but more like a flower springing from the rot on a forest floor? The families, the crosses on the wall, the uniforms of the police, the street signs advising safe speeds, all these things are the nails in a tire long dead and flat, the chants of a vanished religion. The *cholos* with cold eyes, short lives, and the itch to put a bullet through the head are the function. The drugs dusting everyone's life are the way. The hydra-headed monster we seek, the creature killing all over the city, is like sunshine in fact, and this new light falls equally on one and all.

The factories are now the house of death, offering no future, poisoning the body with chemicals, destroying the spirit faster than cocaine or meth.

Juárez is not behind the times. It is the sharp edge slashing into a time called the future. We have made careers out of studying the Juárezes of the world, given them the name Third World. We have fashioned schemes to bring them into our place beside the sacred fire and called these schemes development. Each new building with a wall of glass stands as a temple to our ambitions to pour the mash of human life on this planet into one mold. But always, a place like Juárez is seen over the shoulder, some city glimmering in our own past, a place we have moved beyond, and now, with a few magical tugs of our economic ropes, we intend to bring Juárez and its sister cities around the world promptly into our orbit of power and largess. We count the employment, we tally the exports, we rummage in the till, and we comfort ourselves with these numbers because that is our safe place. We do not wander the *calles*—in Juárez, there is a actually a private bridge so that the masters of American capital can visit their holdings here without squandering precious time in the long lines of machines that are the crossing for the rest of humanity. All our understanding of such places is based on the new buildings and the calming numbers. And we are careful what we count. Every story on Juárez says it has 1.2 million people or 1.4 million even though for at least a decade it has had more than 2 million people. But if it really has 2 million people, then all the numbers treasured by business and two governments are diminished. More taxes must be repatriated from Mexico City, and suddenly a huge shortfall in paved roads, sewers, water, electricity, police, and public transport must be admitted. A simple shift in total population takes Juárez from the column called developing to the column called failure. So we are careful in what we see and what we count and what we admit.

But what if Juárez is not a failure? What if it is closer to the future that beckons all of us from our safe streets and Internet cocoons? Here, boys stand on corners with pistols because there is no work, or if there is work, it pays little or nothing. Here, the girls walk by in their summer clothes, but they do not believe in the seasons or in harvest time. Here, Thanksgiving, Christmas, and Easter come and go without much fanfare save a drunken spree to memorialize a dead belief system. This is the way of bullet-street with graffiti on the walls, steel bars on the windows, faces peering out with caution, and corpses on the shattered sidewalks.

After decades of this thing called development, Juárez has in sheer numbers more poor people than ever, has in real purchasing power lower wages than ever, has more pollution than ever, and more untreated sewage and less water than ever. Every claim of a gain is overwhelmed by a tidal wave of failure. And yet this failure, I have come to realize, is not failure. The gangs are not failure. The corrupt police are not failure. The drugs, ever cheaper and more potent and more widespread, are not failure. The media is increasingly tame here, just as it is in that place that once proudly called itself the first world, a place now where wars go on with barely a mention and the dead are counted but not photographed.

Everything in Juárez will soon be state-of-the-art. For years, the prosperous here have bundled themselves into gated communities, and now these strongholds are not sufficient, and security has vanished from the life of the city. After all, this is a city where the publisher of the newspaper and the mayor and his family live across the line in the United States in order to feel safe. There is no job retraining in Juárez because there are no new jobs to be trained for. The future here is now, the moment is immediate, and the message is the crack of automatic weapons. All the other things happening in the world—the shattering of currencies, the depletion of resources, the skyrocketing costs of food, energy, and materials—are old hat here. Years ago, hope moved beyond reach, and so a new life was fashioned and now it crowds out all other notions of life.

Please be advised that there will be no apocalypse. The very idea of a Götterdämmerung assumes meaning and progress. You cannot fall off a mountain unless you are climbing. No one here is slouching toward Bethlehem to be born. We shall not meet next year in Jerusalem. For years, I thought I was watching the city go from bad to worse, a kind of terrible backsliding from its imagined destiny as an America with different food. I was blind to what was slapping me in the face: the future. A place where conversation is a gun and reality is a drug and time is immediate and tomorrow, well, tomorrow is today because there is no destination beyond this very second.

Things can be fixed now if I can just find a clean needle. After all, heroin is cheap, and the purity is very high. Imagine a world with an absence of work that will pay your bills, a place where gasoline and electricity cost more than a simple fix for your soul. You don't even dream about a room of your own. You don't worry about retirement, either, or how you can pay that dental bill. You don't fret about things like overpopulation. You don't fret, for that matter. Nor do you accept things. You finally live, and life is about what is and what is stares up at you with orphan eyes.

The mayor announces a plan to put three thousand cameras in the banks and schools and businesses of Juárez. The police threaten to go on strike because of abuse from federal officers and from the army. They hold a vigil for two days with family members, and all of them wear masks for security reasons. Want ads in the newspaper recruit students—"We are looking for students with valid passports and visas to work during spring break. We offer well-paying jobs." The authorities advise that these solicitations are placed by people in the drug industry who are seeking drivers to ferry drugs into the United States. The army seizes twenty-two employees of the Chihuahua state attorney's office. They wish to ask them questions. This is in a news release. No report of the answers to these questions has surfaced. The city of Juárez announces a new urban anthem for the populace. The song is titled "Ciudad Juárez, Valor de Mexico," which roughly means "Juárez, Jewel of Mexico." The opening lines go,

Juárez is our city,
the best of the borders,
because it was born with courage
and built its history with great faith and hope.

A city official explains, "We feel that Juárez, despite all its problems has great riches . . . We don't always realize that Juárez is a jewel of Mexico, and has many, many positive things that we should extol."

The violence is explained. It turns out, according to a U.S. official deep in the drug war industry, that all the dead people are turning up simply because the Zetas have hooked up with the Juárez cartel to fight the Sinaloa cartel for the crossing. The official hopes that the Mexican army will now capture the heads of these various cartels. But, he cautions, such tasks are not simple.

"You cut the head off the mother snake," he explains, "and you deal with the babies. Are they poisonous? Sure. But they are babies."

The police arrest a teacher in one of the city's private high schools. He's also a lawyer. Noe Bautista Vega is twenty-four years old, and according to the authorities, he's been playing hooky. They have him down for seven bank robberies.

A bishop announces that the leaders in the drug industry have been kind to the church and generous to their communities. The bishop also heads the Mexican Bishops Conference. He notes that the drug folk help out with public works—things like electricity, telecommunications, highways, and roads—in rural areas, where the government seldom leaves a mark. They also build churches.

"There have been some who have approached us and asked for orientation about how to change their lives," he notes. And he says, they come "from all levels."

A tapestry is woven every day so that there will be no loose threads. Cartels battle in the new fabric, the army restores order, bank robbers are punished, and bishops are reprimanded if they mess up the weave. Mexican Attorney General Eduardo Medina Mora explains away the surge in violence by asserting that all the newly minted dead people simply indicate the waning of the cartels "and how these structures as we knew them are collapsing." Good Friday, clearly, indicates this collapse. Twenty-three Mexicans were executed around the country that day. A musician performing in a town south of Mexico City died when someone opened up on the entire band as they played a set. Some unnamed soul also pitched a grenade into an army convoy on the Gulf coast. All this goes into the loom and is made safe and sane.

We are experts at walling things off. At the moment, the United States is busy building a wall. There will be at least seven hundred miles thrown up along the line, with more on the way. Already, this simple chore is getting complicated. At Columbus, New Mexico, the wall stretches now for miles— fifteen-foot steel poles a few inches apart and plopped into three feet of concrete. Now the cutting begins, an almost daily assault by hacksaws and acetylene and plasma torches. Also, government video cameras have captured images of men with huge ladders who then descend on the other side using bungee cords. In sections, the fence is settling and gaps form large enough for a person to squeeze through. Of course, this is to be expected. Eighty miles to the east in El Paso, facing Juárez, a team of men must make daily repairs in the fence built there.

This is all part of the tapestry. As Juárez spins into a future that cannot be admitted by either government, the wall goes up to contain the mystery of blood and drugs and gangs and gunfire that must be explained away even as they are cordoned off by stout ramparts.

The former captain of the city police, Sergio Lagarde Felix, goes down in a barrage on May 2. He had quit the force in January, the same month comandantes began being killed on the street and the month that the lists of dead cops and soon-to-be-dead cops were posted on the police memorial monument. About noon yesterday in front of an auto mechanics shop, he took a round through the chest and one through the head. Five .40-caliber shells were found around his corpse and two more inside the business. He was forty-four. Formerly, he assisted the chief of police, but now his former chief is in jail in El Paso for setting up a drug deal in the United States.

There was another killing of a man thirty-five years of age. He took six, mainly in the head. He is the same man as the former captain, only in disguise in an earlier report. That can happen here, this shedding of years, this variation in the nature of one's death. This is the place of possibility and it has escaped the stranglehold of simple facts.

They find them in the bright light of morning in late May 2008. Five men wrapped in blankets. The blankets are made in China since global trade has wiped out the Mexican serape industry. Two of the men have been decapitated and their severed heads rest in plastic bags. Beside them is a sign indicating that they died because they are "dog fuckers."

Killing people is fun. There is a feeling of power in slaughtering other human beings. And for many in Juárez, a feeling of power is a rare thing. The men beat their women, and that helps, but it is hardly the same rush of exhilaration that comes from killing another person. If wife beating were really a decent substitute for slaughter, then murder would be all but absent in Mexico. But this is not the case.

No one knows how many assassins live and thrive in Juárez. There are an estimated five hundred street gangs—but our knowledge of these facts is limited since the city police's expert on gangs was executed in January 2008 at the beginning of a killing season that is humming along at more than one hundred corpses a month. Still, assume there are five hundred gangs. Assume that full membership requires murder, be conservative and say there are only ten members in each gang, and then you have five thousand young and frisky killers. To be sure, the Aztecas, one premier gang, have three thousand members, but why exaggerate the number of killers? Let's just say five thousand. This tally ignores the world floating about the gangs, the land of police and soldiers and cartels, where many other murderers find wages and niches.

You have two choices. Either you're going to be straight, get that job in an American factory in Juárez, work five and a half days a week for sixty or seventy bucks, going to do this even though no one can live on such a wage, going to do this even though you know the turnover in the plants is 100 to 200 percent a year, going to do this even though as you were coming up in the barrios you saw the men and women slowly devoured by the plants and then noticed that around age thirty, they were tossed away like old junk, yeah, you're going to do this, you're going to be straight.

Or you are going to take that ride, join a gang, learn to flash the sign, do little errands for guys with more power, get some of that money that flows through certain hands, snort some powder, and have the women eating out of your hand for a few hours in a discotheque, and you'll wear hip-hop clothing, have a short, burr haircut, never smile, stuff a pistol in your oversized britches. A big SUV rolls down the *calle*, you hop in, the windows are darkly tinted, and the machine prowls the city like a shark with its fanged mouth agape, and oh, it is so sweet when you squeeze the trigger and feel the burst run free and wild into the night air, see the body crumple and fall like a rag doll, roll on into the black velvet after midnight, and there'll be a party, fine girls and white powder, and people fear you, and the body falls, blood spraying, and you feel like God even though you secretly stopped believing in God some time ago, and they tell you that you will die, that your way of living has no future, and you see the tired men and women walking the dirt lanes after a shift in the factory, plastic bags of food dangling from their hands, and you caress the gun stuffed in your waistband, and life is so good and the killing is fun and everyone knows who has the guts to take the ride.

Dying is the easy part.

Killing is the fun part.

Taking that first ride is the hard part.

They call him "King Midas" because he owns so many venues. Willy Moya, forty-eight, is a success as he exits his V Bar, one of his many huge nightclubs, at 4 A.M. May 18. The building is the size of a warehouse, and it is but one piece of an empire—Hooligan's, Vaqueras y Broncos, Frida's, Tabasco's, Arriba Chihuahua, Willy's Country Disco, and so forth—that he lords over in the swank part of Juárez. He is standing in the center of his bodyguards when the bullet enters his skull. His bodyguards are unharmed. He is declared dead at the hospital only a block away. Until he falls dead on the ground, he is considered untouchable because he is rich and he is connected to other men with power and money.

I stand in front of his closed empire, and there is a huge, white bow over the door, a framed photo of him by the steps, with a candle and some wilted yellow roses.

Carlos Camacho is a former member of the federal congress, the environmental representative for Chihuahua in Ciudad Juárez and a member of the president's political party. He lives in a very good apartment complex, one with seven units and a parking lot full of fine cars. He is talking to his girlfriend on the phone when he tells her that the army is at the door. That is his last statement. The next day, he and two other residents of the complex are found dumped on the street, strangled, their bodies with signs of torture. No one wants to face this May killing. Camacho is the clean leader, a man widely known and liked. His family says publicly that the army is responsible. And then, they fall into silence.

It is just drug guys killing drug guys, and if it is not, then who is safe?

The Aroma restaurant is fine wood and mirrors and veal chops that go for forty-five dollars. I sample sushi, lobster bisque, and a forty-five-dollar bottle of Chilean red that would cost maybe six bucks in a U.S. supermarket. The café is on a plush avenue next to the rich district of Juárez, an area of mansions and guards and a country club. The rumor is that on May 17, fifty heavily armed men arrived here, took the cell phones of the customers, and told people they could not leave. Outside, the army guarded the serenity of the establishment. Then El Chapo Guzman swept in, dined, and left around 2 A.M. He paid everyone's tab. He is a man with a $5 million reward on his head and is said to be at war with the Juárez cartel. Yet everyone in the city seems to know of this visit to Aroma and believe it. That weekend, at least twenty people were murdered in Juárez as Chapo dined and the government of Mexico waged war on drug cartels.

The waiter brings a form for rating the dining experience. I check off everything as excellent and sign myself as El Chapo.

He is bubbling with energy, but then El Pastor always seems as though he is about to OD on a vitamin B shot. We are sitting in the Golden Corral in El Paso—El Pastor likes a good feed.

But the violence in Juárez is on his mind.

"There is a terror there right now," he says. "People are more kind. They don't honk their horns." Suddenly he is flapping his arms and going *honk honk honk*.

Lately, he's been going with people at shift change to the local police stations in Juárez and leading prayers with the cops.

"They are frightened," he explains. "I saw this woman cop get out of her car for her shift with her two little kids, and they were kissing her and crying because they were afraid she wouldn't come back. They are sending *narco-corridos* on the police radios an hour or two before a cop gets killed. The *sicarios*, the hit men, are kids, so skinny. But they get an AK-47 and they are powerful."

He broods about what drives the violence, where does all the death come from?

"They are fighting for power," he says, and now he is entering that Mexican moment where suddenly an unexplained "they" shows up, that fog of language that protects one's mind from what one knows. He sketches a world where the ruling party, the PRI, ran the country as a smiling dictatorship for seventy years and worked with, and yet had some control over, the drug industry. Then Vicente Fox upturned this order in 2000, when the opposition Partido Acción Nacional (PAN) took power and now, well, no one seems in control. This is a traditional view of things in Mexico, where the hard hand, the *mano dura*, is seen as essential to rule.

For El Pastor it is simple: "The police, the gangs, the governor, the state, now they all want the money. If the cartels agree, all the killings will calm down. We Mexicans know what is going on, but we cannot say anything, because if you say something, they kill you."

He pauses and then changes tone.

"You see birds walking on the pavement in Juárez," he explains, "and their heads dart from side to side because they are waiting for someone to throw a rock and kill them. This is the way it is for narcos."

That is the way explanations of the violence always go. There is the body, or the experience, the woman cop is terrified and so are her children, the *narco-corridos* boom through the police radio, and death is waiting, things are out of control. And then the retreat, the belief that it is a cartel war, or that the government is behind it, no matter, someone is in control and eventually order will be restored. This is the safe place amid the killing.

But El Pastor, the street preacher, has a nagging memory. A man who worked for a nightclub tycoon came to him and said, How much does your work with the crazy people cost? El Pastor said, ten thousand dollars a month. The man said, I can get you twenty thousand. El Pastor said, Is this money clean? The man said nothing.

No matter. A few days later, Willy Moya was shot in the head as he stood amid his herd of bodyguards.

El Pastor told the man he could pray for Willy Moya, but he did not want such money.

"Probably," El Pastor says, "Willy Moya wanted to clean his mind. He probably could feel death tapping him on the shoulder."

Murder Artist

I wait for the phone to ring. The first call came at 9:00 A.M. and said expect the next call at 10:05. So I drive fifty miles and wait. The call at 10:05 says wait until 11:30. The call at 11:30 does not come, and so I wait and wait. Next door is a game store frequented by men seeking power over a virtual world. Inside the coffee shop, it is calculated calm, and everything is clean.

I am in the safe country. I will not name the city, but it is far from Juárez and it is down by the river and it is electric with the life and quiet as an American dream. At noon, the next call comes.

We meet in a parking lot, our cars cooped like cops with driver next to driver. I hand over some photographs of Juárez murders. He quickly glances at them and then tells me to go to a pizza parlor. There, he says that we must find a quiet place because he talks very loudly. I rent a motel room with him. None of this can be arranged ahead of time because that would allow me to set him up.

This is the place he lives, a terrain where the simplest things can kill him. He always studies his rearview mirror. He never turns his back on anyone. Nor does he ever relax. Or trust.

He glances at the photographs, images never printed in newspapers. He stabs his finger at a guy standing over a half-exposed body in a grave and says, "This picture can get you killed." And then he tells me the man in the photograph is Number Two, the strong right arm of the boss.

I show him the photograph of the woman. She is lovely in her white clothes and perfect makeup. Blood trickles from her mouth, and the early morning light caresses her face. The photograph has a history in my life. Once, I placed it in a magazine, and the editor there got a call from a terrified man, the woman's brother, who asked, Are you trying to get me killed, to get my family killed? I remember the editor calling me up and asking me what I thought the guy meant. I answered, "Exactly what he said."

The next time the photograph came into play was at a bar in San Antonio, where I was having a beer with a DEA agent. He told me he knew her, that he'd been watching a stash house in El Paso when she came by. A few hours later, they took down the stash house, and the next day, her body was found in Juárez. He figured they thought she'd snitched off the stash house. But she had not. Her visit was a coincidence and had nothing to do with the case.

Now, he looks at her and tells me she was the girlfriend of the head of the *sicarios* in Juárez, and the guys in charge of the cartel thought she talked too much. Not that she'd ever given up a load or anything, it was simply the fact that she talked too much. So they told her boyfriend to kill her, and he did. Or he would die.

This is ancient ground. The term *sicario* goes back to Roman Palestine, where a Jewish sect, the Celotas, used concealed daggers to murder (*si carii* meaning a dagger carrier) the Romans or their supporters.

Silence is my old friend here, a thing that feels like a hand at the throat choking off all sound. It is not the silence of the grave or the silence of the church, but the speechlessness of terror. Words barely form in the mind. And after a while, even thoughts lose shape and float like ghosts. Things are explained, but the sentences have no subject, only a hint of a verb, and after a while, even the object is a muddled thing. Two men are found dead, showing signs of torture never clearly stated, spent brass around the bodies. Elements are killing people in the city. The authorities express outrage at mayhem and disorder. All this is a form of the silence. Juárez is a place where a declarative sentence may be an act of suicide.

He leans forward and says of the cartel leaders, "Amado and Vicente could kill you if they even thought you were talking."

Yes. Shortly before our talk, a woman—the daughter of that lawyer who posted the sign against dumping bodies or garbage—stands in front of the hotel owned by her family. She is cut down. Federal police are sleeping in a hotel. The building is strafed. But no one fires the bullets, they simply fly, tear through flesh, and eventually, the gunfire dies away and is absorbed by silence.

This photograph can get you killed. Words can get you killed. And all this will happen and yet you will die and the sentence will never have a subject, simply an object falling dead to the ground.

Sitting with the *sicario,* I feel myself falling down into some kind of well, some dark place that hums beneath the workaday city, and in this place, there is a harder reality and absolute facts. I have been living, I think, in a kind of fantasy world of laws and theories and logical events. Now I am in a country where people are murdered on a whim, a beautiful woman is found in the dirt with blood trickling from her mouth, and then she is wrapped with explanations that have no actual connection to what happened.

I have spent years getting to this moment. The killers, well, I have been around them before. Once, I partied with two hundred armed killers in a Mexican hotel for five days. But they were not interested in talking about their murders. He is.

What does he look like?

Just like you. Or me.

You will never see him coming. He is of average height, he dresses like a workman with sturdy boots and a knit cap. If he stood next to you in a checkout line, you would be unable to describe him five minutes later. Nothing about him draws attention to him. Nothing.

He has very thick fingers and large hands. His face is expressionless. His voice is loud but flat.

He lives beneath notice. That is part of how he kills.

He says, "Juárez is a cemetery. I have dug the graves for two hundred and fifty bodies."

The dead, the two hundred fifty corpses, are details, people he disappeared and put in holes in death houses. The city is studded with these secret tombs. Just today, the authorities discovered a skeleton. From the rotted clothing, forensic experts peg the bones to be those of a twenty-five-year-old man. He is one of a legion of dead hidden in Juárez.

That is why I am here. I have spent twenty years now waiting for this moment and trying to avoid being buried in some hole. At that party long ago with the two hundred gunmen, a Mexican federal cop wanted to kill me. The host stopped him, and so I continued on with my tattered life. But I have come to this room so that I can bring out my dead, the thousands who have been cut down on my watch.

We sit at a round wooden table, drapes closed.

He says, "Everything I say stays in this room."

I nod and continue making notes.

That is how it begins: Nothing is to leave the room, even though I am making notes, and he knows I will publish what he says because I tell him that. We are entering a place neither of us knows, a place where the secrets are dragged into the light of day, and yet, neither of us admits this, because it means death. I can never repeat what he tells me even though I tell him I will repeat it. Nothing must leave the room even though he watches me write his words down on sheets of paper.

I lean back and say, "No one will ever know your name or where we are meeting. I will never know your name. When we finish, I will not know how to find you again. But you will always know how to find me. I want the story of your life because you and the others like you are phantoms. I am not here to solve crimes. I am here to explain how the world works. When I publish what you tell me, no one will know your name. They will only know my name, and I will be unable to give you up, because I will not have any way to trace you."

He nods.

He tells me to feel the triceps on his right arm. It hangs down like a tire. Now, he says, feel my left arm. There is nothing there.

He stands, puts a chokehold on me. He can snap my neck like a twig.

Then he sits down again.

I ask him how much he would charge to kill me.

He gives me a cool appraisal and says, "At most, five thousand dollars, probably less. You are powerless and you have no connections to power. No one would come after me if I killed you."

We are ready to begin.

I ask him how he became a killer.

He smiles, and says, "My arm grew."

I feel calm. I realize the lies will finally stop. Of the thousands of executions that I have noted in Juárez, there has never been a single arrest, much less a conviction. Instead, the city copes by floating theories about cartel wars or military actions or police actions or gang actions. At the moment, murder is the leading cause of death in Juárez, outstripping the old leader, diabetes. I have listened to endless explanations of the slaughter. Now I have made it to the killing ground.

Information has all but ceased because of people such as him. Reporters are now being issued bulletproof vests, and articles appear without bylines. One editor of a media Web site was on his way to the funeral of the reporter gunned down in front of his daughter. His cell phone rang and a voice said, "You are next." He immediately fled to United States with his family and left behind his house, car, office, and life. Reporters zeroing in on killings get those warnings from their police radios, "If you get close, the same thing will happen to you." A press photographer runs into a caravan of armed men, but chokes because he knows a single snap of his camera would mean death. Another photographer comes upon armed men, and he cannot tell if they are police or *sicarios*. He snaps shots through his windshield, then puts the memory card in his sock so that if he is killed, there will be a record. He lives, and no, they were not police. Or the press pulls into a gas station, and men are there with long guns and pistols. Six men have just been executed, but the commandos at the gas station seem unworried and unhurried.

The man sitting across the table from me has helped to create such a world.

He takes a sheet of paper, draws five vertical lines and writes in the spaces in green ink: **Childhood, Police, Narco, God**. The four phases of his life. Then scratches out what he has written until there is nothing but solid ink on the page.

He cannot leave tracks. He cannot quite give up the habits of a lifetime.

I reach for the paper, but he snatches it back. And laughs. I think at both of us.

"When I believed in the Lord," he says, "I ran from the dead."

But now we turn to the time he worked for the devil.

"I had a normal childhood," he insists. He will not tolerate the easy explanation that he is the product of abuse.

"We were very poor, very needy," he continues. "We came to the border from the south to survive. My people went into the maquilas. I went to a university. I didn't have a father who treated me badly. My father worked, a working man. He started at the maquila at 6 P.M. and worked until 6 A.M., six days a week. The rest of the time he was sleeping. My mother had to be both father and mother. She cleaned houses in El Paso three days a week. There were twelve children to feed."

He pauses here to see if I understand. He will not be a victim, not of poverty, not of parents. He became a killer because it was a way to live, not because of trauma. His eyes are clear and intelligent. And cold.

"Once," he says, "my father took me and three of my brothers to the circus. We brought our own chilis and cookies so we did not have to spend money. That was the happiest day of my life. And the only time I went somewhere with my father."

His life breaks into two pieces. There is a kind of childhood with no money, not much food, parents always working, and a crowded, small house. He is in high school, aged either fifteen or sixteen, and the state police recruit him and his friends. They get fifty dollars to drive cars across the bridge to El Paso, where they park them and then walk away. They never know what is in the cars, nor do they ever ask. After the delivery, they are taken to a motel where cocaine and women are always available.

He drops out of the university because he has no money. And then the police dip into his set of friends who have been moving drugs for them to El Paso. And send them to the police academy. In his own case, because he is only seventeen, the mayor of Juárez has to intervene to get him into the academy.

"We were paid about a hundred and fifty pesos a month as cadets," he says, "but we got a bonus of a thousand dollars a month that came from El Paso. Every day, liquor and drugs came to the academy for parties. Each weekend, we bribed the guards and went to El Paso. I was sent to the FBI school in the United States and taught how to detect drugs, guns, and stolen vehicles. The training was very good."

After graduation, no one in the various departments really wanted him, because he was too young, but U.S. law enforcement insisted he be given a command position. And so he was.

"I commanded eight people," he continues. "Two were honest and good. The other six were into drugs and kidnapping."

Two units of the state police in Juárez specialized in kidnapping, and his was one such unit. One group would take the person and then hand the victim over to the other group to be killed, a procedure less time-consuming than guarding the victim until the ransom was paid. Sometimes, they would feign discovering the body a few days after the abduction.

That was the orderly Juárez he once knew. Then in July 1997, Amado Carrillo died. This was in his eyes an "earthquake." Order broke down. The payments to the state police from an account in the United States ended. And each unit had to fend for itself.

"I have no real idea how and when I became a *sicario*," he says. "At first, I picked up people and handed them over to killers. And then my arm began to grow because I strangled people. I could earn twenty thousand dollars a killing."

Before Carrillo's death, cocaine was not easy for him to get in Juárez, because "if you cut open a kilo, you died." So he and his crew would cross the bridge to El Paso and score. He is by now running a crew of kidnappers and killers, he is working for a cartel that stores tons of cocaine in Juárez warehouses, and he must enter the United States to get his drugs.

That changed after Carrillo's death. Soon he was deep into cocaine, amphetamines, and liquor and would stay up for a week. He also acquired his skill set: strangulation, killing with a knife, killing with a gun, car-to-car barrages, torture, kidnapping, and simply disappearing people and burying them in holes.

He mentions the case of Victor Manuel Oropeza, a doctor who wrote a column for the newspaper. He linked the police and the drug world. He was knifed to death in his office in 1991.

"The people who killed him, taught me. *Sicarios* are not born, they are made."

He became a new man in a new world.

He mentions a cartel leader in Juárez, "a man full of hate, a man who even hates his own family. He would cut up a baby in front of the father in order to make the father talk."

He says the man is a beast.

His eyes now are very dark, blank eyes, and behind them, I can sense he has returned to the murders, the tortures, all those things that seem so distant from this motel room where the exhaust fan roars and the colors are soft, sedating, and bland.

He is drifting now, going back in time to a place he has left, the killing ground when he would slaughter and then drop five grand on a single evening. He remembers when outsiders would try to move into Juárez and commandeer the plaza, the crossing. For a while, the organization killed them and hung them upside down. Then, for a spell, they offered Colombian neckties—throat cut, the tongue dangling through the slit. There was a spate of necklacing—the burned body found with a charred stub where the head had been, the metal cords of the tire simply blackened hoops embracing the corpse.

He has lived like a god and been the destroyer of worlds. I look down at the thick fingers on his large hands—"my arm grew"—and I can hear the last gasps of the people he has strangled. The room is still, so very still, the television a blank eye, the walls sedated with beige, the exhaust fan purring. His arms at rest on the wood table, everything solid and calm.

And fear. Not fear of me but of something neither of us can define, a death machine with no apparent driver. There is no headquarters for him to avoid, no boss to keep an eye peeled for. He has been green-lighted, and now anyone who knows of the contract can kill him on sight and collect the money. The name of his killer is legion.

He can hide, but that only buys a little time, and time just keeps rolling on and on. One serious mistake, and he is dead. His hunters can be patient. He is like a winning lottery ticket and one day they will collect. The death machine careens out on the streets, guns at ready, always rolling, no real route, randomly prowling and looking for fresh blood. The day comes and goes and ten die. Or more. No one can really keep count any longer, and besides, some of the bodies simply vanish and cannot be tallied.

He stares at me.

He says, "I want to talk about God."

I say, "We'll get to that."

He is the killer, and he does not know who is in charge. Just as he sometimes did not know the reason for the murders he committed. He will die. Someone will kill him. No one will really notice.

No place is safe, he knows that fact. A family in the States owed some money on a deal, so a fourteen-year-old son and his friend were snatched and taken back over. The kidnapper killed them with a broken bottle, then drank a glass of their blood. The man talking to me knows things like this because of what he has done. He knows crossing the bridge is easy because he has crossed it so many times. He knows all the searches and all the security claims at the border are a joke, because he has moved with his weapons back and forth. He knows everything has been penetrated, that nothing can be trusted, not even the solid feel of the wooden table.

The rough edge of burning wood fires at those shacks of the poor, the acrid smell of burned powder flowing from a spent brass cartridge, an old copper kettle with oil boiling and fresh pork swirling into the crispness of carnitas, the caravan of cars passing in the night, windows tinted, then the entire procession turns and comes by again, and you look but still do not stare because if they pause, however briefly, they will take you with them to the death that waits, the holes being dug each morning in the brown dirt of the Campo Santo, the graves a guess and a promise gaping up like hungry mouths for the kills of the morning and afternoon and evening, and four people sit outside their house at night and the cars come by, the bullets bark, two die soon after the barrage and the other two are scooped up by family who drive them from hospital to hospital through the dark houses because no healers will take them in, because the killers have a way of following their prey into the emergency rooms in order to finish the work.

His arms are on the solid wooden table as Juárez wafts across our faces and we do not speak of this fact, we simply inhale life and death and smell the fear of betrayal rising on the wind.

I cannot explain the draw of the city that gives death but makes everyone feel life. Nor can he. So we do not speak but simply note this fact with our silence. We are both trying to return to some person we imagine that we once were, the person before the killings, before the tortures, before the fear. He wants to live without the power of life and death and wonders if he can endure being without the money. I want to obliterate memory, to be in a world where I do not know of *sicarios*, where I do not think of fresh corpses decorating the *calles*. We have followed the different paths and wound up in the same plaza, and now we sit and talk and wonder how we will ever get home.

I crossed the river about twenty years ago—I can't be exact about the date, because I am still not sure what crossing really means, except that you never come back. I just know I crossed and now I scratch like a caged animal trying to claw my way out and reach the distant shore. It is like killing. There are some things that if learned change a person forever. You cannot know of the slaughter running along the border and remain the same person. You cannot know of the hopeless poverty of Mexicans who are fully employed in U.S. factories and remain the same person. And you cannot listen to a *sicario*—who functioned for years as a state policeman—tell of kidnappings, tortures, and murders and remain the same person.

I ask him, "Tell me about your first killing," and he says he can't remember. I know he is not telling the truth, and I know he is not lying. We all remember the first killing, the first love, the first betrayal, and the first moment we knew we would die. But sometimes you cannot reach it, you open that drawer, and your hand is paralyzed. It is right in front of you, your nostrils fill with the smell, the gun is warm in your hand, the little quiver coming out of the throat as your hand tightens, but still you cannot reach it and so you say you don't remember.

We sit there in the quiet room tasting the void that is now Ciudad Juárez.

He is the product of a religion called the global economy, the child of a poor family that had to flee the interior and become factory hands in the American mills of Juárez. The bright man who cannot afford the university. The eager pupil of the FBI.

He is law and order with his training and police uniforms.

He is a *sicario*, and it is trade like other trades. All those bodies found in the dawn, hands and feet bound with duct tape, sometimes the head severed, or the tongue cut out, often signs of torture on the torso—this requires work. The people vanished as if beamed up into the sky by an alien life form, yet more work. These things are seen as mysteries. Now he offers to explain the simple mechanics of the job.

He cannot explain Juárez, because he is too busy being Juárez. In his eyes, the current torrent of murders results from all of his work. The new killers are his children, and now they mimic what he did and operate as independent death machines. All the official explanations—a cartel war, a war between the army and the cartels, a war between the cartels and the government—remain a blur to him. He is one small cog in a big machine, and during his entire career, he never once got to see the whole machine. Nor did he ever know who, if anyone, controlled the machine. Nor was he ever certain who his real boss might be. Now he watches the city disassemble itself. The cars vanish into junkyards to be sold for scrap. The stores are all robbed. Everyone tries to extort money from everyone else.

Something has changed and yet nothing has changed. His life has spilled out beyond his body and now has become the life of the city.

"I will tell you horrible things."

I am in Shadowland, where things come briefly into view and then disappear again, and even the memory of what has been glimpsed is shaky and indistinct. By May 2008, over four hundred people have died. In five and a half months, the murders in the city exceed the number of the entire previous year.

One weekend in the middle of May, three men are taken from a nice apartment complex and turn up dead a few hours later. They are bound and gagged and show signs of torture. The family of one man, Carlos Camacho, says the army took the men. The wife of another man says the army took the men. And this is the first time the newspaper prints what has been on many lips.

Also, there is a story that says reporters track police radio in order to cover the murders, but that now, for the first time, voices are coming over these police channels and over their cell phones, warning them to slow down, to not arrive at the killing scene just yet. Because it is not finished.

The problem is that information only comes in fragments. You learn someone is breaking into police channels and issuing warnings to the press. And then you sit back and you think, Yes, but the report does not say who is breaking into these bursts of police communications. And then you sit back and you say, "But wait a minute, how do I know any of this is happening since the press in Mexico is always cowed and often prints deliberate fables?" And then, you realize how much of what you know is barely on the edge of fact.

When the three men (or more—one report says that the apartment complex has seven units and all the men were taken from each unit) vanish into the hands of what the surviving family members insist is an army unit, the newspaper carefully gives the make and color and year of every car in the parking lot. Why? Because in Juárez, it is a code for narcos, and this code is believed because in Juárez, good cars mean illegal income. But does it? And if it does, is the code accurate in this instance? You don't get to know. The papers famously drop stories after a single mention, and the follow-up on foot can be difficult because survivors have a way of falling silent once the lethal air of the city again fills their lungs.

A long time ago, maybe two months or so before the boys vanished from the apartment complex, two women went to the police and reported that their boyfriends had disappeared. The women and their guys were all from Sinaloa. Then the mystery was solved. The three guys were in the tender care of the Mexican army—suddenly the paper contained a photo of them standing in the sun, looking a little worse for wear, and bracketed by soldiers. Turns out one of the boys allowed that he'd done about sixty executions in Juárez, and the other fessed up to twenty or twenty-five. And then the story vanished. Nothing more is heard of the girls or the boys or their frisky talent for killing.

For a brief moment over the weekend when Willy Moya takes a round in the skull at 4 A.M. in the parking lot of one of his establishments, the silence lifts. Moya, it turns out, lived in El Paso. His ex-wife talks to the newspaper on the record and says her ex-husband was alarmed by the level of violence in Juárez. And then the next day, at the funeral, a family member said, "Perhaps the family needs to know what happened in order to have a little peace and to see those responsible for this disgrace and grief punished by the authorities, but we know that this is not going to happen."

But no name is given. The family has reentered Shadowland.

And we go back to Shadowland, the place where only fragments of fact surface and those fragments are always suspect. Just where are the sixty-five to ninety bodies these two boys say they murdered? And just how far off is the official killing record of the city? And what has the army done with these rascals, and where are the three boys now and are they alive? Or dead? Or are they back on the street working for whoever now controls those streets and patrols them?

"Who sent you?" asks the dying comandante.

I keep making little lists, and I pretend these lists impose some reason on the killing. They do not, but still I scribble them in my notebooks as I sit in cafés drinking coffee and pretending to understand.

On January 16, 2008, Saulo Reyes Gamboa is arrested in El Paso in a drug sting. He is a leading Juárez businessman. From 1998 to 2001, he was the chief of police in Juárez.

On February 19, four men were executed in Ascensión and Palomas in a twenty-four-hour period. The reports describe the killers as armed commandos.

In late February, close to $2 million is found in an SUV entering Mexico, mainly in five-dollar and hundred-dollar bills. The vehicle is driven by a family from Kansas City, Kansas.

On March 1, a man's body is tossed off a cliff around 3 A.M. and lands in a Juárez backyard. The man's hand, feet, and head are bound with tape.

In early April, the Mexican army arrests ten Juárez policemen. The army says they possessed drugs and illegal guns.

Twenty-two employees of the Chihuahua state attorney general's office are taken in by the Mexican army for questioning. The army says it is looking for links to organized crime.

On May 6, a municipal policewoman comes to her door in Juárez. She takes thirty-two rounds.

On May 15, the police bring wounded men to the city hospital in Juárez. Then armed men come and kill four people. The hospital staff calls the authorities for three hours. No one responds.

A new list of police yet to be executed is found outside a police station. At the bottom of the list of names is a simple thought: "Thank you for waiting."

On June 4, two city cops die in a barrage in front of a school as they are dropping off their four- and six-year-olds. The woman is thirty, the man thirty-five.

She is scared of the killings in Juárez and wants to go live with her mom in El Paso. But she does not get out in time. She is sitting in a park with two girlfriends when some guys in a nice new Tahoe snatch them—the men are being followed by killers and want the girls as human shields. The girls make a break for it, and two get away. But Alexia, twelve, doesn't quite make it. She takes a round in the head. The killers disappear with the guys in the Tahoe, and nobody has seen them since. The girl's father insists he is not a narco but a Christian. It is Monday, June 9, and summer has yet to begin.

On Father's Day, three Juárez businesses burn in forty minutes. The newspaper notes that armed commandos arrive early in the morning and torch the places with Molotov cocktails. One of the establishments is the Aroma café where Chapo Guzman dined. The owner is very upset. He says his fine restaurant had only been open a year, and very fine people dined there, people like the archbishop of Mexico. He realizes that someone thinks Guzman recently feasted there. He does not deny this story, but he does say that rich families often come there to eat, and naturally, they arrive with bodyguards who stand outside the building. And sometimes, five or six rich families are dining, and so, one can understand how in such circumstances, there would be a lot of bodyguards standing around outside. People might see such a sight and then start a rumor, perhaps a story that Chapo Guzman is eating inside the Aroma. No matter, he has no time to discuss such stories. He insists that the authorities must restore tranquility. Meanwhile, he figures that he and his family will move to El Paso.

In the last few days, fourteen nice bars and restaurants in Juárez have been torched, many of them once owned by the late Willy Moya, though the Juárez paper fails to mention this fact. Just as the paper reports the kidnapping of a prosperous Juárez businessman. His assailants psychologically torture him for four hours—mainly by driving him around in a car while they point pistols at his head. The businessman notes a curious fact—his kidnappers know every detail of his banking business, all the account numbers and the amount of money he has in each account, facts he does not even share with his family. The story suggests this is only possible if someone inside the Juárez bank is cooperating with the kidnappers. But the newspaper fails to print the name of the bank that works with a kidnapping ring.

We must be careful. Saturday, two were machine-gunned. Sunday, five more. Monday, that lawyer was mowed down. And now, early Tuesday morning, a state cop in his fine Dodge Ram takes a lot of rounds. They have hauled him to the hospital, but this is not a good idea, considering the killers' excellent follow-up capabilities. That is why at least seventeen people have fled to El Paso with their gaping wounds.

Also, the city and state are concerned that so very few Mexicans wear seat belts when they drive. Something must be done to educate the public.

At any time of the day or night, the machine-gun fire can cut you in half. This can happen anywhere. No need to watch your back, to keep eyes peeled. No need to be afraid. And of course, everyone but the authorities knows there is no need to wear a seat belt. Just go about your business and relax.

A few weeks ago, a man was machine-gunned just downriver from Juárez. His daughter went to his funeral. And she was machine-gunned. We do not know more. Nothing has been reported. Just as a few days ago, the government said it seized thirteen hit men in a tiny village just downriver from the city. But again, we have heard nothing more about them.

And then, this very morning, in the middle of June 2008, a group of businessmen put up a short video on YouTube. They demanded that the violence stop, that they would meet violence with violence. They demanded security, they demanded justice, they asked for an awful lot of things. And then, after one minute and twenty-seven seconds, they signed off and forgot to tell anyone their names. Or show their faces. But they did provide nice background music—Beethoven's Fifth Symphony.

The next day, leaders in the business community denied any connection with the announcement. Then, at six busy intersections, banners went up from people purporting to be the business community and announcing roughly the same warning. These were taken down almost instantly. The banners were puzzling. If they really did come from the well-heeled business community, they misspelled El Chapo Guzman's name.

So I relax. It hardly matters that I go to a fine restaurant, and then it is burned. It hardly matters that I drink coffee in a café, and half a block away, a fistful of people go down in a burst of machine-gun fire.

The DEA and the Mexican authorities have told the newspapers that this is a war and it is being won. It seems that elements of the Gulf cartel and the Juárez cartel have joined with elements of the Sinaloa cartel in order to crush El Chapo Guzman and create a mega-cartel. And so once more, killing is done, order will return to the city and the nation, and we can all go back to a good night's sleep. Either way, *la gente* cannot lose, don't you see? Of course, not a single person quoted has spoken with one of the architects of this mega-cartel, and so our knowledge is based on something that we cannot really know. We must trust the authorities, even though they give us no facts that we can verify. Nor will they let us ask them questions. They simply announce things to the press, who then print these announcements for us. The only real facts are the dead people, and they are barely facts since we do not always learn their names, and more and more, we do not even learn that they have been killed.

1. The Bible left open by one of eight or nine killed at prayer in the rehab clinic.

2. And he hears voices that order him to conquer a city with drugs and he has lost his mind to booze, beatings and drugs.

"For those who continue not believing"

3. She's a cardboard target left behind in a death house and beckoning with her gunshot lips.

4. *And they gather with El Pastor in the crazy place.*

5. *The army a few yards from the international bridge when three men die.*

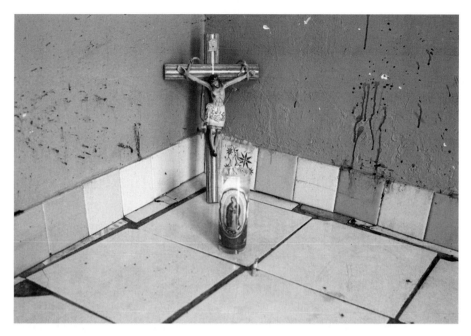

6. Flies buzz on the fresh blood around the cross and candle at a drug clinic.

7. The addicts eat at the shelter waiting for their turn to die.

8. Guns are seized but other guns keep firing.

9. Cops hide behind masks as they protest their torture and kidnapping by the army.

10. *They kill you on the way to the mall.*

11. *They kill you in front of your home and then signal their gang loyalties.*

12. *The doctors protest their extortion and kidnapping.*

13. *The woman washes cars on the street and her friend grieves her murder.*

14. The university student is slaughtered by soldiers.

15. She is pregnant and learns that her husband has been killed.

16. *They kill a professor.*

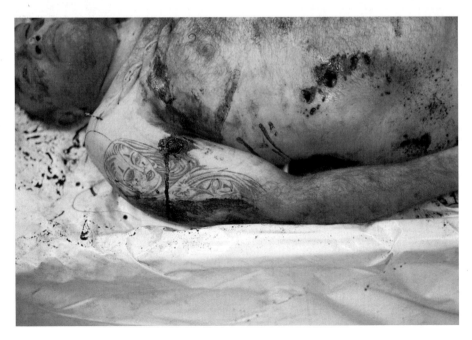

17. *He rests at the morgue with gang tattoos and wounds that mark his journey.*

18. *And then a child goes into a mass grave.*

19. *Then ten go down at another clinic and the government says the dead are criminals.*

20. And red roses for a blue city.

That is why I can finally relax. There is no way to be safe. So there is no reason to worry. And, once the mega-cartel arrives, calm returns. And the army can declare victory.

It is all in the papers.

Besides, it is 106 degrees in the shade and in a few days, we will embrace the solstice and summer will begin. We have planted well in this city, and we can expect a very good harvest.

On the third day of June, a twenty-four-year-old woman is washing cars on the street in Juárez. She has been fired from her job in a maquiladora as punishment for getting pregnant. Besides the child she is carrying as she scrubs down the cars, there are three more at home. She is from Veracruz and is the sole support for the family. A shoot-out with machine guns catches her, and so she and her three-month-old fetus die with water and suds and blood.

Moisés Villeda takes a walk around 2 A.M. after a night working as a reporter. A car pulls up, a guy asks him where a main avenue is, which happens to be three feet away. Then the guy says, get in, and Villeda declines. That is when another guy gets out of the car with a machine gun.

Once the reporter is in the car, they beat his head with the butt of the gun and break his arm. Around 2:35 A.M., the boys dump him out on the street. But first, they call the cell phones of all the other press and tell them where to find their colleague. Also, they fire a burst in the air, so that the federal police standing about a block away will know where to look.

The reporter is taken to the hospital. The morning paper notes the facility is under security now because the killers have made a habit of coming to the hospital to kill survivors.

In the morning edition of the paper, the local businessmen announce that contrary to a video on the Internet, they are not going to take law and order into their own hands, but rather will count on the authorities to maintain peace in the city.

She is forty years old and probably worries about the coming years' taxing her face and her body. Maybe she thinks of Botox treatments. No matter, now. She has full red lips, hair to her shoulders, a white blouse, and a dark coat, and a necklace gleams at her throat. She is the administrative director of the Juárez police department. She had worked in the department from 2002 to 2005, left and then returned in October 2007. Technically, her job put her in charge of human resources.

She lives in a very nice neighborhood, and at about 10:23 P.M. on Monday, June 16, she is murdered in front of her home. A sign thoughtfully left with her corpse explains that she had hired too many people associated with El Chapo Guzman. Her name is Silvia Guzman Molina.

Now she becomes a new woman. Before her murder, she was law enforcement and by the standard of the city, an innocent. But having been assassinated, she now becomes dirty, someone who must have been connected to bad people doing bad things. The police department says she was doing an adequate job, and that is why they are surprised she has been slaughtered. Juárez has these little mysteries about the dead.

Given the standard—that the dead are dirty and the living are innocents—clearly the heads of the major cartels in Mexico are innocents. Since this massive drug war began at the behest of the president of Mexico, they have not had a hair on their heads touched. Also, the killers moving around Juárez with machine guns and big SUVs have also suffered few, if any, deaths. So clearly, they also are innocents.

There is a room no one has filed a report on, and I am not allowed in this room. But I am certain it exists. The walls are turquoise blue and brilliant, the tiles cool Saltillo, the light is soft and caresses the skin. The dead come here, not all of the dead—the innocents, that tiny handful, they go someplace else. The dirty come to this room I know of, the one where I am always denied entrance. I try, but I suspect I am not ready. I still have some patina of stupidity and willful denial and basic fraud about me. I still try to make sense out of things and believe in patterns and rational behavior. I still—and I think this is my unforgivable flaw—not only believe in the system but much worse, I believe there is a system.

If I could get into that room, I would finally find someone to talk to who is not a liar, someone quite different from me.

Someone who really knows the score.

Someone who would stop inventing explanations and give me the sensation of rounds from an AK-47 ripping through their hide, and did it sound loud or was it like being underwater? And when they cut your balls off before they killed you, what were you thinking? And tell the expressions on their faces and give the character of their eyes. And were they wearing uniforms, and if so, what kind—Mexican army, federal police, state police, city police, or their allies from the street gangs?

And does the beer still taste good and cold when you are dead?

They are leaving, and now this fact is finally noticed. By late June, after months of the president of Mexico periodically announcing that the fabled cartels are on the run, after months of the mayor of Juárez periodically announcing that the city is fine, that only bad people die, that there is a lack of tranquility but that peace and joy are on the way, after months of the press timidly probing corpses and finding in their entrails proof positive of cartel connections, the official lid suddenly comes off . . . because they are leaving. The people with money are fleeing to the United States.

The mayor of Juárez keeps a home in El Paso and one in Dallas. The rich are hiring U.S. lawyers to get political asylum. Turns out the burning bars and restaurants are getting demands for protection—or else. Turns out that no one feels safe in Juárez even with the Mexican army close at hand. Turns out the city is in a state of terror.

Except the imaginary city, the golden city, the beautiful city that for years everyone in Juárez clings to when blood flows in the streets. This city is dynamic and fun, full of fragrances and laughter—the real city—everyone has said this for years. The huge slums where the factory workers live, they are not the real city. The bodies left on the street from drug deals gone bad, they are not the real city. The filth, the potholes, the buses spewing black exhaust, they are not the real city. The real city is a tiny zone with nice restaurants and discos, gated communities with armed guards where the rich live in huge houses.

And now the rich are fleeing. Hundreds, perhaps thousands, are moving into the United States, where they have always kept their money, and now they plan to store their lives, also. They have papers, and if they don't have papers, they have something else the U.S. government understands and respects: money. So they move and fill out little documents and live as the rich tend to live everywhere: They live very well. They have been scooting out of Mexico for years, building up their bank accounts in U.S. vaults, buying homes in nice cities, preparing for the day when someone notices that they have all the money and almost no one else has any.

Meanwhile, the killing plods on. No one really pays much mind to it anymore because everyone grows numb. In January, the city was stunned when 40 human beings were executed. In March, almost a 120 crossed over. Then, the army took over and April was such a relief, only 52 dead. So Juárez tasted a solution that was even bloodier than January. May topped 100. In the first nine days of June, 48 souls go to paradise. The missing are no longer counted, and many of the dead remain unidentified, just tossed in those common graves.

The city now is murder, extortion, arson, kidnapping, rape, robbery, car theft, and the sweet haze of drugs and alcohol. The temperature bumps 110, but the marijuana and the cocaine and the heroin and the cold beers save the human heart from the human violence.

I see no problem.

I see a future.

I see the way things will be here now and the way things will be where you live in good time.

I see a city where basic institutions erode and then burn or die, and yet in the morning, my fellow human beings get up, smell the coffee, and continue on with their lives.

I see Alexia's funeral, her little brown twelve-year-old face in the open coffin, her mother weeping and a lot of pink balloons because that was her favorite color, and she was going to graduate from elementary school in three days and so all her friends are there.

A friend of mine is taking photographs at Alexia's funeral when the army comes and grabs him. This could be bad since people who leave with the army tend not to come back. But the crowd holding those flotillas of pink balloons storms over and says, "Hey, leave him alone, go find and catch the bad guys." And the soldiers let him go and so he is fine.

Yes.

We're gonna have us a time.

Juárez is where we are learning the very first steps of the dance that will come sweeping through our lives.

But we turn a deaf ear to the music of Juárez. We think this act will keep us sane and safe.

I sit under towering cottonwoods near the border, and hundreds of birds feed on scattered seed, a squirrel forages under a feeder hanging from a pole, and just then, in the early rays of morning, a Cooper's hawk banks against the stand of carrizo and the air explodes with wing beats as the birds flee for cover. But I notice that the squirrel, busy feeding, does not even look up.

I am sitting with a contract killer, another *sicario*, in that café, and we are eating carnitas as he softly tells me of his work. A few tables away, a trucker in a dirty T-shirt and faded blue jeans shares a meal and beers with a blond woman spilling out of her half-unbuttoned blouse. They drink beers, and it is clear that she is bought and paid for and is by no means a wife. But what I notice as the killer murmurs his account of slaughter and drug movements and gang wars is that they are oblivious to the death machine a few feet away from their carnal dreams.

This is my Juárez, a place that seems normal if you make the effort not to see or hear. Or feel. A place where many die, but they are the bad people and we are the good people and so death will not come to our door because the Lord of Hosts will spare us.

So I sit here and tally the dead, and try to keep an honest count of the killing. But most moments, as the stench and dust of the city floats over me, and I sit in some flyblown café and drink a beer or a cup of coffee, none of the deaths really exist for me, and the violence of the city does not exist either.

I am sure that Miss Sinaloa is sitting outside somewhere and birds are singing in a patio around her and she smiles and cannot really be sure that she was gang-raped in Juárez and then went to the crazy place and met the true love of her life. I understand the feeling. I often have coffee at a small café that is two blocks from where a prominent Juárez lawyer was murdered two years ago in broad daylight. As I sip my drink, I hardly ever recall this killing, and when I pass the very corner where he died, I often fail to remember the event.

That is how we survive.

If we could truly remember, we would not be able to go on. And if we truly forget, we will have a small patch of bliss until that bullet, and it is possibly already arcing through the air, slams into our skull.

But the city itself goes on murdering with or without our memory.

We can only endure the place that kills by pretending the place will not kill us.

She goes into the room, her skin fragrant, and men's eyes light up and their lips say Miss Sinaloa. She is offered a drink, there is a line of white powder on the table top.

Dead Reporter Driving

I am sitting in the Hotel San Francisco in Palomas almost four years to the day since the moment Emilio Gutiérrez destroyed his life. The small restaurant has eight tables, the walls host an explosion of plastic flowers screaming yellow, red, and pink. Carved wooden mallard heads spike out as hat racks for Stetsons. In the lobby is a large statue of San Francisco, and in his hands and at his feet illegal immigrants have left handwritten messages and offerings. The tile floor is the color of flesh. Just five blocks away, the poor plunged through the line and headed into El Norte—none of the notes are very recent. The river of misery has changed course for the moment. Music floats through the air, Bob Dylan singing "Knocking on Heaven's Door."

The notes whisper of people in flight: "Father, help us all who pass as wetbacks. Help us Our Father. Bless us all who think of You, who trust in You.

"And I ask You to bless and help my mother, my father and me and my brothers and sisters and all of my family. In Your hands we place our good luck to pass ALIVE. Adios Our Father."

Or a note says: "Please I ask You with all my heart look after and protect my husband that he pass safely. Amen."

A Bible lies open, and someone has dropped this plea on the page:

> God bless us and protect us
> along the way
> Yonathan
> Manuel
> Tomaz
> Yumbo
> Graciela
> Norma
> Olinda
> Guide us on a good road
> and protect us.

There are no customers here, just these prayers from the height of the migration two years ago and the dust outside in the street.

The walls in the lobby are murals of an imaginary Sierra Madre in an imaginary Mexico. A huge buck deer stands in an alpine meadow, an eagle swoops down on a lake, a caballero in a sequined suit stares with love at the beautiful senorita. In the kitchen, short, dark women chop vegetables for salsa. Their movements are very slow and their faces blank.

Across the street, in a rundown hotel for migrants going north, is where Emilio's life began to end. No one here remembers. Within an hour or two of a killing, there is no one left to describe the murder but the flies buzzing over the drying blood on the ground. This loss of memory is not because of cowardice. It is wisdom that comes with survival. When some townspeople witnessed a night of kidnappings in 2008, familiar faces were recognized. But no one would name these faces. As I leave the hotel and restaurant, Johnny Cash is singing:

You can run on for a long time
Run on for a long time
Run on for a long time
Sooner or later God'll cut you down
Sooner or later God'll cut you down

On January 29, 2005, six soldiers came to the hotel across the street, took food off people's plates, and robbed the customers of their money and jewelry. Emilio got calls in Ascensión, and so he phoned the local police chief and the manager of the hotel. He called the army also, but as is its custom, the army refused to answer any questions from the press. Then he filed a brief article about the incident, one of three he wrote in that period noting similar actions by the army in the area.

That is how he destroyed his life.

Late at night on February 8 of that same year, Colonel Idelfonso Martinez Piedra calls Gutiérrez at home, explains that he is "the boss," and orders him to come immediately to the Hotel Miami in downtown Ascensión. Emilio explains that he is getting ready for bed, and some other time would be better.

The colonel says, "If you don't come, we'll come looking for you at home or wherever you are."

So he puts his then-twelve-year-old son in his truck and goes there. He notices fifty soldiers in the four-block area around the hotel, and two vans full of bodyguards for the officers. He leaves his son in the truck and walks up to the officer. It is a very cold night.

In his mind, he is thinking, "What the fuck are these *cabrones* up to?" Soldiers swiftly surround him. He is in front of the Hotel Miami, but he is in solitary confinement.

The colonel says to another officer, "Look, General, the son of a whore who has written all kinds of stupidities has arrived."

Then the general, Garcia Vega, says, "So you are the son of a whore who is lowering our prestige. You son of a fucking whore, you are denigrating us, and my boss, the minister in Mexico, is extremely bothered by your fucking lies, idiot."

Emilio feels very small, and he cannot think of a way to escape his fate. He tries to form words to excuse himself but he cannot. The general is in charge of all of Chihuahua. He is short, and his uniform is brilliant with gold trim.

Emilio is very frightened, and he says that he only writes what the officials or the victims tell him.

The general says, "No, you have no sources for that information. You made it up. Just how much schooling do you have, asshole?"

Emilio lies and claims two years of communication studies in the university.

The general explains that Emilio lacks an education equal to his own.

To have a general speak to you is not something to be desired. They can hand out death like a party favor.

The general suggests he should write about drug people.

Emilio says he does not know any, and besides they frighten him.

"So, you don't know them and you fear them," the general bristles. "You should fear us, for we fuck the fucking drug traffickers, you son of a whore. I feel like putting you in the van and taking you to the mountains so you can see how we fuck over the drug traffickers, asshole."

The guards now surround him, he can see his son in the truck about fifteen yards away, and the boy looks very frightened and nervous. People walking past the hotel greet Emilio, and he thinks this is what saves him from more curses or a beating.

He grovels, apologizes profusely to the general.

"You've written idiocies three times, and there shall be no fourth. You'd better not mention this meeting, or you'll be sent to hell, asshole."

The colonel tells him he is under surveillance "and should not fuck up."

Then, he is dismissed. He gets back in his truck, and his son asks what is going on. He says, they want to kidnap me. He drives aimlessly and finally calls his boss, who tells him, "This is serious. This is a problem."

He decides his only chance at safety is making the threats known. Because if he remains silent, he senses they will return and kill him.

On February 10, he publishes a third-person account of the incident and files a complaint with the assistant public security minister in Nuevo Casas Grandes and meets with the boss of the ministry, a woman, who warns him, "You better think it over carefully because it is very dangerous getting involved with the militaries." But he is building a paper record to try and save himself. He files a complaint against General Garcia Vega and Colonel Piedra and the soldiers with the National Commission of Human Rights. Three months later, the state police begin an investigation that goes nowhere. The representative of the Commission of Human Rights proposes a conciliatory act between them and the military. Emilio agrees, but he knows this means nothing because he will "continue to be in the eye of the hurricane as the weakest one."

He does not write anything unseemly about the army again. He becomes almost a ghost and hears no evil and sees no evil. He hopes they will now leave him alone. On February 12, 2008, he merely notes in the newspaper that a convoy of seven hundred soldiers and one hundred vehicles sweeps the area from Palomas to Casas Grandes. In Ascensión, they ransack the house of a friend, a guy who runs a pizza parlor. The friend is given the *ley fuga*, the traditional game of the military where they let you run and, if you can dodge the bullets, you live. His friend is mowed down in the street in front of his home. That night, twenty people vanish from the town and only one ever returns, a Chilean engineer who is saved by his embassy. The others simply cease to exist. The reporting of these events illustrates how the press functions: In his first story, Emilio mentions an army convoy sweeping the area. But in later stories about the killings and people vanishing, there is no army, simply armed commandos. That is how an honest reporter tries to avoid becoming a dead reporter.

He thinks, "This is behind me," and he will put it out of his mind.

When the president of Mexico floods his zone with soldiers in April 2008, he learns the army has a long memory.

After midnight, on May 5, 2008, he hears a loud knocking on the door of his home. Fifty soldiers raid the house. Emilio screams, "Press, the Press from *El Diario*," and a soldier says, "Hands up, asshole. On the ground!"

They tell him they are looking for guns and drugs, and separate him from his stunned son. When they leave, the commander advises him, "Behave well and follow our suggestions."

On June 14, he steps out of his house and waters his small garden of squash, cantaloupe, watermelon, and cucumbers. He has a pear tree, also an apricot tree and three roses blooming pink and red. He is going to make his son breakfast, a task he enjoys. It is a Saturday. He notices five guys in a green pickup seventy yards away. They look like soldiers and they are watching him. But he is not certain because there is a store down the block where the soldiers come to buy cocaine, and so he thinks just maybe their presence has nothing to do with him. Then, they start the truck and cruise slowly past him. They are short, dark, and clearly from the south of Mexico. A while later, they come back, but this time in a white vehicle. And they park and watch his house.

Still, he thinks this cannot really be happening. He has behaved properly. Local drug people have offered him money, not to mention the *tiendas* selling cocaine.

He's told them, "Don't worry. You don't have to pay me. I am not going to write about them."

Besides, he knows that both the army and the police are involved in the local drug sales, so just who is he going to inform about these illegal businesses? Instead, he's picked up his extra money by writing publicity releases and selling ads for the newspaper.

But he knows, "The hardest part of the job is to survive on the salary. That is why *sobres* exist." It has been years since he completely trusted anyone he works with.

He goes inside and makes *machaca* with eggs for his boy. He tells his son that he is going to his office and that the boy should keep an eye on the house.

He reads the papers at his desk, then goes three blocks to the police station to talk to a drunk the police have arrested, the usual small moments of a small-town newspaper. Outside, the green pickup is back and watching him. He leaves his office around noon and stops by a friend's welding shop. This time, he realizes the white vehicle is trailing him. Now he is worried, so he and his friend go to a little store, buy some beers, and return to the shop. There is a place nearby where people buy cocaine, and he sees a guy from the green pickup go in there and then come out. He does not like what he is seeing.

He calls home to make sure his son has showered, because he must be at church at 4 P.M. Emilio heads home and brings some food for his son. Then he returns to his friend's welding shop. After a while, he goes out to get some more beers and now the white car is back. It pulls up right in front of the store he is in. Upset now, he calls his friend and tells him to come around to the back of the store. He escapes, and his friend takes him back to his house. A few hours later, Emilio ventures out and retrieves his own truck.

His son goes to church and then down to the plaza to be with friends. Emilio stays at his friend's house, and around eight o'clock, a woman calls and says, "Emilio, I have to see you right now. Where are you? I can't talk over the phone."

He is entering a place he will only recognize later: denial. He is trying to pretend none of this means anything and none of this has anything to do with him.

She comes over and tells him she is dating a soldier and the military people all talk about how they are going to kill him. She is crying. She says, "Emilio, you have to leave now. They are going to kill you."

I t is late June 2008, the solstice has passed, the heat is on, the city boils
at over a hundred degrees. The churches of El Paso announce they are
going to pray for an end to the violence in Juárez. Over the weekend, at
least twelve die. Some guys are drinking, and one of them is machine-gunned.
There is a fiesta to celebrate the baptism of a baby. Two are killed at the party.
Some guys approach a college student, and they ask him to hold some stuff
for them. He refuses. They beat him to death. Most are fairly routine
butcheries—a hail of bullets from machine guns, the thud as a body hits the
ground. Around 3 A.M., a man staggers across the bridge to El Paso. He is
full of bullet holes and would like some medical attention.

On Monday, June 23, a corpse is found on the western edge of the city.
Nearby is a black daypack. It holds the head. There is no identification on
the corpse. He is about thirty-four years old, and he rests on the side of a
Catholic church. Anapra is a place where people squat in shacks on land they
do not own, steal electricity from high-power lines, buy water off a truck, and

work in American factories. They seem to eat sand since the ground here is largely sand. The woman who lost her sister in 1998 to rape and murder and started the campaign to paint utility poles with pink paint and black crosses to memorialize the city's penchant for killing women, well, she was raised here. The sprawling slum also hosts train robbers who regularly hold up the U.S. trains that pass just a few feet across the wire on its northern edge. One dirt track links it to Juárez. Anapra is home to tens of thousands of people who do not exist to those who govern the city.

It is also a touchstone for me, a place where all the pieties of free trade and hands across the border and growing the economy become grit in my mouth. It abuts the United States, and so its residents stare at a world they cannot touch.

But the body by the church, well, the head is really severed and in the daypack. So also the legs and arms, and they are scattered over an area of about ninety feet. The feet wear black socks. Someone has covered the torso with a blanket—green, brown and yellow. The clothing was in a white plastic bag. Children found the body. Adults in the area saw a car going by Sunday night with a man who appeared to be a captive. Someone really cared and put in the extra work.

The authorities say they are investigating.

There is delirium induced by the heat.

I am slowly ceasing to function.

The bodies all blur. The killings merge into one river of blood.

I have reached a serene state where things no longer make sense but simply exist. So much depends on a decapitated corpse with the head in a black daypack in the white heat of June.

The killers hardly matter. What would a solved case really tell me? It would be like having the men who raped Miss Sinaloa explain to me their motives. Because they could. Because they wanted to have her. Because the air is dusty, the city is hot, the houses are small, the smell of sewers is everywhere, the police are not useful, guns are available, killings are possible.

And besides executions, the city kills in other ways. Social services are a phrase, not reality. Blanca Edna Paez Orozco is twenty-two when she dies.

Her brother Abel is twenty and he survives. They are both playing with matches and the house catches fire. This is very bad because they had been tied to the bed that morning when the father, also named Abel and sixty-five years of age, had to leave the house in order to earn a living. The brother and sister are retarded and social services in Juárez mean being tied to a bed with a rope. A small death in the tidal wave of gore.

I think if I ran into some local criminologists, say, on my way to a bar, I would kill them with my bare hands in order not to hear their explanations. I have dreamed of burning the newspapers in both Juárez and El Paso to the ground so that they could write no more stories about mysterious armed commandos or drug cartels that are having a big dust-up in the city, cartels that have not made a single public utterance but somehow are apparently well known to the press and whose motives and members and actions are transparent to those toiling in newsrooms. I have also considered torching the nearest DEA office since it offers battlefield reports on the killings in the city without visiting the battlefield.

Imagine a city with five hundred corpses and not a single shred of evidence explaining their slaughter. No one even knows where those people from the death houses have gone. This last thing gnaws on me. It seems reasonable to me that someone—say, a newspaper reporter or maybe one of the local intellectuals who coat the op-ed pages of the paper—might ask the powers that be just what they have done with forty-five stiffs that came out of the soil of the city.

But I am not bitter. I like heat. And I am focused, like a monk in a Zen garden, on the sheer physical feel of things. I take my bodies one at a time. I do not question why they have been killed. I do not wonder who the killers are.

It is the twenty-fourth day of June, the clock is running out on the first six months of death, and so far 518 have died, 16 of them women. Now I wait for an arbitrary time span, the first half of the year, to end, and an arbitrary measure of life—murders in Juárez—to be tallied.

Like the murdered, I have stopped learning. Yesterday afternoon, in the dull heat two guys entered an insurance office. They left an employee dead.

A reporter leaves a bar and takes twelve rounds. The owners of junkyards are being kidnapped for ransom. They complain to officials. The relative of a U.S. congressman is kidnapped and released when the money is paid. The press totes things up and announces that 28 percent of all the executions in Mexico happen in Juárez.

The old man is walking his dog in his neighborhood in Juárez. Thieves keep breaking into his place to steal the copper pipes. Just a week or so ago, someone blew up a car right in the front of the house. So he and the old lady seldom leave the house together. Someone must stand guard. Just down the street lives an ex-cop. The old man walking his dog sees a white van pull up full of armed guys, and they drag the ex-cop out of his home, and then one of the armed guys says, "*No es él*, it's not him," and they let him go.

On June 21, twenty-one people are murdered in drug killings in Chihuahua, thirty-eight in all of Mexico. Eighteen of the deaths are in Juárez. On June 26, the fifth top commander of the federal police to be slaughtered in thirteen months goes down while having lunch in Mexico City. The killer escapes. Witnesses notice a man videotaping the murder. Then walking calmly away. On June 28 in Juárez, four men are executed in the afternoon. Earlier in the day, a woman's body was found—she was killed inside a burrito café. Another man also took a barrage in his home, plus two fragmentation grenades.

A city policeman explains to American radio listeners how he gets to work: Never obey a stop sign or a red light, because if you do, killers will pull up beside you and pump you full of bullets. This matter-of-fact account purrs across the airwaves on National Public Radio, a lonely message from a forgotten city.

Esther Chávez by June is looking to build a second women's shelter near downtown. Her current facility on the edge of the city is a two-hour bus ride each way for many of the poor. The city tells her of some vacant land she can have. She drives there to discover a bustling slum built out of pallets from the loading docks of the American factories.

No one can keep track of things here, not even of vacant land.

June is running out, and I can't tell if the murders this month are at 120 or 130. Nor can I bear at the moment to go back over my tally. I'll wait for the month to end, and then, as is the custom, the Juárez papers will briefly announce the slaughter, and then, as is the custom, it will vanish from memory.

The woman in the burrito café was forty-seven when the man entered and killed her. Six months ago, I might have wondered about her story. Did she know him? Was he a husband or lover? What did she look like? And was she frightened as she entered the café shortly before midnight? I would have had questions and feelings and sought answers. Now I do not. There are too many, that is part of the problem. But also, the answers seem a way to erase what is happening, a way to explain a death so that in a real sense, it does not matter because, given the explanation, it is inevitable, unique, and irrelevant to my life or your life.

And so, I do not ask. The deaths blur, the names go by too fast. I sit here blinded by the storm and ignorant of the lives that led to the deaths.

The air, feel the air, the sun, rising and warming the skin, the broken sidewalk underfoot, the sewage wafting down the lane, the sounds of cars and buses, there, take it all in, absolute, finite, actual. Swallow the sensation of the city whole, and this will stop the blurring, steady the mind, and make it possible to believe in order and calm. Each murder is explicable. There is a body, and there are killers, there is a time of day or night, the gunman has a reason, or the gunmen were sent by someone with a reason, and even the innocent bystander mowed down by accident, this corpse, too, has an explanation and can be made sense of by tracing the trajectory of the rounds, the entry point of the bullet into the flesh.

But then it breaks down. Over five hundred murders in six months, and still, no one seems to make sense of the murders, and no one seems able to say the names of the killers or to explain who they are, who they represent, and what they want. No matter how many facts and details are assessed, the killings overwhelm simple explanations. There are too many authors writing too many short stories on bodies, there are too many styles of handwriting, and forensic specialists get baffled by all the murderous forms of cursive writing. No matter how clever the examiner, still, there is a door behind whatever explanation is offered. The gangs are sent to kill, but who sends them? The cartels are killing, but who in the cartels gives the orders and why? The army slaughters, but who is behind the army? And what if a person finds the door and opens it and finally gets in the room where the orders are issued, the deaths decreed, yes, walks into that room. And finds nothing but dust, cobwebs, and a cold cup of coffee?

Maybe I am wrong. Maybe that room has skeletons, bones centuries old, and these gleaming white forms run everything and are beyond party or deals or moments, and are—like the sounds and smells of the city—simply part of the very fabric of the thing called life. They are death, these skeletons, and they are life, and so we avoid going into that room because we want an explanation that does not involve our lives and our souls and the very ground we stand on. We want peace and quiet—that tranquility the mayor says is lacking in the city—we want blue skies and the breath of summer as we sit in the shade of a tree and the rose blooms by the doorway. But mainly we want to not know what we know, to forget that this thing within us has always been there, a virus lurking in our being that has now slipped out into the flow of life and ravages not the city, not the people.

But the imaginary life we have always led and now must realize was a lie.

A puddle of blood seeping into the brown earth by the roadside.

The body has just been taken away by the authorities.

I lean over and flies rise up off the blood.

Below, a herd of goats searches for food in a garbage dump. The hillside gleams with shards of broken glass.

The flies rise to my face.

And I can only decide whether to face what I see.

Or turn away.

We are high on the hill in Salt Lake City, and this is good. El Pastor is considering a deviled egg when I point out its name in English and suggest it may be satanic. He laughs, and this is a good sign. It is October now, and Juárez has had about twelve hundred murders so far this year. The business community worries that tourists have stopped crossing the bridges for a visit. So they have put up a new billboard on the U.S. side: "Juárez, Land of Encounters."

In the last, two months, El Pastor has had three messages.

The first time, the federal police came to his office at 6 P.M. Then they returned at 9 P.M. Nothing was ever said.

After that, the phone calls began. A person would say he was with the federal police and he understood El Pastor had a lot of money. After all, it must take a lot of money to run the crazy place in the desert. The second call was similar. And the third.

El Pastor had been given a very nice new car by a man who believed in Jesus Christ, or wanted to believe in Him. This man was a friend of a state policeman in Juárez, a law enforcement agency that handles public safety, killings for the cartel, and also moves drugs. El Pastor began to worry about his fine car because everyone told him that only a narco could own such a car.

So he stopped driving it.

And he stopped coming to Juárez on a schedule.

Now he comes without warning and leaves without warning and struggles to create no pattern. He has long kept his wife and family across the line, where there is less violence. Now he stays home more than he had planned.

And so he is in Salt Lake City giving talks to raise money for the people in the crazy place. He tells the audiences of Jesus, he tells them how Mexicans only want to come north to do dirty jobs Americans do not like.

He asks people, "Do you want to go to the fields and dig potatoes? We will. I don't think you will."

He also laughs a lot and smiles and explains how he was a drunk and drug addict and chased a lot of women, and finally the U.S. government got weary of his escapades and threw him back into Mexico. And then he lived on the street, was very dirty, did anything he could find, ate out of garbage cans. Until Jesus saved him.

He feels good here. True, almost everyone is white, and El Pastor is brown. And no one here even knew there is a secret city within this city until one day, when at least eighty thousand illegal Mexicans marched in the streets of Salt Lake asking for a little respect and a lot less pressure from the U.S. government. We are both taking a little holiday from death. Not an escape, because the power of Juárez and the scent of Miss Sinaloa always draws us back.

We sit in the nice house on the hillside, while the fall leaves rustle in their last frolic before the killing season comes and they tumble down yellow and brown and taste life no more. In this exact moment, the poetry of Juárez continues ceaselessly in the daily newspaper of the *ciudad*:

Body
found in western Juárez
A man turned up dead
in an abandoned lot
of the colonia
21st century
in the western part of the city
around
2:00 P.M.
The victim's hands were tied
behind his back
and he was thrown face down on the ground.
Personnel
from the Forensic Medical Service
arrived at the scene
to take away
the body
and collect evidence
that might have been left
around him.

There is a beauty in this killing, music, a sonata perhaps, but an extremely loud sonata.

Yet people here listen to El Pastor's message in the safe city in the safe valley where harm is outlawed—everyone says so—by the flag, by God and the local police. When they see images of the people living in the crazy place, they feel bad, and they give him money. When they see the video of him in the yard at the crazy place calming people with his embrace, they give him money. And when he goes into one of the rebar cells and tells an enraged toothless woman to be calm "in the name of Jesus," and she slowly stops screaming and yelling and follows him out into the yard as he chants the name of Jesus—when the people at the fund-raiser see that footage, they don't know what to say, but still they give him money—a hundred here, a hundred there.

And no one here is threatening to murder him, or calling on the phone with scary messages.

El Pastor is reconciled to death and being reunited with his Savior. After all, he has it all planned—the huge barbeque, lots of meat, music, and song.

He can handle death because it means he will be with Jesus.

It's just that when the car comes, and they take him away to be murdered, he hopes they do not torture him.

He hopes they will not apply fire to parts of his body or stick in an ice pick and run it along the bone in a local ritual called bone tickling. And should they desire to cut off his head, as some do, he hopes that at this point, he is dead. He also hopes he is dead when they decide to cut off his hands or feet.

He can handle being murdered.

He will then be with the Lord.

But the torture part, that makes him very upset.

We have the numbers. Since January 1994, there have been 3,955 murders in Juárez. Since January 2008, there have been 540 murders. It is the last day of June, and there is still time. The numbers that give us comfort, those dates and tallies, these numbers are still tumbling in. We can write them in columns on white paper and install order in our minds.

But still, that door must be opened.

On the last day of June, bees attack seven people. On the last day of June, a fifty-four-year-old woman pulls into the parking lot of a convenience store after withdrawing eleven thousand pesos from a bank (found on the body) and is shot dead with ten rounds. On the last day of June, a man says his wife and children are missing. On the last day of June, the total number of murders for the month hits 139, and the total for the year reaches 541. Or 543, depending on which paper one reads. The numbers blur now. No one knows how many people have been snatched, nor what became of them. Just as no one knows where to file the corpses from the two houses of death.

On the last day of June, I see and taste and feel the fully mature culture of death. Death from low wages, death from drug deals, death from unknow-able wars, death from going to the bank, death from riding down the street, death from every direction. Death is blamed on all the factories that have brought the poor to the city where they now live in a carpet of slums. Death is blamed on the drug industry that has brought violence to the city as heavily armed men move white powder and billions of dollars. Death is blamed on the Americans who want cheap goods and so create warrens of slaves, who want strong drugs and so create cartels of machine guns. It has taken decades to transform a sleepy border town into a city of death, but now the work is done and the thing has a life of its own and that life is murder. Death has aged and is now the bony hand on the shoulder, the culture when the sun rises and when the sun sets.

The city is fiestas, dust, cantinas, discos, and people savoring the week-ends and dreaming of the nights when love will find them. There is song in the air. The culture of death becomes a life. The slaughtered die fast, the rest grind out time in dust, poverty, and bouts of terror. Only six months ago, everyone was horrified when forty people were slaughtered in one month.

Now a hundred a month seems acceptable because in the culture of death . . . life goes on.

In March, according to a poll, 90 percent of the people of Juárez supported the army. By the end of June, 30 percent of the local people, according to a poll, said the military occupation of the city was of little or no consequence. The general in charge said that those who questioned the army's success were either narcos or worked for narcos. Besides, he thought narcos probably paid for the poll.

Life goes on.

The family comes with the body, and they are a half hour late for the funeral. They do not come into the church but have a benediction said in the parking lot. They are afraid more people will be killed if they linger with the corpse of their murdered family member.

She sits on the piano bench, her black hair clean and shining as she bends over the keys. The moon is full and rides the sky hunting for more bodies. Two days ago, they killed seven. Yesterday, in the afternoon sometime in October, six went down. Or was it seven? It is getting very hard to keep track of the daily or monthly count. Even the grand total for the year seems like a smear of blood on a wall. No matter how hard I work at my tally, I fall behind. I write down numbers in my black notebook, and then take a sip of coffee in the dawn light, and before I return the cup to the immaculate white saucer, the number is gone. Juárez, even now as I sit in the room, wine in hand, moonlight playing off the walls, yes, at this very moment Juárez marauds through my mind: corpses, ghosts, bullets, knives, severed heads, all manner of carnival moments, a parade from a lively hell, shapeless, formless, and often meaningless. She leans forward flicking her fingers on the white keys as the rhapsody pumps so much energy and hope into the room.

So I sit, glass of wine in hand, as she strokes the keyboard and plays "Rhapsody in Blue." The opening is bold, the bellowing of a young century and a cocksure country. She stumbles on parts and apologizes, but there is no need for such comments. Her playing is beautiful, as her black hair and fair skin glow in the moonlight washing over the dark room. The moon walks through the window and plays on the white wall. Branches and leaves dance as shadows.

It was like this. Three cars arrive and empty out. Six human beings are lined up against the wall of a gymnasium in the bright light of the afternoon. Or the dimming light of early evening. Facts are slippery here, perhaps, because of the blood. The men were taken from Colonia Azteca and brought to this location. One of them is said to be a former policeman, but we cannot be certain of this. Here is what we can be certain of: Six men line up against a wall, their faces turned to the blocks. Children are playing in the street. There is a settling of accounts about to take place. The men are in their twenties or thirties, they wear jeans of various colors and T-shirts. Except for one guy in gym shorts. Then, the guns fire and now the men lie side by side on the ground. Spent cartridges, at least a hundred spent cartridges from AK-47s and AR-15 rifles and .40-caliber and 9 mm pistols litter the ground around the bodies.

The locals later remember a few things. They said the shooting lasted ten minutes, but my God, they insist, it seemed like ten hours. The police are called, but it takes them a very long time to arrive.

Later, one local says, "We don't understand how it is that the police did not catch them, because the bullets sounded very loud, and it went on for a long time."

What fills the air is not sirens but this: cries of pain, voices begging for mercy, the roar of guns. Then silence. But this pure and sacred silence is broken by moans and screams. And so more shooting is required. Finally, it is finished.

The shooters have thoughtfully brought a sign that they leave by the bodies.

MESSAGE FOR RATS: THIS WILL CONTINUE.

About the same time, in another part of the city, a carpenter sits outside his house. Neighbors later report that the carpenter was a peaceful and hard-working man. This could be true. It hardly matters. Reasons are for people who seek to avoid the killing. The rest of us, those truly committed to death and slaughter, we need no reasons.

So a man has lived forty-three years and he is a carpenter. A car comes down the street and moves very slowly.

When the police finally do bother to come, they find eleven cartridges. And the body.

But, I am remiss in my counting. I need the wine, the music pouring from her fingers as she strokes the keys and fills the room with that famous rhapsody in blue.

Because then I forget what I see and smell and feel. I forget that it is cold in the night now, and the woman is twenty-two and she has four small children and one is six months old and another one died last year at birth and, ah, tell me if the lovers are losers in the shacks and rough lanes, go ask the twenty-two-year-old who was raped as a child and now has doomed children to fill her hours and she lives in a city where the rapist is free, more free than she will ever be, since he was never charged and he has never carried a child and feeds no young and hungry mouths, and the woman has no man and all of this loving family goes hungry and the floor is dirt, there is no heat, and I must listen to my rhapsody, the one called blue, maybe code blue, and enjoy the wine and refuse all explanations of the violence as the city storms into my mind with the hunger that will never be filled by anything but screams.

I see the fourteen-year-old who is pregnant, the forty-year-old woman with six children, a shack, a baby in her arms, no food, no doctors, nothing but the cold in the night, and the men who come and go and leave the litter of young lives in their wake. And I must say it is their fault, they breed too often, they have careless ways, they should read more and improve their minds.

I have found the place where theories die, where explanations are stabbed with sharp knives and flutter down the *calles* like litter created by the world that will not come here and will not listen to ignorant cries of people busy dying and calling it fate or God's will or the way things are and have long been and the only way they know.

The cars with tinted windows prowl the streets, the guns go off, the authorities hide, and death without end, amen.

The counting, I will get to later.

Yes, I will.

The man found incinerated in a car, that burned corpse with a sign saying he was a thief, well, I will get to him in a while and return to tabulating things. But in passing we should note that the remnants of a dragon tattoo still glow from his charred chest. Just as I will acknowledge that three or four hundred local cops had to be let go because they failed various tests, and it turns out they were actually criminals and drug addicts. But they have been replaced by yet more cops, and so life will continue in the approved fashion.

But now, right now, I need this red wine, I need her dark form leaning over the piano in the moonlight, I need the music flowing through my heart.

I imagine a city as a living organism with electricity, gasoline, and propane firing through its arteries along with heroin, alcohol, cocaine, and meth. The humans, the creatures such as myself, think we are the city, but we are merely servants of the organism, and we can be dispatched without any warning by bullets, and yet the city will continue because it functions for our pleasure and our safety. Where the energy we have unleashed plays out like a tidal wave and levels everything in its path, levels the army, levels the police, levels the cartels, levels the gangs, levels the woman walking home from work, levels the man careening out of the midnight saloon. The general and the thief face the same giant wave. One thinks power safeguards him from the wave, and one thinks the delirious visions of the drug shelters him from all storms, and all learn that something they never imagined has come to pass.

Once, their worst nightmare was that they were not in control.

Now, their real nightmare is that no one is in control.

There is an afternoon and six men are put against a wall and executed in broad daylight. There is a morning and three prison guards at the bus stop are machine-gunned on their way to work. There is the man burning in the car.

There is a midday when two men fall dead in a hail of bullets.

The moon streams in, the fingers fly, I become "Rhapsody in Blue," and ignore the killing ground until the notes fade away.

The black boots came with Miss Sinaloa. She arrived that December afternoon with shiny black boots reaching almost to her knees, the heels thick, the surface acrylic as it threw light back up toward the heavens. The rest of her was skin, skin with bite marks all over her breasts, skin with handprints all over her ass. There were marks of beatings, also.

That was some weeks ago, when she had hair flowing down to her ass but had lost all of her wardrobe, save those boots. And lost her mind.

I sit here looking at a photograph taken in the yard of the crazy place. She has now been in her cage for some weeks, and her hair has been shorn. She is calming down and can be let out into the yard at times, a safe-conduct moment in which she struggles to rejoin the human race.

So she stands in the bright sunlight, boots gleaming, and she wears a satiny green dress and a black leather jacket. She holds a microphone in her right hand, and she is singing love songs. Behind her is the black amplifier and behind the equipment are her neighbors in the crazy place, and they look here and there and pay no attention to Miss Sinaloa singing of the heartaches that women must endure as they seek love in the world of men.

Her face is round and perfectly made up. Her cheeks shine, lips underscored with liner, eyebrows narrow and finely stated. Her body is solid and, to foreign eyes, might even look fat, but here in her native country, she looks good, a woman with some flesh, a woman a man can get a hold of as the night passes on sweat-soaked sheets. She is battered, she is still healing, she is half crazy, but it is clear to even my ignorant eyes that Miss Sinaloa is back, and men are simply creatures God created to worship her.

One member of her audience sits with head bowed and hands clasped between his knees. Another man wears a huge peaked hat such as the kind favored by Merlin in the ancient tales. A short man in a beige sport coat looks out with an idiot grin.

She sings because to fall silent is to die.

Even here, the world is about love or the world is about nothing at all.

I have learned many things from her, and because of this, I love her and her songs.

I think at times I need her music even more than she does.

Those red lips mean so much in a world of dust and blood.

They must pretend to have a monopoly on violence. So in the autumn of the killing season, six hundred military police and two hundred state and local cops converge on the prison that sits on the southern edge of Juárez. They come for their prey at 6 A.M. The prison is controlled by three local gangs: the Aztecas, the Mexicles, and the Artistas Asesinos—the Murder Artists. Some leaders are shipped away to another facility. There is a show of force until the veil drops again and the prison falls back into itself.

The entire raid is like a laboratory experiment that mirrors the city itself. The state parades as the real power. Inmates briefly cower and then return to violence and gangs and a world without a center. The newspapers note the assertion of order, then fall silent again as killing walks every pathway in the city.

It is a careless time.

Nothing you do can make you safe, and nothing you do can put you in danger. So, relax. You are in play, and all the neighborhoods are the wrong neighborhood, and all the bars are the wrong bar, and every minute of the day and night offers slaughter. This is not some breakdown of the social order. This is the new order. And we will adjust to it and it will be fine.

We are in a forever war, only it is not a war. It is not a crime wave. It just is. And we are. And this is it.

A kind of poetry falls out of the mouths of people as this new reality sinks in. The head of a local citizen's group says,

We are living the consequences
of the war that has come to the city
and unfortunately
we are also realizing
that the presence of the
police
and the military
has not managed to lessen the number of
homicides at all.

The head of the local bar association says,

To what the people already know,
the fight against narco-trafficking
that has generated a war
between groups
and is a factor in the
incidence of criminality.
Another factor
is that we have not been able to have a structure
for
the efficient procurement of justice
demanded
by the size and quantity
of the crimes.

The state attorney general's office offers,

For the Prosecutor's office,
the most important thing
is to carry out
the greatest effort to lower these statistics.

I feel the dust blowing across Juárez, sip a beer, hear the humming of the gears in the murder factory, watch the police prowl and hunt. Serenity comes once you relax and accept the product. There is so much work to be done and so many willing hands. Those hundreds of gangs, also the gangs that wear police uniforms or military uniforms, the polished professionals of the fabled cartels, as well as volunteers from the bars and sad marriages—all are willing to help with the slaughter. And all of those failed gods line up like tired whores to give whatever support they can.

Black velvet, yes, that is the feel of the sky, the feeling of the darkness coming down as I spiral into the embrace of death on high heels wobbling through the bullet-shredded night. The lipstick bright red, the scent a bouquet snatched from a fresh grave.

Feel the rush of fresh air as people vanish, and space becomes available.

Take the present for granted.

And the night.

A long time ago, back when the world made sense to me and everything was appetite, I walked across the room at a party toward a woman with fine breasts and a "hello fella" smile and a singer floated out of the speakers saying, "Ain't it just like the night to play tricks when you're tryin' to be so quiet."

A long time ago, I walked into a motel room covering my first murder and saw blood on the concrete block wall, a dull brown-colored stain against the gleam of the latex paint.

A long time ago, I broke into a neighbor's house because she had not answered the phone or door for a day and I found her sprawled on the kitchen floor, eyes open and mouth with an expression of mild surprise.

A long time ago, I did not have to live in the future.

Nor did Miss Sinaloa.

I hold her hand, and, to be honest, neither of us pays much attention to the murders. We've lost count and ignore the details of the slayings.

The headline says that a commando re-kills a guy at the local Red Cross.

Around 8 P.M., a man arrives in a Montero jeep with Texas plates and a bullet hole in his thorax.

A few minutes later, three cars arrive, and two guys with rifles walk in, and as a doctor watches, they pump three rounds into the patient, two in the chest, one in the head.

Then they leave, and all three vehicles melt back into the traffic of the city.

For two hours, the Red Cross is out of commission, though the parents of the dead guy come by to see how he is doing.

Like I said, Miss Sinaloa and I have lost track of the killings and become lazy these days.

Round up the usual suspects.

What we have here is a failure to communicate.

There are a million stories in the naked city.

Death be not proud.

"You are a mist that appears for a little while and then vanishes," James 4:14.

True grit.

Suck in yer gut, we're gonna whup it.

Don't complain, don't explain.

Are you feeling lucky, punk?

I have this desire to hear out a killer, to get down some torrent of speech on the work, a cascade of meanings and theories about killing people. I will be in a room sitting on a hard chair, notebook in hand, and the killer will start speaking and go on and on, and I will never write down a word, I will never hear a word. For a moment, I will be stunned by this dereliction of duty, and then a vast calm of indifference will descend, I'll pour another drink, turn my back on the killer, watch a bird on a wire, think of a recipe I wish to cook, hum a favorite hymn as he prattles on and on trying to give meaning to a life he has emptied of meaning.

I have lost all appetite for explanations since they stalk truth and love and shove us all into a coffin of lies.

In the end, we are in the future. Or some of us are.

Miss Sinaloa moves closer, and I feel the warmth of her body.

Murder Artist

He always has time for a little prayer. He was raised Catholic and he believes in God. So he makes it a rule to give them two minutes for a prayer. They are handcuffed, blindfolded, half-starved, and badly beaten. They are ready. And so they pray. And then, he strangles them, feels their bodies fight for air, struggle to retain some hold on life, and there is this ebbing, he can feel this in his hands, as they slide away into eternity.

He wants me to know this as we sit in the room, drapes pulled shut to keep out prying eyes, black coffee steaming in his hand, his voice level, and the sentences direct and with a simple eloquence. He is speaking for a trade, the *sicarios*, the professional killers, and he wants the world to know the work, and he wants the other *sicarios* out there to know that it is possible to leave the work. And come to God.

He has a green pen, a notebook. He has printouts from the Internet, mainly things about myself. He has spent ten hours researching me. Like so many pilgrims, he is in the market for a witness who can understand his life. He has decided I will suffice. He is at ease now. Before, his body language was hunched over, shoulders looming, hands ready, those trained and talented hands. He wore a skullcap that hid his hair, and he seldom smiled.

Now he is a different person, a man who laughs, his body almost fluid, his eyes no longer dead, black coals but beaming and dancing as he speaks.

"We are not monsters," he explains. "We have education, we have feelings. I would leave torturing someone, go home, and have dinner with my family, and then return. You shut off parts of your mind. It is a kind of work, you follow orders."

For some time, his past life has been dead to him, something he shut off. But now it is back. He thinks God has sent me to convey his lessons to others. Like all of us, he wants his life to have meaning, and I am to write it down and send it out into the world. Of course, he must be careful. When he left the life two years ago, the organization put a contract on his life of $250,000. He does not know what the contract currently is, but it is unlikely to be lower. At the moment, God is protecting him and his, he knows this, but still, he must be careful.

Just the other day, a man and a woman from El Paso went to Juárez for the funeral of the woman's sister who had been murdered the previous week. They both worked in the El Paso hospital where gunshot patients from Juárez are often brought for their own security. At about noon, two cars cut the couple off from the procession. Twenty rounds were pumped into the front seat, killing the man and the woman. Two people riding in the backseat were left unharmed. As so often happens, no one really saw anything, and so the killers in their two cars rode away as if they were invisible.

Such incidents can never be far from his mind. He is almost a scholar of such actions, since for about twenty years he performed them.

"I don't do bad things anymore," he says, "but I can't stop being careful. It is a habit I have. That's how I ensure security for myself. They killed me twice, you know."

And he lifts his shirt to show me two groupings of bullet holes in his belly from when he took blasts from an AK-47.

"I was in a coma for a while," he continues. "I weighed two hundred ninety pounds when I went into the hospital, a narco-hospital, and I shrunk to a hundred twenty pounds."

It was all a mistake. The organization believed he had leaked information on the killing of a newspaper columnist, but it turned out the actual informant had been the guy paid to tap phones. So they killed that guy and "apologized to me and paid for a month's vacation in Mazatlán with women, drugs, and liquor. I was about twenty-four then."

He sips his coffee. He is ready to begin.

He notes that when I asked him earlier about his first killing, he said he couldn't really remember because he used so much cocaine and drank so much alcohol. That was a lie. He remembers quite well.

"The first person I killed, well, we were state policemen doing a patrol," he begins. "They called my partner on his cell phone and told him the person we were looking for was in a mall. So we went and got him and put him in the car."

Two other guys get in the car, identify the target, and then leave. They are the people paying for the murder.

He and his partner have a code: When the number thirty-nine is spoken, it means to kill the person.

The guy they have picked up has lost ten kilos of cocaine, drugs that belong to the other two men.

His partner drives, and he gets in back with the victim.

The target says that he gave the drugs to his partner, and at that moment, his partner says, "Thirty-nine," and so he instantly kills him.

"It was like automatic," he explains.

They drive around for hours with the body, and they drink. Finally, they go to an industrial park, pry off a manhole cover, and throw the body in the sewer. For his work, he gets an ounce of coke, a bottle of whiskey, and a thousand dollars.

"They told me I had passed the test. I was eighteen."

He checks into a hotel and does cocaine and drinks for four days.

"The state police didn't care if you were drunk. If you really wanted to be left alone, you gave the dispatcher a hundred pesos and then they would not call you at all."

After this baptism, he moves into kidnapping and enters a new world. Soon he is traveling all the country, he has a pilot and plane assigned to him. He is nineteen and on top of the world. He is working for the police, but whenever an assignment comes up, he gets leave.

A few of the kidnappings he participates in are simply snatches for ransom. But hundreds of others have a different goal.

"They would say, 'Take this guy, he lost two hundred kilos of marijuana and didn't pay.' I would pick him up in my police car, I would drop him off at a safe house. A few hours later, I would get a call that said there is a dead body to get rid of.

"This was at the start of my career, after I passed my test. For about three years, I traveled all over Mexico. Once, I even went to Quintana Roo. I always had an official police car. Sometimes we used planes, but usually we drove. We got through military checkpoints by showing an official document that said we were transporting a prisoner. The document would have a fake case number."

He becomes a tour guide to an alternative Mexico, a place where citizens are transported from safe house to safe house without any records left for courts and agencies. When he arrives someplace, the person has already been kidnapped. He simply picks him up for shipment.

Controlling them was simple because they were terrified.

"When they saw that it was an official car and when I said, 'Don't worry, everything will be fine. You'll be back with your family. If you don't cooperate, we'll drug you and put you in the trunk, and I can't guarantee then that you'll see the end of the journey.'"

The drive is fueled by cocaine. He and his partner always dress well for such work—they get five or six new suits from the organization every few months. They are seldom home but seem to live in various safe houses and are supplied with food and drugs. But no women. This is all business. They hardly ever do police work, they are busy working full time for narcos.

This business looks almost normal on the surface—snatch under the guise of police work and then collect money owed to the organization. But the real product is vanishing people. Hardly anyone who is taken ever returns to the world.

This is his real home for almost twenty years, a second Mexico that officially does not exist and that operates seamlessly with the government. In his many transports of human beings to bondage, torture, and death, the authorities never interfere with this work. He is part of the government, the official state policeman with eight men under his command. But his real employer is the organization. They give him a salary, a house, a car. And standing.

He estimates that 85 percent of the police work for the organization even though on a clear day he could barely glimpse the cartel that employed him. He is in a cell, and above him is a boss, and above that boss is a region of power he never visits or knows. He also estimates that out of every hundred human beings he transports, maybe two make it back to their former lives. The rest die. Slowly, very slowly.

In each safe house, there would be anywhere from five to fifteen kidnap victims. They wore blindfolds all the time, and if their blindfold slipped, they were killed. At times, they would be put in a chair facing a television, their eyes would be briefly uncovered, and they would watch videos of their children going to school, their wife shopping, the family at church. They would see the world they had left behind, and they would know this world would vanish, be destroyed if they did not come up with the money. The neighbors never complained about the safe houses. They would see police cars parked in front and remain silent.

And the money. They might owe a million, but when the work was finished, they would pay everything, their entire fortunes, and maybe, just maybe, the wife would be left with a house and a car. People would be held for up to two years. They were beaten after they were fed, and so they learned to associate food with pain. Once in a great while, the order would come down to release a prisoner. They would be taken to a park blindfolded, told to count to fifty before they opened their eyes. Even at this moment of freedom, they would weep because they no longer believed it possible for them to be released, and they still expected to be murdered.

The prisoners memorized the individual footsteps of their keepers and knew when a hard beating was coming.

"Sometimes," he notes, "prisoners who had been held for months would be allowed to remove the blindfolds so they could clean the safe house. After a while, they began to think they were part of the organization, and they identified with the guards who beat them. They would even make up songs about their experiences as prisoners, and they would tell us of all the fine things they would make sure we got when they were released. Sometimes, after beating them badly, we would send their families videos of them, and they would be pleading, saying, 'Give them everything.' And then the order would come down, and they would be killed."

Payment to the organization would always be made in a different city from where the prisoner was held in a safe house. Everything in the organization was compartmentalized. Often, he would stay in a safe house for weeks and never speak to a prisoner or know who they were. It did not matter. They were a product, and he was a worker following orders. No matter how much the family paid, the prisoner almost always died. When the family had been sucked dry of money, the prisoner had no value. And besides, he could betray the organization. So death was logical and inevitable.

He pauses in his account. He wants it understood that he is now similar to the prisoners he tortured and killed. He is outside the organization, he is a threat to the organization, and "everyone who is no longer of use to the boss, dies."

He is now the floating man remembering when he was firmly anchored in his world.

"I want it understood," he says, "that I had feelings when I was in the torture houses and people would be lying in their vomit and blood. I was not permitted to help them."

He is calm as he says this. He alternates between asserting his humanity and explaining how he maintained a professional calm while he kidnapped, tortured, and killed people. He says he is feared now because he believes in God. Then he says he could make a good grouping on the target with his AK-47 at eight hundred yards. He would practice at military bases and police academies. He could get in using his police badge.

The work, he insists, is not for amateurs. Take torture—you must know just how far to go. Even if you intend to kill the person in the end, you must proceed carefully in order to get the necessary information.

"They are so afraid," he explains, "they are usually cooperative. Sometimes, when they realize what is going to happen to them, they become aggressive. Then you take their shoes away, soak their clothes, and put a hot wire to each foot for fifteen seconds. Then they understand that you are in charge and that you are going to get the information. You can't beat them too much, because then they become insensitive to pain. I have seen people beaten so badly that you could pull out their fingernails with pliers, and they wouldn't feel it.

"You handcuff them behind their backs, sit them in a chair facing a hundred-watt bulb, and you ask them questions about their jobs, number and ages of children, all things you have researched and know the answer to. Every time they lie, you give them a jolt from an electric cattle prod. Once they realize they can't lie, you start asking them the real questions—how many loads have they moved to the United States, who do they work for, and if they are not paying your boss, well, why not?

"They will try, by this point, to answer everything. Then we beat them, and let them rest. We show them those videos of their family. At this point, they will give up anything we ask for, and even more. Now you have the advantage and you use this new information to hit warehouses and steal loads, to round up other people they work with, and then you video their families and begin the process again. You know the families will not likely go to the police, because they know the guy is in a bad business. But if they do tell the police, we instantly know, because we work with the police. We're part of the anti-kidnapping unit. Sometimes the people kidnapped are killed immediately because, after we take their jewelry and cars, they are worthless. Such goods are divided up within the unit, between five and eight people. The hardest thing is when you kill them, because then you must dig a hole to bury them. Most people make two mistakes. They don't pay whoever controls the plaza, the city. Or they dreamed of being bigger than the boss."

But none of this really matters, because he never asks why people are kidnapped, or who they really are. They are the product, and he is a worker. Their screams are background noise to the task at hand. Just as calming them or transporting them is just part of the job. He is not living in evil, he is living beyond evil and beyond good.

He has dug two hundred fifty graves. He knows where at least six hundred corpses are hidden in Ciudad Juárez alone.

There is a second category of kidnapping, one he finds almost embarrassing. Someone's wife is having an affair with her personal trainer, so you pick up the trainer and kill him. Or a guy has a hot woman, and some other guy wants her, so you kill the boyfriend to get the woman for him.

"I received my orders," he says, "and I had to kill them. The bosses didn't know what the limits were. If they want a woman, they get her. If they want a car, they get it. They have no limits."

He also resents people who like to kill. They are not professional. Real *sicarios* kill for money. But there are people who kill for fun.

"People will say, 'I haven't killed anyone for a week'. So they'll go out and kill someone. This kind of person does not belong in organized crime. They're crazy. If you discover such a person in your unit, you kill them. The people you really want to recruit are police, or ex-police, trained killers."

All this is a sore point for him. The slaughter now going on in Juárez offends him because too many of the killings are done by amateurs, by kids imitating *sicarios*. He has watched the disintegration of a professional culture he gave his life to, all in the last two years or so, when this new wave of violence began. He is appalled by the number of bullets used in a single execution. It shows a lack of training and skill. In a real hit, the burst goes right where the lock is on the door because such rounds will penetrate the driver's trunk with a killing shot. The pattern should be very tight. Twice he was stymied by armored vehicles, but the solution is a burst of full-jacketed rounds in a tight pattern—this will gouge through the armor. A hit should take no more than a minute. Even his hardest jobs against armored cars took under three minutes.

A real *sicario*, he notes, does not kill women or children. Well, unless the women are informants for the DEA or the FBI. And of course, anyone who informs to the Mexican police is immediately reported to the organization.

Here, he must show me. A proper execution requires planning. First, the Eyes study the target for days, usually at least a week. His schedule at home is noted, when he gets up, when he leaves for work, when he comes home, every thing about his routines in his domestic life is recorded by the Eyes. Then the Mind takes over. He studies the man's habits in the city itself. His day at work, where he lunches, where he drinks, how often he visits his mistress, where she lives, and what her habits are. Between the Eyes and the Mind, a portrait is possible. Now there is a meeting of the crew, which entails six to eight people. There will be two police cars with officers, and two other cars with *sicarios*. A street will be selected for the hit, one that can easily be blocked off. Time will be carefully worked out, and the hit will take place within a half dozen blocks of a safe house—an easy matter since there are so many in the city.

He picks up a pen and starts drawing. The lead car will be police. Then will come a car full of *sicarios*. Then the car driven by the target. This is followed by another car of *sicarios*. And then, bringing up the rear, another police car.

During the execution, the Eyes will watch and the Mind will man the radios.

When the target enters the block selected for the murder, the lead police car will pivot and block the street, the first *sicario* car will slow, the second car of *sicarios* behind the target will pull up beside him and kill him, and the final police car will block the end of the street.

All this should take less than thirty seconds. One man will get out and give a coup de grâce to the bullet-riddled victim. Then all will disperse.

The car with the killers will go to the safe house no more than six blocks away and will pull into a garage. It will be taken to another garage owned by the organization, repainted, and then sold on one of the organization's lots. The killers themselves will pick up a clean car at the safe house, and often they return to the scene of the murder to see that everything has gone well.

He sketches this with exactness, each rectangle neatly drawn to delineate a car, and the target's car is filled in and blooms on the page with green ink. Arrows indicate how each vehicle will move. It is like an equation on a chalkboard.

He leans back from his toil, the look of pride in craftsmanship on his face. This is how a real sicario performs his work. No one is left behind alive. If anyone in the group should be injured, he goes to one of the organization's hospitals—"If you can buy a governor, you can buy a hospital."

"I never knew the names of the people I was involved with," he continues. "There was a person who directed our group, and he knew everything. But if your job is to execute people, that is all you do. You don't know the reasons or names. I would be in a safe house with the kidnapped for a month and never speak to them. Then, if the order came to kill them, I would. We would take them to the place where they would be killed, take off their clothes. We would kill them exactly the way we were ordered—a bullet to the neck, acid on the bodies. There were cases where you would be killing someone, strangling them, and they would stop breathing, and you would get a call—'don't kill them'—and so you would have to know how to resuscitate them, or you would be killed because the boss never makes a mistake."

Everything is contained and sealed. In the 1990s, they used crazy kids to steal cars for the work, but the kids, about forty of them, got too arrogant and started bragging in the nightclubs and selling drugs. This violated an agreement with the governor of Chihuahua to keep the city quiet. So one night in 1998, fifty police and one hundred fifty guys from the organization, who were to ensure the job was done, rounded up all the kids on Avenida Juárez. They were not tortured. They were killed with a single headshot and buried in one hole.

"No," he smiles at me, "I will not tell you where that hole is."

He has trouble remembering everything.

"I would get up in the morning and do a line," he explains, "then have a glass of whiskey. Then I would go to lunch. I would never sleep more than a few hours, little naps. It is hard to sleep during a time of war. Even if my eyes were closed, I was alert. I slept with a loaded AK-47 on one side, a .38 on the other. The safeties were always off.

"Do I know of the death houses?" he asks. "It would take a book to do the death houses. After all, I know where six hundred bodies are buried in safe houses in Juárez. There is one death house they have never revealed, which I know has fifty-six bodies. Just as there is a rancho where the officials say they found two bodies, but I know that rancho has thirty-two corpses buried there. If the police really investigated, they would find bodies. But obviously, you cannot trust the police."

But he especially wants to know what I know about the two death houses uncovered this spring. I say one had nine bodies, the other thirty-six.

No, no, he insists, the second one had thirty-eight, two of them women.

He carefully draws me the layout of this second death house. One of the women, he notes, was killed for speaking too much. The other was a mistake. These happen.

But he keeps returning to the death house with the thirty-eight bodies. It has memories for him.

I remember standing on the quiet dirt street as the authorities made a show of digging up the dead. Four blocks away was a hospital where some machine-gunned people were taken that spring, but the killers followed and killed them in the emergency room. Shot their kinfolk in the waiting room, also.

"The narcos," he wants me to understand, "have informants in DEA and the FBI. They work until they are useless. Then they are killed."

He pauses.

"Informants for the FBI and DEA die ugly."

He explains.

"They were brought handcuffed behind the back to the death house where they found thirty-eight bodies," he rolls on. "A T-shirt was soaked with gasoline and put on their backs, lit, and then, after a while, pulled from their backs. The skin came off with it. Both men made sounds like cattle being killed. They were injected with a drug so they would not lose consciousness. Then they put alcohol on their testicles and lit them. They jumped so high—they were handcuffed, and still I never saw people jump so high."

We are slipping now, all the masks have fallen to the floor, the veteran, the professional *sicario* is walking me through a key assignment he completed.

"Their backs were like leather and did not bleed. They put plastic bags on their heads to smother them and then revived them with alcohol under their noses.

"All they ever said to us was 'We will see you in hell.'

"This went on for three days. They smelled terrible because of the burns. They brought in a doctor to keep reviving them. They wanted them to live one more day. After a while, they defecated blood. They shoved broomsticks up their asses.

"The second day, a person came and told them, 'I warned you this was going to happen.'

"They said, 'Kill us.'

"The guys lived three days. The doctor kept injecting them to keep them alive, and he had to work hard. Eventually, they died of the torture.

"They never asked God for help. They just kept saying, 'We will see you in hell.'

"I buried them with their faces down and poured on a whole lot of lime."

He is excited. It is all back.

He can feel the shovel in his hand. Smell the burned flesh.

We seem to take things for granted, to take the dust for granted, to take the drugs for granted. And to take the killing for granted. Soon we will come to expect our own murder and not even worry if it arrives on schedule.

That is the way El Pastor was years ago when he moved out into the desert and built a hut as the initial act of his decision to create an asylum for the destroyed people. He had a burro, and he gathered dead wood in the sands for a fire.

He looked up at the mountains where the giant Uffington horse spread Celtic mystery over the Chihuahuan desert. Some days the wind blew and the sand came up and hid the mountain. But there were times, wonderful times, when the stars came out at night, and the sun fell down like honey on his mission.

These were the wonder days for El Pastor. He had nothing, the hut did not even have a real roof, just canvas spread over the adobe walls. He was living the life of the early Christians, and I'm sure his soul was full of Jesus and his mind full of anxiety.

He noticed that a giant iguana had been sketched on the mountain in the same manner and scale as that of the Uffington horse. Everyone knew and whispered that the big horse was the gift of Amado Carrillo, the head of the Juárez cartel, to the mountain. And of course, El Pastor knew that the big iguana was the symbol of the Juárez cartel, a kind of trademark, and having it on the mountain told everyone that the city belonged to them.

Sometimes during the day, and also at night, El Pastor saw helicopters landing right by the iguana.

So one day, he went up there to see what was going on.

Men with guns told him he did not belong there and that he should not come back. Perhaps the fact the he was a man of God spared him more than a verbal warning.

No matter, El Pastor went back to his work and prayer and eventually built the compound that became the temporary home of Miss Sinaloa when she lost her mind through the rapture of a party with cocaine, whiskey, and rape.

The giant iguana itself became like the dust storms and hot days, something so commonplace as to be beneath notice. Just part of the natural landscape of this city of the future.

I have this kind of vision as I eat dust in the wind. All the dead since January 1 will gather in this special place. They will sit in rows of chairs just as the dead sit in rows in Thornton Wilder's play *Our Town*. There will be a thousand or more separate tales of how they loved things and enjoyed life and how they were murdered and who murdered them. Even the forty-five corpses recently dug from death houses will be there to share their stories. Perhaps the governor and the police forces and the army officers will attend to hear the stories of the unofficial Juárez.

I have not chosen this spot for the performance, it has demanded to be the venue. It earned its place in the late afternoon of August 13, when eight people were murdered here in the largest single killing in the history of Ciudad Juárez. The event passed with as little public notice as possible. No one said out loud that this was the biggest single slaughter on record. No one said much of anything.

On that bloody day in August, at 7:15 P.M., four or eight men drive up and park their trucks, a red Chevrolet Avalanche and a Chevrolet Suburban. Down the street—about fifty yards, or in one report, just a few yards—waits a detail of seven or eight soldiers wearing the red beret of an elite unit in a white Ford Lobo pickup. The men enter CIAD No. 8, a center for the treatment of drug and alcohol problems. Prayer fills the air because a group of evangelicals—the deacon, the woman preacher, and five members of the congregation—have arrived to lead a religious service for the recovering addicts. They belong to a family worship center called Jesus Christ Blessed Works.

They are in the back *sala*, a room maybe fifteen feet wide and thirty-five to forty feet long, and are just at the point in the service when they make the call for people to come forward and give their lives to Christ. All the worshipers have their hands up in the air for Christ, their faces lifted up toward heaven, the woman leading them from the podium. In all, there are about thirty-five people in the facility when the men enter through the office. They have black hoods on their heads, wear body armor, and carry AK-47s. They remain about fifteen minutes and leave sixty spent cartridges on the ground. The preacher says, "They began to shoot, right and left in all directions, meanwhile I was crying out to God to send His angels to protect us, and I saw the young people falling injured all around me and others who managed to run for their lives."

They take four people out of the *sala* and execute them on the ground in the patio. The director of the center jumps atop a pregnant woman—the wife of one of the visiting evangelicals—to protect her. He dies, she is wounded but lives. Some people flee to the tiny bathroom in the back of the room and pile up atop each other. Others flee to the roof, tear out a cyclone fence, and jump. The secretary is pursued down a narrow passageway, round the corner, and to the top of the stairs, where he is mowed down. When the fifteen minutes are up, there are eight dead and five wounded, among them the secretary. When the shooting begins, neighbors go out and alert the army detail parked just outside, but the soldiers ignore them. Some neighbors call the Emergency Response Center. But there is no response. Except for that barrage of bullets. The army detail leaves once the shooting starts—though the military later denies that they were present. The killers stroll out and drive away. And then comes the silence. The police do not come for a long spell, and even then, they simply cordon off the area, but do not offer any relief to the wounded. Ambulances do not come. No one comes. Finally, the survivors load up the wounded in old vans and drive them to hospitals. One boy dies en route.

Forty-one hours later, the street is midday sun and dust. Broken buses line one side, where men tinker to get them ready for one more bumping journey down the rutted lanes of the city. I am here against my will. I had decided that six months of killing was enough for me and everyone else, and that anything beyond that merely meant repeating what was already known. I had determined I could not look at one more corpse, that I was ill, and that the toxic elements floating through my cells and through my mind came from this city and this slaughter. I had determined to leave and stay away and never return, eat wholesome food, drink bottled water, fill bird feeders religiously, and keep the slightest tremor of stress at bay and barred from my life. But people slaughtered while praying bring me back.

The street is broken earth, rock, and ruts. On one side is a row of vans from Sonora, the drivers sitting with stone faces and anxious eyes. On the other side, the buses. The drug rehab center itself is muted, its name whitewashed out since the killings. Dogs bark and snarl from behind iron gates of the houses lining the street. Trees struggle, leaves limp in the summer heat. A few blocks away, the cement plant towers over the barrio. It is thought that the people who jumped from the roof were fleeing toward the cement plant. Just down the road is the prison. And the military base for the city. On the walls everywhere, spray paint spells out "LOCOS 23," the local gang. Everything here is coated with fatigue, all the faces, the machines, the tiny houses, the plants, everything. The sky itself sags with fatigue, and the sun seems to struggle not to fall to earth.

From here each day, the addicts would spill out into the city selling candy and gum to earn their keep in rehab. Mexico is not a good place to need help. The average wait for entry into a rehab facility for substance abuse is ten years. Other problems mean even longer delays in treatment—people with anxiety disorders wait in line thirty years before their first treatment. What this means is that treatment for most Mexicans means absolutely nothing at all. The government has programs, the government makes pronouncements, the government produces studies, but if you are a Mexican with a problem, you must take care of it yourself because no one else is going to help you. Or you find this strange treatment center where they give you a bunk bed in a dormitory and talk you down and then send you out to peddle candy and gum to pay for your room and board. And you will be grateful for a spell as you find shelter from the streets that are killing you.

But the nature of life here does not seem to penetrate the minds of people in other places. They seem to think that there is treatment available here, but because of the poverty, it is just more austere than in the wealthier zones of the earth. They talk about police corruption, but seem to think in terms of a place like Chicago, and so they do not perceive this as a real problem. They read about the murders, but tell themselves that murders are high in Detroit. They know people are poor, but convince themselves that the people are slowly rising and soon things will be fine. They read that the Mexican army can be rough, but never grasp the fact that the Mexican army historically has been stationed all over the country in order to repress and terrorize the people of Mexico.

Sometimes I think I am living in a hall of mirrors like those I saw as a child in the carnival funhouse—huge mirrors that distort every form and yet retain enough of the actual form so that you think you are seeing a kind of visual riff on actual reality. And so we learn to pretend that what is happening is not really happening. Or we learn to pretend that what is happening is merely some kind of high range of normal experience, a slight exaggeration of what we already know. And so we kill both the slayers and the slain and make them go away by insisting they are part and parcel of the world we already know.

There is a body in the coffin. He is nineteen years old, small, faint moustache, proud member of Locos 23. He is in the kitchen, the sink full of dirty pots and pans. He sleeps, his face under glass, a pink-and-white striped shirt on his chest. Rosaries dangle from the coffin lid. A young mother hoists her baby up to look at the body. She stares, eyes wide.

He was one of the eight cut down in the drug center at around 7:15 P.M. as dusk slowly descended on the city by the river.

I stare into the baby's wide, dark eyes and try to make out what is and what will be. A golden crucifix, Christ with arms outstretched in His agony, floats over the face so still now, the eyes closed. The baby stares with round eyes of wonder.

I look into two versions of myself, the body in the coffin and the babe in arms. I am possibly past due for the coffin, but I remember through the haze those early glimpses of life when I was younger than I can even recall, those blues and greens, the smell of fresh apples, the feel of the grain in the floor-boards in the old farmhouse, the cluck of the chickens, the strange sounds coming from the mouths of adults. So I am in a small room full of people, the body is against the wall in a glass-topped coffin, the baby looks down at the still, dead face, and I can smell fresh hay from some forgotten summer when I first caught the light gleaming into my eyes. And I know that my early days were somehow similar, that bodies were still displayed in the house, that wakes were home affairs, the children and babies were not sheltered from the fate of all living things, and that all of life that mattered took place in the kitchen.

The city's fatigue seeps into my pores, the midday sun bakes my mind, and I wander between the coffin and the killing ground, and this is easy because the boy in the coffin lived next door to the rehabilitation center where he was murdered.

The gate is open to the center, and I enter. Men are tearing the place apart, and they seem frantic in their work. They are all from Sonora, and the story is very simple and clear. A week and a half earlier, armed men came to one of their three clinics in Juárez and herded fifty people into rooms, and then they took the director and a visitor out and executed them. The group, centered in Cananea, Sonora, decided to close all three facilities and leave the state of Chihuahua. They painted the word CLOSED on the center where the murders occurred. They called the police and army in Juárez and told them they were shutting everything down as fast as they could. They asked both the police and the army to give them protection until they could close down the centers—this request was denied. They piled into vans and drove over on Wednesday, their plan to load all the beds and office equipment into the vans and flee back to Sonora. The group arrived two hours after the killings.

He stands on the roof looking down at me in the small patio of the center. He refuses to give his name. Yet he cannot stop talking. They came through the office, he says, and then entered this patio. I look around and see a row of rooms—office, infirmary, lounge, detox, kitchen, *sala*—all open onto this concrete slit called the patio. He points to the corner of the patio—yes, there, there is where they took four from the *sala*, put them on the ground and executed them. I see the bullet holes.

He is a solid man in his forties with cropped hair and quick eyes. He has worked for the centers for six years, and he refuses to give his name. This last fact is to be expected. The neighbors quoted in the newspapers about that night also remain nameless. Only the dead get to have names. Everyone else—killers and survivors—are without identity. He says, "Come here, come here," and he leads me from his rooftop perch into a narrow defile between the concrete block center and the wall sheltering it from the street. The passageway is less than three feet wide, and down this corridor the secretary ran with AK-47s firing at him. The man on the roof makes me look at the steel casement around a window—the bullet holes through the metal are the size of a quarter. Then I turn the corner and see the staircase ahead and, on top of the building, the cyclone fence that is torn apart where desperate patients leapt from the roof to some hope of survival on the ground below. The secretary himself made it to the top of the open staircase before he was cut down by gunfire. He now is near death in a hospital. Terror lingers in the narrow passage. I climb up the stairs and enter the little rooms that line the roof and functioned as barracks for the addicts. On the walls are photographs—a pinup of a singer, a 1970 Mercedes convertible, and a velvet painting of a Mexican *águila*, eagle. On the floor is a book touting creationism over evolution, a workbook that teaches parenting without anger problems. It is still. No one is coming back for their things. And no one on site can really tell if these remnants belong to the quick or the dead.

Men tear apart metal beds—there is the screech of hacksaws and banging of hammers—a manic act of salvage. Other men carry out piles of blankets—the cheap Chinese ones made of synthetic fiber that have inundated Mexico. Today, two men were found wrapped in such blankets, their hands cut off and left by their sides, the bodies showing signs of torture. So the men carry out mounds of these blankets, but they do not put them in the vans. They toss them into trash barrels and say nothing. That scent of what were once people coming off the blankets they slept in every night, this fragrance of a life lost, is more than even the men salvaging materials can bear. So they stick to saving metal and trash the blankets.

I look up at the man on the roof, and he says, "They don't want us in Chihuahua. We get the message."

I enter the *sala*, the killing chamber where people were raising their hands to God when the gunmen entered. Flies buzz, and the sound sizzles in the empty room. In back is the tiny bathroom where people piled atop each other in some fantasy of escaping death. On the front wall are the twelve steps to curing addiction in Spanish. Also, the Serenity Prayer, Reinhold Niehbur's contribution to sanity in World War II when it fluttered across American life.

DIOS CONCEDEME SERENIDAD PARA ACEPTAR LAS COSAS
QUE NO PUEDO CAMBIAR

It is posted in the front of the room, where the woman stood at the podium soliciting the addicts to come forward for Christ. On the floor, the tiles are brown, red, white, gray, and beige. A map of the Holy Land is underfoot. A crucifix leans in the corner, a candle sputtering before it.

VALOR PARA CAMBIAR LAS QUE SI PUEDO

There are three bullet holes in the floor, and the wall has dribbles of blood and one red palm print. The floor has been mopped, but still, there is the blood on the wall and the blood that has seeped into the grout between the tiles. The flies buzz and buzz.

SABIDURIA PARA DISTINGUIR LA DIFERENCIA

The man from the roof tells me, "I believe the police are scared. Our own people started pulling people into the vans because no one came."

Yes, amid the noise, the men hurrying to load the vans, everyone is quite alone here. The largest slaughter in the history of the city, and there is no yellow police tape, no visible investigation of the crime scene. A set of clinics for addicts is leaving the city because of terror, but there are no reporters, no cameras. Just silence. And this sense of being alone.

Luis Angel Gonzalez Corral was nineteen years old and a member of Locos 23 and had a habit of sniffing glue—a habit that was getting the best of him. So a week or two ago, he went next door and joined the rehab program. On Wednesday night, his family heard the shooting next door and hid during the fifteen minutes of thundering gunfire. Then emerged and found a dead son.

The yard is dirt with a vine trailing over a leaning fence to the north. Two poles support big sheets of canvas and provide shade for the mourners sitting on old chairs or concrete blocks. They are mainly women, and the oldest is maybe in her forties. The ancients that should be clogging such a wake have been left behind in the country. This is a barrio of people driven off the land,

and of people barely surviving in the new world of the city. Only one woman wears a dress. Everyone else is in clean shorts or jeans and T-shirts. Voices are muted, a kind of murmuring floats across the ground. The faces are tired, the eyes glazed. There are few males in attendance: just gang kids come to honor one of their own and two or three older men. It is early afternoon, the men are either at work or looking for work. This is also a barrio where each day is an effort to find some way to provide food. There is no future here, but a constant struggle in the present.

The small house of three little rooms shares a common wall with the abandoned center. The body lies in the kitchen. A sheet blocks the window and has been painted with a message of support from Locos 23. Women sit in a row of folding chairs before the sheet and face the coffin. They are also very tired and pass for the matrons of this street of dust.

One woman lost her son six weeks ago. She says he was twenty-five years old and did work now then as a plasterer or drywall hanger. They came in the night, and she did not see them, she says, because she was in bed. The next day, his body was found. He had been tortured. Neighbors told her he was taken away by the municipal police. Four young men of this area have been executed in the last few months, four who lived within a few blocks of each other. Her voice is soft and flat as she recounts the loss of her son. Little or no emotion colors her tale, perhaps it would be too taxing on the soul. Here, getting killed is part of growing up for young men.

I ask the mother of the dead boy who rests in the glass-topped coffin what he planned to be when he grew up.

She stares at me silently as if slowly digesting the question.

Then, she holds her hands out palms up and shrugs at the implication of such a question. Ambitions do not grow here, and the future does not exist here. At least not in a way recognized by governments. Ambition is displayed on the sheet where Locos 23 states its claim to the dead boy. It is in the eyes of the people at the wake who see death but expect no justice beyond a life lived and ended by slaughter. A girl in tight black pants and a black lacy blouse enters the kitchen, gets a soft drink from the refrigerator, and smiles at friends. She is pregnant with the dead boy's child, and for a few hours this afternoon she is the center of a kind of mild attention. Just as the mother dressed in black holds a kind of low-key standing in the heat, flies, and dust.

The boy had been in treatment before, and failed. Then, last Friday, the family could tell he was on drugs again, and so they took him next door and put him in the center. He'd basically been raised by his grandmother. After the shooting, the boy was one of the wounded put in a van for transportation to the hospital. He didn't make it and was left on a street corner. His grandmother found him and wailed. His head was a mess, he was covered with blood, and he seemed very still to her. He was gone. The old woman had planned to take him out of the center that Saturday. Thursday morning, she was taken to the hospital with a heart attack. And now, at the wake on Friday afternoon, everyone is quiet and tired and the mother shrugs when explaining what ambition her son might have harbored.

There is nothing puzzling at the wake next door to the slaughterhouse. The killers give no reason for killing, they simply fire. The army parks down the street and does nothing. The neighbors hide during the fifteen minutes of murder. No one wants a real name publicized. The police do not come, the ambulances stay away. Gang kids paint a sheet, drift into and out of the wake, and look at the body with blank eyes. The girl, maybe sixteen years old, is pregnant, and she sips Seven-Up a few feet from her boyfriend's body. The mother answers questions with a flat voice. And a whisper begins: that the church deacon killed had a premonition that he should not come. That he froze when he was to read a Bible verse and could not speak. Soon other signs will be remembered, and somehow the blood and the flies will be erased and made smooth by legend. The baby leaning over the coffin—the glass top now covered with rosaries brought by local people, the base surrounded by carnations and gladiolas and daisies and roses—will grow up learning tales and stories and miracles associated with the killing, and this will be part of being alive on this street with the dust in the air. After all, one pregnant woman at the meeting survived—the dead deacon's body was draped over hers. She will be proof of God or the devil or some force besides the flies and dust and sun, the water that fails, the electricity that comes and goes, the police who might kill you, the army who might kill you, the gangs that might kill you. And the gang that is all you have or ever will have in your short life. After all, there is that photo of you and your friends taped on your coffin lid, and you are all tossing out gang signs with your fingers.

So much depends on a blue carnation and fingers flicking messages into the void. The white carnations have a blue dye by the body resting in the coffin. And I think, okay, this is what it is about, doing the best, the very best one can do under the circumstances. So much depends on the people in the neighborhood, who say the gunshots could be heard for blocks and blocks. About the time of the killings at the center, the government announced that there have been about 839 murders in the Juárez area this year, but only eighteen people have been charged.

So much depends on the worker at the center who is busy loading the vans so that all can flee Juárez, and I ask him, just what do you think is going on here? and he says, "Something evil. Something very, very evil."

To ask what your son wanted to become is to imagine a world that is not a thought in the yard with the dust, the canvas hoisted on poles for shade, the vine wilting on the fence in the afternoon sun, and the coffin resting in the kitchen by the dirty pots and pans.

On the kitchen wall, the tear-away calendar has stalled at August 13/14, the night of the killing. But of course, time goes on, and the boy in the box will not be the last to die, nor the last member of Locos 23. We are in a place without beginning or end, and all the ways to tell the story fail me and repel me. There are many dead, and they each have a tale. Beyond that, the efforts to explain are to me efforts to erase truth or deny truth or simply to tell lies. I don't know what is going on, nor do the dead or the living. But there are these stories of the killings, there is the tortured flesh, the individual moments of horror, and I rest on those moments because they are actual and beyond question.

Dead Reporter Driving

The woman and Emilio collect his son. They stop by his house to get some clothes and then flee to a small ranch about six miles west of Ascensión, where he can hide. He is terrified. Later that night, a friend takes him back to his house once again. He wears a big straw hat, slips low in the seat. He sneaks into his house and gets vital documents. A friend delivers a small black car out at the ranch.

All day Sunday, he tries to think of a way to save his life. He comes up with only one answer: flight. No matter where he goes in Mexico, he will have to find a job and use his identity cards and the army will track him down. He now knows they will never forget his story from 2005, that he cannot be redeemed.

He tells his boy, "We are not going back to our house. The soldiers may kill me, and I don't want to leave you alone."

Monday morning, he drives north very fast. He takes all his legal papers so that he can prove who he is. He expects asylum from the government of the United States when he crosses at Antelope Wells, New Mexico.

What he gets is this: He is immediately jailed, as is his son. They are separated. It is a common practice to break up families to crush the will—often jailing men and tossing the women and children back over the fence. He is denied bond, and no hearing is scheduled to handle his case. He is taken to El Paso and placed in a private prison. Had he entered the United States illegally and then asked for asylum, he would have been almost immediately bonded out. But since he entered legally by declaring his identity and legal status at a port of entry and applied for asylum, he is placed in prison because Homeland Security declares that Emilio has failed to prove that "he does not represent a threat to the community."

It is possible to see his imprisonment as simply the normal by-product of bureaucratic blindness and indifference. But I don't think that is true. No Mexican reporter has ever been given political asylum, because if the U.S. government honestly faced facts, it would have to admit that Mexico is not a society that respects human rights. Just as the United States would be hard pressed, if it faced facts, to explain to its own citizens how it can justify giving the Mexican army $1.4 billion under Plan Merida, a piece of black humor that is supposed to fight a war on drugs. But then, the American press is the chorus in this comedy since it continues to report that the Mexican army is in a war to the death with the drug cartels. There are two errors in these accounts. One is simple: The war in Mexico is for drugs and the enormous money to be made by supplying American habits, a torrent of cash that the army, the police, the government, and the cartels all lust for. Second, the Mexican army is a government-financed criminal organization, a fact most Mexicans learn as children.

Emilio Gutiérrez becomes a new kind of man, one who has lost his career, failed to protect his son from jail, a man with no clear future. He is deloused, given a blue jumpsuit, and set to work scrubbing floors for a dollar a day or an apple. He has tried to enter the United States legally and now makes less than what the illegal migrants who work in the country make. He also remembers all those bribes, all those *sobres*, he refused for years. He thinks, "If I had taken bribes, I wouldn't be here in prison." And of course, he is right, because if he'd been dutifully corrupt, he'd be safe inside the system and still living and writing in Ascensión, Chihuahua, with his son. Instead, he is surrounded by 1,200 to 1,300 Africans, Middle Easterners, East Indians, Russians, and, of course, Mexicans swept up in the increasing Immigration and Customs Enforcement (ICE) raids. The Mexicans are forlorn because the raids have separated husbands from wives and parents from children.

"The Mexicans," he explains, "are treated the worst. The staff curses us and calls us rats, narcos, and criminals. The work of the prison is done by the Mexicans and Central Americans. It is ironic, the illegals are arrested for working and then put in prison and made to work for nothing."

When he crossed, he imagined that the U.S. government would take him to some safe house, perhaps guard him and protect him. He did not expect jail. Now he feels impotent. He is angry at the United States because they criticize other nations for human rights abuses, and when he flees for his life, they treat him like a criminal. He has nightmares of being deported. And he is desolate because he cannot learn anything about his son. He remembers those moments he loved: making his son's breakfast, washing his son's clothes. Now he can do nothing for him. Emilio cries a lot.

For a month, he is not allowed to speak to his son. He is tormented by the fear that the boy is being mistreated. He worries that older boys might molest him. The prison officials refuse to tell him anything. Finally, he gets a ten-minute phone call. The boy says he is doing okay. Emilio tells him they will not be able to go back to Mexico. He can sense his son is bitter—he has lost his home, his friends, even his dog. Emilio wants to hug him and kiss him as he did each day at home.

Eventually, they get to talk briefly twice a month, and the boy has his fifteenth birthday in a cage. Emilio finally gets a lawyer, but often he cannot even talk to him when he visits because he is too depressed.

The lawyer explains the facts of life to him. He says, "Maybe the United States does not want you, but we know Mexico does not want you. Think of your son."

The prison is haunted by a Cuban ghost. Twenty years before, the man hung himself in the shower. And now at night, sometimes all the showers come on, or the toilets are emptied of water. Security cameras see the Cuban in the library in the middle of the night reading. There are sounds of a guitar playing. The ghost is a message that tells Emilio what prison can do to a man.

His son is released to relatives in El Paso after a few months in jail. He tells his father not to give up. He tells the press, "I really miss him, and I miss my home, too, but for me, my dad is more important. Because if something happens to him, I think that I would die. Because he is the only person I have, and I love him more than anyone in the world."

At the end of January 2009, Emilio Gutiérrez is suddenly released from prison without any warning. When they called him to the office, he assumed he was being shipped to another prison in the American gulag. His lawyer, Carlos Spector, also had no indication of the release.

Now Emilio sits in the sun and tries to teach me Mexico as it is today. He has a hearing coming up in March, but this could be postponed because the U.S. government loves postponing such hearings in the hopes that migrants will give up and go back home. Emilio cannot even work, because the U.S. government has yet to give him a work permit. He stays with friends.

"Mexicans," he explains, "know the army is a bunch of brutes. But what is going on now is a coup d'état by the army. The president is illegitimate. The army has installed itself. They have become the government. They are installed in all the state governments. They control the municipal police. They are everywhere but the Ministry of Education—after all, they are too illiterate to run that. The president has his hands tied, and he has tied them."

But Emilio is a creature of hope. He does not think he will be deported. He has faith in the new U.S. administration because "the race Obama belongs to has been enslaved. I think he shares this history of discrimination with Latinos. And he will realize the huge human rights abuses in Mexico. There are thousands of people like me here. There are thousands of abandoned homes in Juárez alone. If I am sent back to Mexico, I might live a day or a few years. The army may kill me immediately or wait for my case to grow cold."

But if he loses his asylum case, he does have the right to pick a third country for his deportation. He is thinking maybe Cuba or Venezuela because perhaps they will take him for the pleasure of humiliating the United States on human rights grounds.

He is a man who has moved into a reality I cannot reach. He is almost beyond everyday concerns because he has lost everything and eventually may lose his life.

He tells me, "I have learned to like myself, to be thankful to God, to love my son even more. The only happy people in Mexico are the politicians and the army officers."

Two days later, Emilio holds a press conference with two other Mexican nationals, Jorge Luis Aguirre, the creator of a Web site of gossip and news in Juárez who has also fled for his life, and Gustavo de la Rosa Hickerson, the supervising attorney for the State Committee of Human Rights in Chihuahua. They are forming an organization, Periodistas Mexicanos en Exilio (Mexican Journalists in Exile, or PEMEXX). They all say the same thing: that the Mexican army is terrorizing the nation and killing people out of hand.

One reporter asks Jorge Luis Aguirre if he will also apply for asylum, and he answers that he has to think carefully about it since Emilio was jailed for seven months. He says that there is a kind of discrimination by the American government toward Mexican journalists in terms of asylum. Aguirre was on his way to the funeral of a reporter murdered in Juárez when he received a call over his cell phone saying he would be next. He promptly fled to El Paso.

And then Carlos Spector says, "This is precisely the reason we formed this organization. Jorge's fear is legitimate and his concerns are real. . . . We couldn't even talk about this until we got Emilio out. This was part of the Bush administration's 'Guantanamization' of the refugee process. By locking people up, especially Mexican asylum applicants, and making them, through a war of attrition, give up their claims there at the camp. I've represented ten cops seeking asylum, and not one of them lasted longer than two months. Emilio lasted seven months. On the basis of he had his son and he knew he was going to be killed. There was nowhere that he could go and practice his profession."

There are forty reporters in El Paso—print, radio, and television. Only one or two tiny reports are published by any of them. And the matter of the Mexican army killing innocent Mexicans is not mentioned at all. Like the U.S. government, they apparently believe the Mexican army is some force of light in the darkness of Mexico.

Spector is a man on fire. He is fifty-four, red-haired, big, El Paso born and raised. He has built an immigration practice. He's half Jewish, half Mexican in ancestry. In his twenties, he moved to Israel under the law of return and lived on a kibbutz. But eventually, the border claimed him. He has been looking for a case like Emilio's for years, a case of a clean reporter seeking political asylum from the government of Mexico. Now he thinks he has it and can make precedent.

When Emilio was taken into U.S. custody, he was interviewed at length on his motives for fleeing Mexico. He gave a long statement about why he believed the Mexican army would kill him and why he could not stay in Mexico in any capacity and stay alive. Accidentally, without knowing U.S. law, he made Carlos Spector's case.

Political asylum is only possible under U.S. law if the applicant has some immutable characteristic—say, the person is a homosexual in a place where government persecutes homosexuals, or has a religion whose members the government slaughters. A policeman fleeing for his life would not be eligible, because the U.S. government would insist the cop could become, say, a plumber and live happily ever after. But Emilio's deposition gave him an immutable characteristic: those three stories he filed in 2005 about the army. After that, he apologized. He ceased writing anything bad about the army, even when he witnessed them killing and disappearing people in his town in February 2008. None of this helped him. When the army returned in force in April 2008, they came after him and planned to kill him.

Spector says, "The concept of revenge is part of the Mexican political system. Emilio has insulted the institution, and it has an incredible memory. The only thing worse he could do, he has done also—to leave the country and denounce it."

So Emilio Gutiérrez has an immutable characteristic: He wrote the truth about the Mexican army, and now they will kill him, even if it takes forever. He just told the truth about the Mexican army to the U.S. press, and they will ignore him forever.

Surely, such a man cannot be allowed to live in my country.

After all, a man whose high school classmate was raped, tortured, and murdered by the Mexican army, who has taken note as people were murdered in his town and disappeared by the Mexican army, and who has been sentenced to death by the Mexican army cannot be trusted to tell the truth.

But what lingers in my mind is not that he cannot live in Mexico but that he cannot live within any American understanding of Mexico. He is the unacceptable face of the border. He can be championed by U.S. organizations devoted to defending the rights of reporters, but what he says about corruption in Mexico—corruption in the government, corruption in the military, and corruption in the press—this remains out of bounds and falls on deaf ears.

On Tuesday, March 3, four Mexican army officers visit a friend of Carlos's in Juárez. At that instant, Spector moves from knowing Mexico to feeling its breath on the back of his neck. In the photograph that the Mexican army officers show to his friend, Carlos is wearing a blue suit and entering the El Paso county courthouse. The photograph was taken the previous Thursday, when he appeared for a hearing.

The officers say, "Your friend is a criminal, and we are looking for him. Tell him to get a hold of us."

Outside the house, more men wait in a Hummer.

Carlos takes the call from his friend and falls through space into his new life. He is a knowing player, he spent half his childhood living in Juárez. He is the man who moves freely and easily in two worlds. And now this seamless web is slashed in half.

He must think, he decides. So he drives to a Starbucks and has a cup of coffee. He looks out the window and notices two Ford Expeditions full of men, and then he remembers them behind him in traffic as he drove here. He leaves, and suddenly they are in his rearview mirror and the men in the vehicles are on their cell phones. He turns sharply and then executes a U-turn, and suddenly, he is behind the Fords. They bolt, but he notes the Chihuahuan license plates.

He is learning new facts.

His problem is all connected to representing Emilio Gutiérrez.

This problem is real—his friend in Juárez flees with his family to a distant part of Mexico.

And he can no longer have the life he once enjoyed.

"It feels like an out-of-body experience," he says.

He has joined his client, and they live in a place beyond courts and laws and the illusions of the United States of America.

He has become a Mexican, body and soul.

Emilio says, "Carlos is now an exile, also."

Yes, we will have the performance here at the abandoned rehab center. Surely, ghosts can't take up that much space, and if we run short of space, we can use the kitchen next door since the boy will be in his grave in a few short hours. It will be a quiet performance—the voices soft, the audience will not applaud, and music will not be played this time. The street noises will also fall away—the backfires from old cars, the rumble of buses, the random gunshots, the shouts, and, especially, the suffocating sound of all the silence that cloaks the city after the killings begin.

We will not allow anyone with answers to be present. Explanations will be killed on sight. Theories strangled by my own hands. No one can speak of cartels if he is not a member of a cartel or, at the very least, has not spoken on the record with a member of a cartel. No one will be allowed to speak of the army's war with the cartels unless he has taken a combat role in that war. Academic commentators must show video of themselves at the killings or having beers with the killers before they will be allowed to say a single word.

No, it will be a different kind of show with a different kind of speaker. Just bodies, severed heads, bullets, these can attend. It is time to listen and look and feel.

There are a few ground rules. If you say, the killings make you sad, well, you will be killed—a bullet right into your head. If you say, it is terrible how people live in Juárez, how the poverty is awful, well, you will be killed—a bullet right into your head. If you say, it is all caused by American imperialism, you will be killed—a bullet right into your head. If you say, it is really an issue of femicide, you will be killed—a bullet right into your head. If you say, it is all the result of NAFTA, you will be killed—a bullet right into your head. If you blame American drug consumers, you will be killed—a bullet right into your head. If you say, it is all because of a war between cartels, you will be killed—a bullet right into your head.

There is no telling how long the show will go on. Every hour new cast members are created. Just now as I sit here, four men turn up. They were kidnapped and then, a few moments later, taken to a vacant lot by an industrial park in Juárez.

They are between twenty-five and forty years of age.

They are arranged carefully on the ground.

They have all been shot multiple times—twenty empty cartridges are found by the bodies.

They each received a shot to the head, the *tiro de gracia* given as a courtesy.

They shuffle to the end of the line that already reaches far out the door and trails off into the city.

Ah, in back are three guys from a good home. One of them is a motocross champion. The fine home is gray and rose-pink with white bars on the windows and a clump of three fine palms in front. The lawn is green and neatly manicured. This is the safe place in a city of violence. All the big houses have huge garages.

The doors and bars on the windows have been pried loose, according to the police. The three men have been shot in the head.

Now one by one they roll out on gurneys and are wrapped in white sheets. The attendants bounce them down the steps in front, boom, boom, boom, and even this does not stir them from their slumbers. The late afternoon light feels soft on the street, and the colors on the fine houses glow, the green trees and grace seem to embrace life and wrap around every human being and give comfort. A cluster of city cops with their blue uniforms stands in the street talking and staring back at the killing ground. All is being taken care of.

Lights, blue and red, flash atop police vehicles.

The dead go down those steps one bump at a time.

The forensic people arrive to haul the corpses away for further study.

There are men with guns and uniforms and helmets. There are men with clipboards, and they wear fine latex gloves and note down everything so that this incident of blood can be translated through records into an incident of order.

The three men, of course, shuffle to the back of the line and await their turn to speak.

Or it is a poor neighborhood and the body lies in the street wrapped in a white sheet.

The light is much harsher here.

Men in blue stand at a distance and talk. A white bus hauls people to the factories as if to say the work of the city must continue. The official vehicles are here also flashing red and blue lights.

A car drives past the corpse, the woman in the passenger seat has black hair, dark skin, and she stares at the body without expression.

A boy rides by on his bicycle.

There are very few trees here, and everything is dust.

The body has seven bullets in the chest and one in the head.

The body wears Nike shoes.

And blue jeans.

The corpse in the white sheet also takes his place at the back of the line.

It will be a long night at the performance.

The city evolves just as scholars have always told us. The basic institutions falter—police, fire, government in general. Even the Red Cross recedes. First, when gunmen came and killed four at their emergency care center, they began shutting the facility at 10 P.M. Then, their ambulance drivers began getting radio warnings not to come the scene of shootings, or they would also be killed. Now they ride with cops. The next step, of course, is not to come at all, a response that is already advanced in the police and army.

I will sit with Miss Sinaloa, and I know I will be mesmerized by the accounts, and she will remain a mystery. Her perfect face will be blank. So will her beautiful eyes cocooned in makeup. By now her hair will have grown out, though I doubt it will cascade to her fine ass. The handprints on her buttocks will have vanished. She will retain nothing but barbed memories of her fine time at the Casablanca when she was doing cocaine and whiskey and then was gang-raped for days. Perhaps she will share with me her memories of the crazy place.

The dead sit in rows and wait their turn to speak. They look more alive than the audience because they are totally committed to the play. It is the major performance of their lives, and I can tell they don't want the curtain to come down. Also, they are confident of their lines.

My name is Ernesto Romero Adame, and I am thirty-three. I was driving my 2007 black Volkswagen Jetta and the bullets entered my neck and chest. It was New Year's Day.

Then I hear another chair scrape, and a voice says softly,

Braulio Omar Casillas Arrendondo. And on the fourth of January, I was twenty-five. They wrapped my head and hands, as you can see, with duct tape. And then put some nine-millimeter rounds in my brain.

He sits, and slowly another form rises:

They never figured out my name, and so I'm not going to tell you. It was simple: January fifth, maybe two hundred feet from the Avenue of the National Army, a couple of nines right in the head.

This other guy stands up next to him and says,

*Same day. Bunch of nines in the heart. Name—Luis Alberto Villarreal Vargas,
twenty-five, and no longer counting.*

A man cuts him off and says,

*My hands are bound with wire. Took some forty-fives to the chest. Drove a Dodge
Intrepid. Jesus Felix Laguna, every day of thirty-six.*

Another guy says,

*Let's finish off the fifth of January. No name, doesn't matter much now, anyway.
Two in the head. Found me in a vacant lot.*

I realize this show is going to take a while. But no one waiting to speak
seems anxious or fidgeting. They all look relaxed, especially when you consider the large number of the cast with holes in their heads. Miss Sinaloa
is harder to figure. She seems attentive, and yet I cannot read her lovely
face at all. I can't tell if she is merely being polite, or if she is caught up in
the play.

*Mario Antonio Martinez Hernandez, thirty-eight. Owned a junkyard. The wife
came to pick me up, and I climbed in when suddenly two guys got out of a black
Yukon and tried to open my door. I grabbed it and held it shut. This was January
tenth. They stepped back and started firing.*

I lean back and close my eyes. I simply listen and swim in the stories that
fall from the pale lips.

*Look, I went down the next day. They dumped me in a vacant lot after the torture.
Some nines in the head. No name, please.*

I took some rounds in the chest. I hobbled over to a security guard and asked for help. Then I died.

Enrique Enriquez Armendariz, fifty-one. A lot of torture, but I'll skip over that. Hands and feet tied with duct tape. Dumped near a subdivision.

It's a family thing. I'm a cop and so was my brother—he caught his back in May 2007. I took twenty-two rounds of 5.27x28 mm. I'm Police Captain Julián Cháirez Hernández, thirty-seven. I was on patrol at that moment.

I was coming out of my house to go to work when this van rolls up. Took thirty-five rounds from an AK-47. Never made it to the job. Francisco Ledesma Salazar, thirty-four, city police. Back then I drove a Ford Expedition.

They came for me on January twenty-first, ten of them wearing ski masks and toting machine guns. It was over a week before anyone found me. Some nines were scattered around my body. My name is Fernando Javier Macias Rivera, twenty-three.

They found my body next to his. Luis Carlos Contreras, twenty-one.

José Luis Piedra, thirty. They kidnapped me and then gave me six from a .380 in my neck and head.

I was just driving. They pulled me out of my car at an intersection. Seven in the chest. Juan Garcia Vazquez, thirty-two. That's about it.

I guess I'm the change of pace. Javier Leal Saucedo, thirty-three. Beat me to death.

Me too. Bernardo Rafael Hernandez Vasquez, thirty-nine. Beaten to death.

Look, I don't even know if I should talk. I was out driving with my wife in my white pickup. Then they took me. No reports about me since then, so I think I'll leave it at that.

Well, I'm different. Raymundo Daniel Ruvalcaba, twenty-nine. They put a plastic bag over my head and duct-taped my hands and feet. Then they wrapped me in a blanket. The people who found me saw pools of blood around my body.

I open my eyes, and it looks as though there are still hundreds waiting their turn to speak. I notice the brevity of the people speaking. Name, age, wounds. They don't really say much. Maybe they think no one cares. Or maybe they think everyone already knows. You will die. You will not really see it coming, no matter what warnings or signals you have received. You will ignore the warnings because you will think bad things happen to other people and not to you.

Jesus Duran Uranga, thirty-one. Put me in the trunk of a ninety-five Ford Escort. Finally, the neighbors complained of the smell, and that's how I got found.

I'm thirty. Francisco Macias Gonzalez. Shot in the head in my Dodge Ram with a Hemi. Hands tied behind my back with those plastic handcuffs the cops use.

Look, I work for the state prosecutor's office. I drive a Durango. That's where they shot me.

So you will die and be surprised, and yet you will die and expect to die. The explanations other people crave hardly matter to you because the cause of your death is just a detail. You fucked up, or someone wanted your business, or maybe, just maybe, you looked too long and too hard at the wrong woman. That would actually be kind of nice—to die for love. But in the end, you will die because killing is part of life here, and all the things called motives and reasons don't tell you much in the end, because you can imagine a different kind of place where you behaved in the same way, and you would not be murdered in this other place.

I drift off. I listen and don't listen, in the same way a person sits in a bar and takes in the band and yet is hardly aware of the music.

Of course, nothing Miss Sinaloa knows matters to most people. Just as the dead of Juárez will vanish from memory.

As I watch the new *Our Town* in the abandoned rehab center, I see one little image in my head, a fragment that whispers of a murder. There is a barrio near here where people scavenge old televisions and bits of metal from both Juárez and El Paso and sell them. The barrio is poor and is a place that eats the cast-off entrails of a richer world. A man sells cocaine on the street, and he is warned to stop, but he is in his thirties and has no other livelihood. So he persists and then armed men come with masks and blow his brains out, and he falls on the street near his mother's house. That is not the image in my mind. What I see is his mother. It is night now, the body has been taken away, and there is a light on, the screen door is pushed open, and an old woman with a blank face stares down at the street, and she is there all alone and her son is not coming home, and her face is as inscrutable as a block of stone. Her arms are crossed, and she is a portrait of grief Juárez-style, silent, enduring, and doomed.

I am eight years old. They poured two hundred and fifty rounds into my dad's truck and killed him. They shot my arm off. And then I died.

I am a disabled police officer in a wheelchair, my partner is legally blind, and we were making sure no one was using parking spaces for the handicapped when we were machine-gunned.

My name is David Miranda Ramirez, I'm thirty-six, and I was driving patrol in an industrial park at 10:30 A.M. when at least twenty rounds ripped through my car and my body.

I have no name now. They found my body in a kettle used for frying pork.

December's children arise. First, four cops killed in their stations and cars in a coordinated attack during the night. They say they were merely doing their duty. They sit with over sixty dead cops slaughtered during the year.

Four guys sit near them, also machine-gunned during the same day as the four cops. One holds his head in his lap, the severed skull wearing a Santa Claus hat. It is nearing Christmas, and everyone has the spirit. The kills have streaked past 1,500 for the year.

This program will take some time.

Miss Sinaloa tosses her hair and takes in the show.

God brought her to this city, you know, so that she would suffer and lose her mind, go to the crazy place and meet her true love, who slipped food into her cell and talked sweetly to her. It was meant to be. She knows this. And may know other things.

Did I tell you about her eyes? They see through you to the other side.

Scent wafts off her as we sit and listen and yet do not listen. We are being told what we already know and, in my case, refuse to understand.

Of course, Miss Sinaloa is different.

Her skin is so white, her hair long and glossy, the lips red as ripe fruit.

Murder Artist

He is calm now. The kidnappings, the tortures, the killings, brought back a sense of self he could not control, the workman's pride that fills a man when he sees the wall, the house, or perhaps even the church he has built. True, he would express regret, tell me such things give him nightmares, and he tries as a rule to put them out of his mind. He would indicate that he is revisiting this evil time simply for my benefit.

He takes his various drawings—how to do a hit, where some people were buried in a death house—looks at the green schematics he has created and then slowly tears them into little squares until the torn heap can never be reconstructed.

His life is relatively peaceful until late 2006. He worked all over Mexico for different groups, and the various organizations generally got along. There were small moments such as when others tried to take over Juárez, and it was necessary to burn their heads with tires. But his life in the main was peaceful.

So peaceful, he did not need to know certain things.

Such as who he really worked for. Such knowledge could be fatal.

"I received orders from two people. They ran me. I never knew which cartel I worked for. Now there is Vicente Carrillo against Chapo Guzman. But I never met any bosses, so when the war started around 2006, I did not know which one I did the killing for. And orders could cross from one group to another. I am living in a cell, and I simply take orders. In thirty minutes in Juárez, sixty well-trained and heavily armed men can assemble in thirty cars and circulate as a show of force.

"Then at my level, we began to get orders to kill each other."

He is kidnapped but let go after an hour. This unsettles him, and he begins to think about escaping his life. But that is not a simple matter, since if you leave, you are murdered. As the war quickens, he begins to distance himself from people he knows and works with. He tries to fade away. By this time, a third of the people he knows have been disappeared—"they were seen as useless and then killed."

He doesn't know the boss, he is still not even sure who his boss is. He drinks at home. The streets are too dangerous. New people arrive, and he does not know them. He is not safe.

So he flees.

He confides in a friend. Who betrays him.

He pauses at this point. He knows he is guilty of a fatal error. He has violated a fundamental rule: You can only be betrayed by someone you trust. So you survive by trusting no one. Still, there is this shred of humanity in all of us, and in the end, we feel the need to trust someone. And this need is fatal. It is the very need he has exploited for years, the need he used when he put people in the police car and told them they would be all right if they cooperated, would be back with their families in no time if they were calm. And by God, they did trust him and rode across Mexico, went through checkpoints and said nothing, never told a single soul they had been kidnapped. They would trust him as they were tortured in the safe houses. They would promise him fine things when they were returned to their families. They would help mop the floors, clean up the vomit and blood. They would compose songs. They would trust him right up to that instant when he strangled them.

So his friend gives him up. He is taken at 10 P.M., and this time, he is held until 3 A.M.

But something has changed within him. And some things have not changed. Four men take him to a safe house. They remove all of his clothing but his shorts. They take pool balls in their hands and beat him.

But he can tell they are amateurs. They do not even handcuff him, and this is almost disturbing to him. He is the captive of third-raters. As they beat him, he prays and prays and prays. He also laughs because he is appalled by their incompetence. They have not bound him, and their blows do not disable him. He sizes them up and in his mind plans how he will kill them, one, two, three, four, just like that.

And at the same moment, he is praying to God to help him so that he will not kill them, so that he can stop his life of murder. He has been sliding toward God for some time now, brought to the fact of Christ by one of his first mentors when he joined the state police and became a professional killer. As he sits in the room, sipping coffee and recalling this moment, his face comes alive. He is passionate now. He is approaching the very moment of his salvation. Some people pretend to accept Christ, he says, but at that moment, he could feel total acceptance fill his body. He could feel peace. And yet there was this tension within him. He prays so ardently, and still at the same time he cannot stop laughing at his captors. He knows that in the Christian faith, the lamb is a symbol of belief and of redemption. But he also knows he can never be a lamb. If he is to be a Christian, he must be a Christian wolf.

They point rifles at him. He cannot stop laughing.

"I was afraid," he explains. "I realized I would have to kill them all. I said to God, don't do this to me, I don't want to do this anymore. God, give me time."

Two of the armed men leave. Another guy goes to the bathroom.

Here is his chance. The chance he is praying that God will not let him use. He can see no way out but killing, and now he knows that is no way out.

He looks at the remaining captor.

"The guy says, 'I don't have a problem with you. Once, you told me to be careful or they would kill me. You did me a favor.'

"So, I am praying to God, help me! I don't want to kill these people. And I know I can do it rapidly.

"The guy turns his back on me and says, 'Get out, go.'"

He opens the door and runs without his shoes or clothes. He goes to his home, takes his family out the back way, and sends them to different parts of Mexico. He knows that his killers will not go after his family, because they still fear him and know he can raise some men and kill their families.

"I had no one but God now. I still had some assets. I had a pilot assigned to me, I had knowledge of the organization. I had lived fully. I had risen. Often, I would simply supervise. I might fly to a distant city on a Saturday. Then on Sunday, I would supervise an execution and make certain the individual died. Sometimes, I would give the coup de grâce. I was on a monthly salary. I had a house, a good car, all that I needed was given to me. The boss is like God because everything comes from him. You worship him. When I was kidnapped, I finally realized I had been worshipping a false god. And I turned to the real God."

His face is stern now. He has come to the place, the very moment that has permitted him to recount the kidnappings, the tortures, the killings. He is selling, and what he is selling is God. He is believing, and what he believes, based on his own life, is that anyone can be redeemed. And that it is possible to leave the organization and survive.

"I learned more as I was running. I asked God, if I am such a tough guy, why are they letting me go? I realized no one is a tough guy. I start seeing billboards in Juárez that said you must turn toward God, actual billboards. They had always been there, but I had been blind.

"After the second kidnapping and my escape, I asked God to help me so I didn't have to kill. Tell me, God, how are you going to get me out of this? I was trained to kill. Back in that house, I knew which one I would kill first, and it would have been easy. But I was crying, crying out of fear, because I did not want to kill. One of the kidnappers was the son of a boss, and I knew if I killed him, then I would lose my family because with such a killing, no one would respect my family. The guy who let me run, he was a rich kid, he was just there for the fun.

"There were people who would tremble when they saw me because they knew I was violent. I could go to the door of a bar and simply beckon for a guy to go with me, and he would come because he knew he had to come. I was feared. But my captors, they were only playing."

And so he lives, and now he must explain to himself why he lives, and now he must somehow redeem himself from his earlier life. But he cannot simply denounce this life: He was feared, he was trained, he was the good soldier in his war.

"I had never had free will, I had just followed orders. You never had time to think of the killings, of the executions. If you did that, you might feel remorse. But because of the way I worked, I could leave a torture scene, I could close off my mind. Also, I was using a lot of drugs. I always had to be awake, I always had to be aware of talking on the street, of what was being said about the people I worked with."

His thoughts are a jumble as he speaks. He is telling of his salvation, and yet he feels the tug of his killings. He feels the pride in being feared. Back at the beginning, when he first starts with the state police, that is when Oropeza, the doctor and newspaper columnist, is killed. And his killers, he now recalls, were his mentors, his teachers. He remembers after the murder, the state government announced a big investigation to get the killers. And one of them, a fellow cop, stayed at his own police station until the noise quieted, and the charade ended.

He is excited now, he is living in his past.

"The only reason I am here is because God saved me. I repented. After all these years, I am talking to you. I am having to relive things that are dead to me. I don't want to be part of this life. I don't want to know the news. You must write this so that other *sicarios* know it is possible to leave. They must know God can help them. They are not monsters. They have been trained like Special Forces units in the army. But they never realize they have been trained to serve the Devil.

"Imagine being nineteen years old and you are able to call up a plane. I liked the power. I never realized until God talked to me that I could get out. Still, when God frees me, I remain a wolf. I can't become a lamb. I remain a terrible person, but now I have God on my side.

"I don't carry a gun now.

"I carry God."

His eyes are glowing now. He is on fire.

"God will get them out when they are ready.

"You leave without money.

"You need faith. And prayer."

He stares at me as I write in a black notebook.

His body seems to loom over the table.

This is the point in all stories where everyone discovers who they really are. Do you believe in redemption? Do you believe a man can kill for twenty years and then change? Do you even believe such killers can exist? In every story, there is this same moment when all you hold dear and believe to be true and certain is suddenly called into question, and the walls of your life shake, the roof collapses, and you look up into a sky you never imagined and never wanted to know. I believe his conversion to Christ, I believe he can change, I believe he can never be forgiven. And I am certain my knowledge of his life and his ways will haunt me the rest of my days.

He says, "I have now relived something I should never have opened up. Are you the medium to reach others? I prayed to God asking what I should do. And you are the answer. You are going to write this story because God has a purpose in you writing this story.

"God has given you this mission.

"No one will understand this story except those who have been in the life. And God will tell you how to write this story."

Then we embrace and pray. I can feel his hand on my shoulder probing, seeking the power of the Lord in me.

I have my work to do now.

And so we go our separate ways.

In the parking lot, he moves with ease, in a state of grace. The sun blazes, the sky aches blue. Life feels good. His eyes relax and he laughs. And then I see him memorize my license plate in a quick and practiced glance. He has told me he is bathed in the blood of the lamb, but his eyes remain those of the wolf.

The pace roars in December, and then, just around Christmas, there is a faint slowing. But on December 30, three go down. Number 1,600 is a man who resisted a robbery in an auto repair shop. After him, a guy is murdered on the street when he walked out of a money exchange. Another person is snatched, and his fate left to the imagination. Then, a man is murdered in his boutique dress shop. His customers are beaten and robbed. By New Year's Eve, 1,602 are dead and 195 people had been slaughtered in December, a month rivaling August, when 228 died.

Then, they go down until just minutes before midnight on New Year's Eve, and then there are 1,607 dead. The final body is an act of love, according the Juárez tabloid, *P.M.*:

> *A man who began celebrations to welcome the New Year with a woman was shot to death near midnight in the colonia Plutarcho Elias Calles thus becoming the last mortal victim of 2008, number 1,607.*

According to residents of the neighborhood
just a few days ago, the woman broke off her relationship with another man
who had been planning some kind of revenge fueled by jealousy
and thus, he could be the author of the criminal act.

It is said that it could have been a crime of passion, although state
authorities will investigate
to find out if this was the motive of the aggression.

It occurred near the stroke of midnight marking the end of 2008 and the
beginning of the New Year
at the intersection of Isla Santo Domingo and Isla Quisca streets in the
aforementioned colonia.

According to first reports to Emergency 066, three individuals who looked
like cholos
one of them riding a bicycle
shot at a white car where a man and woman apparently were
resulting in the death of the man.

The deceased, identified by the nickname "El Mango," twenty-eight years old
received several gunshot wounds in different parts of his body
including the head according to witnesses
who said they had seen the woman's ex-boyfriend among the aggressors
and so now, the authorities are looking for him.

They added that the woman who accompanied the victim was not injured
and she managed to get out of the car and hide in her house which was near
the scene of the crime.

According to some sources, "El Mango" had intended to get some
bodyguards

but these guys abandoned him and after running a little way
they fell dejected and downhearted in the street.

State agents came to the scene and it is presumed that they interviewed the
surviving woman
in order to get some facts about the possible identities
of the aggressors.

At 2:40 A.M., the first person is gunned down in the New Year. The next kill comes at 4 A.M. The year of our Lord 2009 is launched.

The next morning, the city is spent. Green, yellow, red, orange, blue, and white balloons flap from a palm tree in front of the club Beach, and the sidewalk is littered with confetti and garbage bags broken open with their reeking contents attracting clusters of pigeons.

On January 6, the day of the three wise men, a huge holiday sweet bread that is over a mile long feeds fifteen thousand people in a park in Ciudad Juárez. Late that afternoon, Mario Escobedo Salazar and his son Edgar Escobedo Anaya have visitors to their law office. The elder Escobedo Salazar, fifty-nine, is killed at his desk. The son runs and is slaughtered just down the block. His own brother, Mario Escobedo Anaya, was executed by the Chihuahuan state police in 2002 after representing a defendant accused of the murder of a group of women found buried in a cotton field. His law partner, Sergio Dante Almaraz, also represented one of the accused in that case. He was executed in January 2005 in downtown Juárez. Almaraz had publicly predicted his murder and said he would be killed by the Chihuahuan state government. Some message has been delivered, some circle closed, but the only part of the statement fully understood by everyone is death.

There is supposed to be an answer to such a number of killings. Some kind of explanation and then, following this explanation, a solution achieved through an orderly series of steps. I go to see El Pastor, and he prays for me, a thankless task for which I thank him.

The year has not been easy for El Pastor. He watches his city die around him. He has men come with guns demanding money. He is at a stoplight one afternoon and sees a man executed three cars ahead of him.

I ask him, "Tell me what the slaughter of the year 2008 means."

He says, "Not even in the Mexican revolution did they kill so many in Juárez. This year of death shows the brutality inside the Mexican government— death comes from inside the government. Not from the people. The only way to end the violence is to let organized crime be the government.

"The crime groups are fighting for power. If the toughest guy wins, he will get everything under control.

"Now there is no respect for the president.

"People now say to the president, 'Fuck you, man.'

"I am a miracle, but I am not a martyr. I don't want to be killed."

We sit outside his house. His red car stares at us with a front plate that says, WITH GOD, ALL THINGS ARE POSSIBLE.

As we enjoy the blue sky and the warmth falling from heaven, more die in the city.

That is the answer.

Both the sun.

And the blood.

Miss Sinaloa goes on and on. Her name changes as does her face. Every day, week, month, she shows up in the city with a new identity with her face made up, her high-heeled shoes, tight skirt, and fragrance. And each time she comes to the city, she is adored, raped, thrown in the trash, and lives on with a maimed mind. She never forgets, and the city always forgets her.

She has those lush lips, that long hair and fair skin. She can never be important. She is not the drug industry, she is not free trade, she is not national security.

She is the blood and dreams of a people.

I will never forget her.

Just as she will never be remembered.

Afterword

At one point, I was hanging around Palomas, a border town an hour or so west of Juárez, and near Palomas is Ascensión, where an ice chest arrives at police headquarters.

The chest was shipped as freight (properly encased in shrink-wrap) via a bus company and addressed to a local clinic. But one by one, the clinics checked their records and realized they had not ordered any drugs or other vital materials that must be shipped on ice and shrink-wrapped. The chest winds up at the police station by a kind of default mechanism. The cops open it and find four severed human heads.

The newspaper says an investigation has been launched.

At the same time, two laborers on a local ranch stumble into some armed men and are promptly cut down.

I read the World War II memoir of Eric Severeid, a son of Velva, North Dakota. At that time, he was a CBS radio correspondent. Later, he was part of television news and for years read brooding and vague commentaries each evening, a voice sandwiched amid the mayhem of nightly items.

He went off to his war as a young man who believed in a raft of ideas labeled progressive, who believed that people were basically decent and wanted to live in peace in democratic societies.

The war threatened his beliefs.

He found an appetite for murder, and he had trouble with this fact. He saw U.S. soldiers kill prisoners without a qualm. He saw average people, French and Italian, turn into killers once the fragrance of "liberation" floated over their towns and villages.

On the American election day, a man is found against the metal bars of a window, arms spread in the crucifixion style, feet firmly on the ground, his face hidden by a pig mask. Children walk past on their way to school. A few days later, a man is found at dawn dangling from a bridge. His severed head is located wrapped in a black plastic bag at the Juárez monument to newsboys in the Plaza of the Journalist.

Like many such tales in the city, it was written up for the daily paper by Armando Rodriguez, who has this very morning, a week after the severed head was left at the monument to journalists, filed his 907th story of the year, and then he takes ten hits from a 9 mm as he warms up his car, his young daughter beside him, in order to take her to school.

The burned body is dumped at the police station, arms severed at the elbow, each hand holding a grill lighter.

He has been strangled and then burned with cigarette lighters.

He has been shot with an AK-47.

A message left with the carcass denounces the dead man as an arsonist.

At the time the crisp body is found, the local police get death threats over their radios.

The cops take down the blanket on which the accusation against the dead was painted, that he was an arsonist.

Then a message comes over their radios to put it back up, pronto.

They do.

This police district is very productive in producing dead policemen.

Since the killing began warming up last January and the first message was posted of cops to be killed, this area has been rich in dead police.

Back then, the message, placed over a funeral wreath of flowers, contained the names of seventeen agents, identified by surname, code, and sector.

For those who continue not to believe: Z-1 Juan Antonio Román García; oficial Martín Casas, Z-4 del distrito Aldama; Adán Prieto, Z-3 del distrito Babícora; Eduardo Acosta, Z-4 del distrito Chihuahua; oficial Arvizu, Z-6 del distrito Aldama; oficial Rojas, Z-5 del distrito Benito Juárez; oficial Rojas, del distrito Cuauhtémoc; Originales Z-4 del distrito Cuauhtémoc; oficial Balderas, Z-3 del distrito Aldama; oficial Villegas, Z-3 del distrito Delicias; oficial Casimiro Meléndez, del distrito Babícora; Evaristo Rodríguez, oficial del distrito Cuauhtémoc; oficial Silva, Z-5 del distrito Cuauhtémoc; oficial Vargas, del distrito Cuauhtémoc; oficial Guerrero, del distrito Cuauhtémoc; Gerardo Almeralla, agente de Vialidad; y el oficial Galindo, del distrito Aldama.

Since that greeting, many on the list have died. Or quit. Or fled.

This is something new and yet something old. This is what Eric Severeid saw in June 1944 on the day Rome was liberated from the Germans. He was thirty years old and battle hardened by all the reports he'd filed from China and Britain and North Africa and Italy. He'd bailed out of a plane on the Chinese/Burma border into jungle controlled by the Japanese and made it out alive. He'd seen men die. He'd learned there was a chasm between his educated beliefs about the war and the feelings of the soldiers who had to fight and die in the war. So when Rome was liberated, he already knew about killing and evil and violence and things he never really wanted to know, and now knew he could never forget. He left a brief page in his memoir, *Not So Wild a Dream*, published in 1946:

At midnight I wandered toward my hotel and in the moonlight came upon two tired American paratroopers from Frederick's regiment, who were sitting disconsolately on the curbing. They were lost, had no place to stay. . . . I took them to my room and they stretched out on the floor. We talked a while, and one of them, a brawny St. Louis man who had been a milk-wagon driver, said: "You know, I've been reading how the FBI is organizing special squads to take care of us boys when we get home. I got an idea it will be needed, all right. See this pistol? I killed a man this morning, just to get it. Ran into a German officer in a hotel near the edge of town. He surrendered, but he wouldn't give me his pistol. You know, it kind of scares me. It's so easy to kill. It solves your problems, and there's no questions asked. I think I'm getting the habit."

*Esther Chávez Cano died on Christmas morning 2009.
She lived to help heal the wounds of Ciudad Juárez,
she insisted on justice from those in power.
And demanded action from the rest of us.*

For our struggle is not against flesh and blood,
but against the rulers, against the authorities,
against the powers of this dark world....

Afterword for the Paperback Edition

He shakes the glass ball as golden flakes cascade on the mounted and armored knight holding a lance. I have never seen him more tired, though his face briefly lights up at the sight of the warrior in the glittering storm. His car broke down at the foot of the bridge leading from Juárez to El Paso, so I had picked him up and taken him to his home down by the river.

José Antonio Galvan is known in the streets of Juárez as El Pastor. He's the man who runs through this book like a river of love, and his will to live and work is being ground down by the massacre of his city. He's a former illegal, a former high-steel worker, a former convict, a former drug addict. He has four adult children who are all college graduates. He works the streets of Juárez trying to bring love to a city of death.

El Pastor tells me he is sixty now and does not wish to live to be eighty. He wants to be in heaven with the angels, where he will no longer hear so many people in pain. A black and white cat lounges on the sofa, a ball of fat that requires daily diabetic medicine. The owner is the man's son, who is now gone for a year to Afghanistan, his third or fourth tour in Special Forces.

"He's not in the field now," the man says. "He's just training local people to kill people. He's like me, a warrior."

A pall hangs over the room this Sunday afternoon because on Friday evening, a massacre occurred. It managed to shock people in a city that had already slaughtered twenty-six hundred people this year.

Francisco Lopez had been deported from El Paso ninety days earlier and brought over his six children, five of them U.S. citizens, and his wife and rented a home in Horizontes del Sur, a working-class barrio in Juárez. On Friday night, he held a birthday party for his son who turned fifteen. The fiesta went awry because of a mouse. Three cars arrived with gunmen who entered searching for *El Raton*, the mouse. No one knew such a person. Among the dead were four teenagers and six women, one of them Francisco's wife. Three minutes after the shooting, the wounded tried to flag down a passing federal police car in front of the house. It ignored them, a fact never mentioned in the U.S. press. Thirty minutes later, help began to arrive. The dead numbered fourteen, the wounded nineteen.[1] Many of them belonged to a religious society at Señor de los Milagros, the church of miracles.

The government has announced an investigation. But there were only thirty-seven arrests last year for around twenty-seven hundred murders, and most of those arrested were released soon after for lack of evidence.[2]

This killing contains within it all the elements of the terror that thrives beneath our national talk of a U.S. war on drugs—the crackdown on illegal immigration, Plan Merida, the Mexican war on the cartels, and NAFTA bootstrapping poor Mexicans up into the bounties of free trade and globalization. Beneath these policies, death lives and terror lives and poverty lives in a vast silence.

A family is deported from the United States because the father is illegal, although five of the six children are U.S. citizens. They move into a working-class neighborhood in Juárez, a place where parents congregate to keep their kids out of gangs. There is no hope that such people will get political asylum in the United States, because people are not eligible for that status unless they can prove they belong to a group the Mexican government cannot protect. It is unlikely that the United States will recognize being a poor Mexican citizen as a qualification for political asylum.

Pastor Galvan sitting on his couch tells me to read Ephesians 6:10–18.

I think, Well, it is worth a shot.

Over seven thousand people have been killed in Juárez since January 1, 2008. It is clear to everyone that the total for 2010 alone will exceed three thousand, but no one wants to say this out loud, because there are limits to what the heart can bear. At least eighty-three thousand jobs in border factories have been lost, 40 percent of the retail businesses are shuttered, 27 percent of the houses are abandoned, at least five hundred street gangs prowl the *calles*, several hundred thousand people have fled (no one knows the real number). The recent mayor says you can hire your own killer for fifty bucks a week, and the U.S. government applauds President Felipe Calderón's announced war against drug cartels.

The violence—while more severe in Juárez than in the rest of Mexico—has spread along the border and into the interior. No one knows its level, since reports from the countryside have increasingly ceased because the press has been murdered or silenced. A friend of mine in Juárez says we are witnessing grassroots violence, meaning it stems from the lives of battered Mexicans and not from some mysterious capos pulling strings in vast narco-mansions. I think he is right. We had drinks Friday night. He was robbed Saturday night.

I've been giving speeches around the United States for most of this year. At first I was promoting this book, and then I drifted into some strange terrain—one much like my friend Pastor Galvan—and to my horror, I realized I had become a missionary and the heathen I was preaching to were the American people.

My sermon reveals the following lies told by the U.S. government to its citizens.

That the president of Mexico is fighting a war against drug cartels. This is nonsense. Over forty thousand Mexicans are now dead, almost all of them poor people. Their murders have not been investigated, and the only thing really known about these people is that they are no longer alive. In the meantime, the drug industry has not been touched—there is no shortage of drugs in the United States and no price rise. If the industry were touched, Mexico would become an economic ruin, since the $30 to $50 billion a year it earns in foreign currency is the largest single source in the Mexican economy. This is a war *for* drugs, not against it.

That NAFTA is a success. Wages in maquiladoras peaked around 1983 and in real pesos have steadily declined since then. Workers in Juárez earn forty to sixty dollars a week, a slave wage. Since NAFTA's passage, the largest migration on earth has streamed out of Mexico as the treaty crushed peasant agriculture and small industry.

That the Mexican army is fighting the drug industry. Under Plan Merida, the United States gives Mexico half a billion dollars a year, mainly for the army. This has resulted in mass murder and government death squads, all while the flow of drugs north continues unabated. In over three years, the army has lost maybe two hundred soldiers—this does not include the tens of thousands who have deserted to the drug industry—and thousands of complaints have been filed by Mexicans against them for robbery, rape, torture, extortion, kidnapping, and murder. The recent seizure of 134 tons of marijuana in Tijuana means exactly this: that the product of one harvest from eighty-nine acres has been burned (well, maybe burned—we only know that something is burning in the photographs). Seizures of heroin and cocaine, the really money products of the drug industry, have been minuscule.

That violence is spilling across the border. This lie is beneath contempt but not beneath being used by the American political class. U.S. border communities have had declining crime rates for a decade and are actually safer than much of the rest of America. The truth is that the violence is spilling south because of the U.S. prohibition on drugs, and because of economic policies that create slaves in the maquiladoras, a situation that in turn creates children with parents absent in the factories and left to the streets.

That there is a river of iron flowing south from U.S. gun shops. In reality, most of the guns seized in Mexico are not from America. There is no way to identify the majority of them, because the army refuses to let the seized arsenals be inspected—almost certainly because they come from the Mexican army itself. There is no U.S. gun shop, for example, peddling hand grenades, although they can be bought for about six and a half bucks apiece in Central America as the legacy of our dirty little wars there.

That the wall will stop illegal migrants and drugs and terrorists. This is absurd: The wall stops nothing but wildlife. There are no terrorists trudging north with prayer rugs. The drugs cross through our ports of entry, thanks to corruption. And the poor continue to come as best they can, propelled by our drug policies that have made their world a killing zone and our economic policies that have destroyed their ability to survive.

I could go on, but I've grown weary of the questions.

We have helped in part to create a disaster, and our only response seems to be to continue the same policies that feed the disaster. We wall off the poor, we fight drugs, we give money to the army—the largest single gang in Mexico—we talk of an insurgency in Mexico (cue up the music for the School of the Americas), and in countless interviews and speeches, I am asked for the solution.

Here is the answer: Tell me the problem.

The largest migration of the poor on earth is heading north because of the corruption of Mexico, because of our economic policies, because of our drug policies, and because of overpopulation. I'll skip global warming, which seems to hurt everyone's head. Until these facts are faced, the talk of walls or open immigration or "Let's legalize just marijuana" or Plan Merida are pointless. This time, the blind men examining the elephant are the U.S. experts, but what they are really examining are their own lies, and what they are really doing is insisting their lies are the truth.

In Ephesians 6:10–13, it is written: "Finally, be strong in the Lord and in his mighty power. Put on the full armor of God so that you can take your stand against the devil's schemes. For our struggle is not against flesh and blood, but against the rulers, against the authorities, against the powers of this dark world and against the spiritual forces of evil in the heavenly realms."

I can see El Pastor watching the gold flakes swirl around his knight in shining armor. Ephesians is starting to make more sense to me than my government.

My friend who was robbed tells me not to be alarmed. He was going to a birthday party and had made all the normal preparations. He carried only about 120 pesos, around ten bucks. He left his credit cards at home. And all they took was his cell phone. This is normal life in Juárez. He said they were very young.

They call them *Ninis* in Juárez. No work, no school.

They are the new citizens of the future. Along with the ten thousand new orphans in Juárez alone. And of course, the hundred thousand dogs abandoned in the last three years by people fleeing.

The truth is that there is no war on drugs in Mexico, because such a war would destroy the Mexican economy. There is a war for drugs and power being waged by the Mexican government against elements of the drug industry. So far, the drug industry is doing better than the government, and the Mexican people are roadkill in this war: They are also killed by neighbors, street gangs, and anyone else who feels the need for vengeance, since there is no functioning justice system in the country. In Juárez, for example, only 2 percent of the murders have been solved, and by *solved*, the government means that someone is charged (forget convictions) or that it has figured out the crime, though nothing is actually done.

Into this fray, American policy experts charge with drones, agents, counterinsurgency tacticians, and various traveling salesmen for judicial reform. No one talks about poverty. No one talks about creating workers' rights. No one talks about raising wages in the American-owned factories, and no one talks about the vicious war on drugs that imprisons Americans, kills Mexicans, and terrorizes American addicts. No one says that our answers to poverty and drugs and migration have been failures and have, in fact, increased the problem.

I'll give you two things I know.

I have spent fifteen years on one murder case. The man was murdered in El Paso, the killer came from Juárez. I knew this from the beginning, though I could never prove it. Now it is late at night, and I am riding around El Paso with the *sicario* who runs through this book like a river of gore. We speak of many things, and I accidentally touch on the killing. He comes alive. He knows the guy who trained the assassin, knows names and addresses, knows where the order came from—that fabled Juárez cartel. And also knows why, in a real sense.

Speaking of the man who ordered the hit, he says, "He knows how to really hurt people."

He is certainly right. I have watched the unsolved death put a family through agony for fifteen years.

Now I learn how it was planned, the missteps and corrections. The night flows past the car window as he drives, the dash gauges are a comforting green, and all the little details finally land and arrange themselves and there is an order to the slaughter of one human being. He tells of a school that some kids are put through. They are beaten, tortured, and if they cry out, they are killed because it is clear they are not up to the work. Those who make the grade become killers, such as the figure who has haunted my life for fifteen years. Almost with admiration, the sicario says that these new kids, these manufactured variations on the traditional human being, are "ruthless."

Nothing will come of this knowledge, most likely. But at least I can close the book, and the family, denied justice, can at least know the truth.

There is another moment.

Pastor sits on the sofa by the fat diabetic cat and swirls all the golden glitter around the knight in armor.

He says, "I have had this dream for many years. I am this knight riding and there is this swirl of glitter and I am riding toward injustice. This knight comes from my dream, he is exactly what I see. Sometimes the dream is different. I am in Rome in the Coliseum, and the emperor and the crowd are there, and I am the Christian fighting for my life. That is my other dream."

So this is what I have learned. Walk out of the room once the experts weigh in. Never carry cards or money on you in Juárez. Read Ephesians. Be patient when your loved ones are murdered, it can take fifteen years for an answer or, more likely, forever. Be a knight in shining armor, a man in the arena fighting for the Lord. Don't stick around until you are eighty.

And don't expect peace anytime soon. This one's coming right out of the ground, and from the sky too if you believe in global warming. It will not be over soon. Give it at least ten years in Mexico.

You can bank on it, since the U.S. government is paying for a lot of it and cheerleading the rest of the slaughter. And the wall between Mexico and the United States, between reality and fantasy, gets longer every day. School is out now, and it is time to go into the streets with our new understanding. And should you object to that suggestion, do not worry, the streets will come to wherever you choose to hide. We're past talk. We now live on the killing ground.

On Desolation Row, "Everybody's shouting, 'Which side are you on?'"

Thanksgiving Day, 2010

Notes

1. Elisabeth Malkin, "Death Toll in Juárez Attack Rises to 14," *New York Times*, 24 October 2010, www.nytimes.com/2010/10/25/world/americas/25mexico.html?_r=1.
2. William Booth, "U.S. to Embed Agents in Mexican Law Enforcement Units Battling Cartels in Juárez," *Washington Post*, 24 February 2010, www.washingtonpost.com/wp-dyn/content/article/2010/02/23/AR2010022305560.html.

After That Year

More troops arrive and more corpses arrive. By the summer of 2009, Juárez looks back on the slaughter of 2008 as the quiet time. This book began because I was astounded by the killings of January 2008—48. This would have spelled out to 576 murders a year, almost double the previous record of 301 in 2007. Now a murder rate of 100 a month would feel like the return of peace to the city. July 2009 is the bloodiest month in the history of the city, with 244 murdered. In August, 316 more go down. There are at least 10,000 troops and federal police in the city, with the murders, 1,440 to date, surpassing the 788 for the same date in 2008—an increase of 83 percent. Small businesses fold all over the city as the extortion rates rise. Forty percent of the city's restaurants close. The city now has an estimated 150,000 addicts. El Pastor believes that 30 to 40 percent of the population depends on drug money for income.

MONTHLY MURDER TALLIES
FOR CIUDAD JUÁREZ, 2008–2009

	2008	2009
January	46	154
February	49	240
March	117	73
April	55	85
May	136	127
June	139	221
July	146	260
August	228	316
September	118	310
October	181	324
November	192	
December	200	
Total	**1,607***	

From various Juárez press sources.

* This total does not include the 45 bodies recovered by federal agents in February and March in clandestine graves in two houses. With these added, the total rises to 1,652.

I am sitting with a Juárez lawyer at a party, and he explains that there has been a failure of analysis. He tells me criminology will not explain what is happening, nor will sociology. He pauses and then says that we must study demonology.

Some blame the violence on a war between cartels, some blame poverty, some blame the army, some blame the army's fighting the cartels, some blame local street gangs, some blame drugs, some blame slave wages, some blame corrupt government.

But regardless of the blame, no one can figure out who controls the violence, and no one can imagine how the violence can be stopped.

But everyone grows numb. Murders slip off the front page and become part of the ordinary noise of life. By early December, 2,400 have died.

Juárez is rated by some counts to be the most violent city in the world.

ON AUGUST 13, 2008, EIGHT PEOPLE WERE KILLED BY ARMED COMMANDOS AT CIAD #8, A
DRUG REHABILITATION CENTER FOR THE POOR IN COLONIA PRIMERO DE SEPTIEMBRE IN
CIUDAD JUÁREZ. THEY WERE HOLDING A PRAYER MEETING. THE BOY IN THE COFFIN, LUIS
ÁNGEL GONZÁLEZ, "SIGNO," 19, A MEMBER OF LOCOS 23 GANG, HAD CHECKED IN FOR
TREATMENT FOUR DAYS BEFORE HIS MURDER. THE MEXICAN ARMY REMAINED OUTSIDE THE
REHAB CENTER WHILE THE SLAUGHTER WENT ON FOR FIFTEEN MINUTES, WITNESSES SAID.

APPENDIX

THE RIVER OF BLOOD

People with brown skin are next door to invisible.

—George Orwell, 1939

At first, it is simply a clerical task. Read the papers and put down the names, if given, and the time and cause of death. Then the volume grows, and the reports get sketchy. People disappear, and their fates never get reported. Nor are there any real numbers on the kidnapped since families hardly ever report such events, because they are afraid of being murdered. Then, the killings per day get larger, the reporters more and more threatened. By June 2008, the city cannot handle its own dead and starts giving corpses wholesale to medical schools or tossing bodies into common graves. The list of the dead becomes a dark burden as solid information dwindles. And so it finally trails off, a path littered with death and small voices whispering against the growing night. But it gives a sense of the rumble of daily life as the bullets fly and the killers roam unimpeded. In January and February 2008, newspapers and voices on

the streets all marveled at the horror of more than forty killings in a month—
a number never before recorded in Ciudad Juárez. By May 10, the work becomes unbearable, and the tally of that moment records only a fourth of the
slaughter the year would bring. Of course, all this happens before things get
really bad in the city. By the end of 2008, the monthly totals reached beyond
two hundred. By summer 2009, more than three hundred murders in a month
became normal in Juárez.

JANUARY

El Diario, Ciudad Juárez, January 1, 2008
State agents know the nickname of the murderer. "El Popeye" shot César Seáñez
to death in Colonia Chaveña Sunday night. The assassin, known by the nickname "El Popeye," at this time has not been arrested by the Ministerial Police.

El Diario, Ciudad Juárez, January 3, 2008
EXECUTED MAN IDENTIFIED IN PASEO TRIUNFO
The man shot to death in his car on the Avenida Paseo Triunfo de la Republica
was identified yesterday by his family. The victim, Ernesto Romero Adame, 33,
bled to death from bullet wounds in his neck, face and thorax. One bullet per-
forated his aorta, causing rapid death, said the spokesman for the State Prosecutor's Office, Mario Ruiz Nava. The homicide occurred on December 31, 2007
at 3:00 A.M. in the Avenida Paseo Triunfo de la Republica. . . . According to
witnesses, the victim was pursued by an armed commando traveling in several
late-model vehicles until they caught up with him in front of a hotel.

La Polaka, Ciudad Juárez, January 5, 2008
FIRST LITTLE DEATH OF THE DAY
A homeless man was found this morning with his head destroyed by a large
rock next to a wall in the Colonia Hidalgo. The first murder this Saturday

occurred at 9:00 in the morning. . . . The body was thrown into some abandoned ruins near the corner of Costa Rica and Tepeyac . . . causing alarm to the neighbors who said they were fed up with the crime in the zone and the lack of police protection.

El Diario, Ciudad Juárez, January 10, 2008
TUESDAY'S MURDER VICTIM WAS A JUNKMAN
The man executed by gunfire in front of a dozen workers at a construction site Tuesday afternoon in the *ejido* Salvárcar was identified yesterday by his family. The victim, Rodolfo Martinez Vazquez, 32, was apparently the owner of a junkyard.

La Polaka, Ciudad Juárez, January 12, 2008
JUST 16 THIS MONTH
This morning the mutilated body of another executed man was found along with two other gang members murdered during the night. The 16th homicide victim of the month was found this morning about 1:30 in a field near the intersection of Sabino Hinostrosa and Ejercito Nacional.

El Diario, Ciudad Juárez, January 14, 2008
18 INTENTIONAL HOMICIDES IN 13 DAYS; TWO KILLED YESTERDAY
Two men were killed in separate incidents yesterday. The first victim died from several bullet wounds, presumably from a group of gangsters, and the other person was stabbed to death apparently during a robbery attempt. These crimes bring to 18 the total intentional homicides committed in Ciudad Juárez in the first 13 days of 2008.

El Diario, Ciudad Juárez, January 17, 2008
385 ARREST WARRANTS FOR HOMICIDE UNSERVED
More than 200 arrest orders remain pending under the old penal justice system, according to a report from the State Prosecutor's Office. Of the total

historic backlog of judicial orders issued in the last 14 years, 385 are for intentional homicide. In addition, from 1995 through December 31, 2007, 844 murder cases remain unresolved and continue to be investigated under the traditional justice system, according to official reports.

El Diario, Ciudad Juárez, **January 18, 2008**
WOMAN BEATEN TO DEATH
Last night a woman was found dead, apparently from a beating, inside her home located in the Colonia Anahuac. The body was found around 11:00 at night in a house located in Churubusco Street near the corner of Melchor Muzquiz, according to reports from the Secretary of Public Security. The first agents who arrived at the scene reported that the victim was severely beaten. Family members of the victim arrived at the house and identified her as María Guadalupe Esparza Zavala, 34. They added that their relative lived alone and they did not know who could have killed her.

El Diario, Ciudad Juárez, **January 21, 2008**
14 POLICE MURDERED IN 13 MONTHS
The municipal policeman murdered yesterday morning is the 14th police homicide victim in the past 13 months, according to media reports. . . . Yesterday, the agent killed Sunday was officially identified as Captain Julián Cháirez Hernández, 37, who worked in the Aldama district. Before this murder, another 13 agents had died in similar circumstances since January 2007. Of the 14 victims, 13 were killed by gunfire while one was intentionally run over by a car.

El Diario, Ciudad Juárez, **January 22, 2008**
AS OF TODAY NO ARRESTS
The State Prosecutor's Office reported that as of today, no arrests have been made in the murder of a 10-year-old girl in her house located in Parajes de San Juan in the southeastern part of the city. The victim, Mirna Yesenia Muñoz

Ledo Marín, was alone at the time of the murder. Her stepfather was at work and her mother had gone out to take another of her children to the doctor.

El Diario, Ciudad Juárez, January 23, 2008

At the Gravesite, Seeking Justice for Mirna Yesenia

The body of Mirna Yesenia Muñoz Ledo Marín lies in a white casket in the center of a room in a small adobe house in Colonia Mexico 68, watched over by her family and friends. The house belongs to Celia Moreno Portillo, grandmother of the 10-year-old girl, where she and her family lived for the past year. . . . Pain and anger provoked demands for justice, that the authorities find the person who took the life of the innocent little girl. "We want to find who is responsible; the authorities must do their work," said Faustino and Mayra Luisa Marín, half-brother and sister of the child. They indicated that their mother and stepfather had gone to live in Parajes de San Juan in order to find a better life and never imagined that they would lose Mirna Yesenia, the youngest of 7 children.

El Diario, Ciudad Juárez, January 24, 2008

Officials Seek Genetic Profile of the Young Girl's Murderer

The State Prosecutor's Office is processing the fluid found on the girl's body. DNA will be compared with a series of suspects. Last Tuesday, the state authority confirmed that Mirna Yesenia Muñoz Ledo Marín was sexually assaulted. The child died from a laceration to the heart after being stabbed in the chest with a sharp object.

El Diario, Ciudad Juárez, January 25, 2008

Corner Peanut Vendor Murdered

According to witnesses, a peanut and pumpkin seed vendor was shot yesterday at midday by a man traveling in a car similar to those driven by the State

Investigative Agency. . . . The crime took place at 2:30 in the afternoon when the man, identified only by his nickname, "Freckles," was selling peanuts at an intersection in the eastern area of the city.

El Diario, Ciudad Juárez, January 25, 2008
CHURCH PLEADS FOR PRAYER TO STOP THE VIOLENCE IN JUÁREZ
Catholic church leaders in Ciudad Juárez asked the community and priests to join in prayer for justice and reconciliation.

El Diario, Ciudad Juárez, January 26, 2001
IDENTIFY AUTHORS OF POLICE AGENTS' MURDERS
CHIHUAHUA—The State Prosecutor's Office has identified the presumed authors of the recent murders of the ministerial agents and the attack on Commander Fernando Lozano and is ready to issue arrest warrants, informed the State Attorney General, Patricia Gonzalez Rodriguez.

El Diario, Ciudad Juárez, January 27, 2008
" . . . FOR THOSE WHO CONTINUE NOT BELIEVING"
A cardboard sign with the names of 4 elements of the Secretariat of Municipal Public Security recently assassinated, of another who is presumed to have been abducted, and of 17 active agents, was placed at the Police Monument located at the intersection of Juan Gabriel and Sanders Avenue. This death threat was registered a few days after a series of attacks began against police chiefs of the different corporations. The list was placed in a funeral wreath on the wall where memorial plaques honor agents killed in action. The message, similar to those found on the bodies of assassinated persons, read: "For those who did not believe: Cháirez, Romo, Vaca, Cháirez and Ledezma." It also warned 17 active agents, identified by surname, code and district: "For those who continue not believing."

El Diario de El Paso, El Paso, Tx., January 28, 2008
U.S. APATHY TOWARD NARCO-TRAFFICKING CREATES MORE VIOLENCE IN MEXICO

The U.S. government has not stopped drug traffic to the interior of the country and this has generated an increase in violence in Mexico, especially along the border, said Charles Bowden, author of *Down by the River,* a book about the drug trade.

Norte de Ciudad Juárez, January 28, 2008
TRAVEL TO JUÁREZ PROHIBITED FOR U.S. MILITARY PERSONNEL

Commanders at Fort Bliss announced that military personnel stationed in El Paso are prohibited from traveling to Juárez due to the recent outbreak of violence there related to organized crime. Since last Saturday, the base commanders have suspended issuance of passes to visit Juárez due to the "unacceptable risk to health, security, well-being and morale" of the soldiers.

Norte de Ciudad Juárez, January 28, 2008
SIX MORE MURDERS OVER THE WEEKEND

This weekend, police reported finding the bodies of six murder victims in separate incidents; four were shot.

El Diario, Ciudad Juárez, January 28, 2008

The secretary of Municipal Public Security, Guillermo Prieto Quintana, ordered the arrest for 36 hours of the agent assigned to guard the Monument to the Fallen Police Officer. The agent was charged with negligence because he was on duty when the funeral wreath and list of 4 murdered policemen and 17 targeted for killing was left at the monument. The officer testified to his superiors that he did not see who left the threat, but unofficial sources say it was left by a group of hooded men in a dark pickup. The agent charged left his post when his replacement arrived but did not tell him or anyone about the threatening note or funeral wreath left at the monument. "It was an act of negligence because the agents assigned to guard duty fall into a routine and think that the job is not important."

FEBRUARY

El Diario, Ciudad Juárez, February 1, 2008
BODY FOUND IN CAR TRUNK; VICTIM JESUS DURAN HAD BEEN
MISSING SINCE JANUARY 19
The body of a man was found yesterday in the trunk of a car abandoned on the street in the southeast area of the city. The victim had been reported missing to the State Investigative Police a week before his body was found. This was the second of four bodies found yesterday in different places in the city.

El Diario, Ciudad Juárez, February 1, 2008
TWO MORE EXECUTED VICTIMS FOUND
The bodies of two men were found yesterday in Rio Champoton Street in the Cordova Americas neighborhood where more than a dozen bodies have been abandoned. Both men were found with their hands tied with adhesive tape, one with hands behind his back and the other with hands in front. The two bodies were found lying a few meters apart and the heads were bloody. Five 9 mm cartridges were found at the scene.

Norte de Ciudad Juárez, February 1, 2008
HOMICIDE RECORD BROKEN; MORE THAN 40 VIOLENT DEATHS
DURING THE MONTH OF JANUARY
January broke a record for intentional homicides. According to official statistics from the State Attorney General, the violent deaths registered at the end of January surpassed those registered during any of the previous 12 months.

El Diario, Ciudad Juárez, **February 1, 2008**

January Breaks 1995 Homicide Record

Forty-three murders were committed in January 2008, more than in any other month in the history of Ciudad Juárez. The previous record was set 13 years ago in September 1995 with 37 murders reported. Just yesterday, four more murder victims were found, after being captured, bound, shot and left in various places around the city.

Fernando Macias Gonzalez, about 30, was found inside a pickup. . . .

Jesus Duran Uranga, 31, was in the trunk of a car located around midday in the Los Arcos neighborhood.

The third and fourth victims, unidentified, were left in a vacant lot in the Cordova Americas neighborhood. All had been shot.

Four of the January murder victims were women and 39 were men.

Notable murders this month in the city include Municipal Police Captain Julián Cháirez Hernández and a 10-year-old girl, both killed on January 20. The next day, the operational director of the municipal police, Francisco Ledesma Salazar, 34, was shot to death in front of his home as he left for work. . . . On the same day, a woman about 34 weeks pregnant was murdered with an ax by her brother-in-law, who later turned himself in to authorities. The victim, Erika Sonora Trejo, 31, was attacked in the presence of her two children aged 11 and 6. Her unborn child also died.

El Diario, Ciudad Juárez, **February 13, 2008**

Three Dead and 14 Abducted in Palomas, Ascensión and Nuevo Casas Grandes; Police Corporations Under Siege in the Northwest After the Assassination of the Subdirector and Two Other Persons

NUEVO CASAS GRANDES—After the violent night in which heavily armed groups left three people dead, one injured, and at least 14 abducted and missing in Nuevo Casas Grandes, Ascensión and Palomas, a psychosis has taken over the Public Security agencies. The towns find themselves besieged by elements of the Army, the Federal Police, and Police Intelligence (CIPOL).

In one of the incidents, Carlos Mario Parra Gutiérrez, Subdirector of Public Security of Nuevo Casas Grandes, was killed after the presumed *sicarios* set his house on fire. Almost simultaneously, several groups killed another two persons in Ascensión and Palomas, where at least 10 more were abducted; this number could be higher because at an apartment complex, the attackers destroyed the locks on all the doors and captured an unknown number of people.

Parra Gutiérrez had tried to fight the fire when he was struck by a bullet in the head, and though he managed to call for help to get to the hospital, he died while receiving medical treatment. The official's coworkers said that he had worked for Municipal Public Security for 12 years.

Another of the victims was identified as Vidal Arámbula Avelar, a storekeeper who owned a wine and liquor store. Vidal Arámbula was violently taken from his home on Puebla Street, and after being handcuffed, he was apparently told to run for his life (*la ley fuga*) and was then machine-gunned in the street. His body was left lying on Avenida Mexico in front of a taco stand.

As of the close of this edition, the authorities had no leads as to the identities of those responsible nor of those persons who remain missing.

El Diario, Ciudad Juárez, February 14, 2008

Heavily armed men in two vehicles exchanged gunfire as they traveled to different areas of the city. The confrontation left at least one person injured and several were abducted at the scene. After the shoot-out, dozens of agents from the army, the State Investigative Agency, the Center for Police Investigation, federal and municipal police surrounded a luxurious residence in Pradera Dorada. Unofficial sources inside the police agencies said the shooters retreated into this house.

Norte de Ciudad Juárez, **February 15, 2008**

Jesús Muñoz Fraire said that his family's home was robbed during a military operation in a neighboring residence. He accused the soldiers of stealing two televisions, a home theater and jewelry belonging to his wife.

El Diario, Ciudad Juárez, **February 16, 2008**

PRADERA DORADA "BUNKER" FORGOTTEN BY AUTHORITIES

Despite the arsenal found inside the residence in the luxurious Pradera Dorada neighborhood, no investigation has been initiated and the house at 3202 Rancho Las Cabras has not been secured. Neighbors interviewed thought that the house had been abandoned. Military authorities reported the confiscation of 25 rifles, 5 pistols, 7 fragmentation grenades, 3,493 cartridges of various calibers, 142 ammunition clips, 14 bullet-proof vests, 13 mesh vests, 8 radios and 5 vehicles, 3 of them with Sinaloa plates.

El Fronterizo, Ciudad Juárez, **February 16, 2008**

MILITARY AND FEDERAL FORCES RETURN TO PRADERA DORADA HOUSE

At about 7:00 P.M., military personnel in at least two tanks as well as federal and state agents moved in on the house again and remained for several hours. Soldiers closed the roads and searched all the cars that passed by.

El Paso Times, **February 18, 2008**

Officer Juan Hernández Sánchez, a 12-year veteran of the force, was last seen Feb. 11, according to his colleagues and his family. His car was still parked at the police station.

Sunday, a homeless man found a bag at Venezuela and Ignacio Zaragoza streets, containing what appeared to be the belongings of Officer Hernández. There were uniform pants and a uniform jacket embroidered "J. Hernández," and an undershirt with what appeared to be a blood stain. There was also some clear and gray adhesive tape, police said. Another officer, Jesús Enríquez Solís Luévano, also vanished, although the circumstances of his disappearance were not clear Monday. That case is also in the hands of state investigators, city police officials said.

Norte de Ciudad Juárez, February 19, 2008
FOUR MEN EXECUTED IN ASCENSIÓN AND PALOMAS IN 24 HOURS BY ARMED COMMANDOS

Martín Gonzalo Palacios, 35, alias El Cuiltra, and Horacio Ontiveros Muñoz, alias El Carolino, were taken before dawn, their bodies found along a dirt road.

In Palomas, the bodies of Javier Ortega Miranda, alias El Boby, and Adán Alonso Pérez Fuentes, alias El Oscuro, were found inside a Cadillac Escalade.

Due to such incidents, army troops now patrol the region searching for killers who have sown terror in these communities.

El Diario, Ciudad Juárez, February 20, 2008

Twenty-one men detained by the army last Saturday in a house in Campestre Arboleda declared that they were beaten by agents they cannot identify since they were blindfolded while being tortured. In their declaration before a judge, they retracted their confession to manufacturing small doses of drugs in the house as they had confessed to while being tortured.

Asrael Govea, one of the detainees, said to the judge: "The officers said to us, 'Who hit you?' And I said, 'The officer.' And they hit me again and again and kept asking me, 'Who hit you?' Until we finally said to them, 'No one, Sir!'"

The uniformed and shackled detainees gave their declarations in a hearing room inside the state prison. When they raised their shirts, in addition to large purple bruises, some had pre-Hispanic symbols and the word "Azteca" tattooed on their bodies. Most said that they worked construction or sold things on the street and earned between seventy dollars and ninety dollars per week.

New York Times, February 21, 2008
DEADLY BOMB IN MEXICO WAS MEANT FOR THE POLICE

MEXICO CITY—Juan Manuel Meza Campos, 44, was trying to plant a bomb in a police official's car when it blew up and killed him on a busy avenue here last week. The blast unsettled residents of the capital, which had so far escaped much of the drug violence that has racked other parts of the country. Mr. Meza, who went by the nickname El Pipén, had links to drug dealers in a high-crime neighborhood called Tepito, where there is a lively trade in drugs and contraband goods.

El Diario, Ciudad Juárez, February 21, 2008

Before dawn yesterday the Mexican army arrested 8 men at different locations in the city who were supposedly working as spies for the criminal organization known as "La Linea," composed mainly of current and former police officers. Unofficial sources said 12 were arrested.

The detainees were identified unofficially as: Luis Carlos Ramírez, César and José Vizcaíno, José Inés González, Juan Rojas, Juan Muñoz, César and Javier Ledezma, Manuel Padilla, Mario Ricardo Martínez Rosales, Francisco Muñoz Escobedo, Ricardo Ramírez.

Fearing retaliation, family members of some detainees demonstrated at the military installations, demanding that the authorities provide information on the whereabouts of their relatives. They were denied entrance and no representative of the military spoke with them. They then went to the offices of the Federal Attorney General asking where their relatives had been taken, but they were informed that they were not there.

El Diario, Ciudad Juárez, February 26, 2008

Federal officials reported that five bodies, two heads and three thoraxes were found buried in four clandestine graves in the patio of a house-warehouse in the Cuernavaca neighborhood at 1847 Cocoyoc Street. The house has been sealed off since January 25 when authorities confiscated 1.8 tons of marijuana.

Las Cruces Sun-News, **February 27, 2008**

Javier Perez Mendiola, alias "El Indio," 41, and Adrian Juárez Juárez, 25, were putting gas in their Dodge Ram pickup at a station just a few steps from the border in the town of Palomas when assailants wearing ski masks pulled up in two cars and opened fire on them. Investigators had made no arrests and were trying to determine a motive for the killings.

Houston Chronicle and El Paso Times, **February 27, 2008**

Agents Seize $1.9 Million Hidden in SUV on Border; Mexican National Jailed in El Paso in One of the City's Largest Cash Seizures Ever

Saul Sanchez, 42, a Mexican national living legally in Kansas City, Kansas, was arrested by ICE agents on charges of currency smuggling. Agents at the Bridge of the Americas used a density meter to inspect the doors of the 1992 Ford Expedition and found $1,858,085 in cash.

International Herald Tribune, Associated Press, **February 27, 2008**

MEXICAN POLICE FIND PARTS FROM AT LEAST 8 BODIES IN PITS NEAR BORDER IN CIUDAD JUÁREZ

A statement from the prosecutor's office said authorities found five complete bodies, three limbless trunks and two heads in four pits.

El Diario, Ciudad Juárez, **February 27, 2008**

Bodies found in a clandestine grave now total nine, according to federal police authorities. A report stated that digging will continue and that it is not possible to say exactly how many human remains might be discovered.

El Diario, Ciudad Juárez, **February 28, 2008**

An agent of the mounted police, José Guadalupe Cruz Cisneros, known to his neighbors as "El Tyson," was executed just a few meters from police headquarters. He died instantly in a hail of AK-47 gunfire. His wife and 12-year-old son and other close family members arrived at the scene. Cruz Cisneros left work at 7:00 P.M. and drove toward home in his 1989 Datsun pickup. He was chased by several armed men in two vehicles; one closed him in as the occupants of both vehicles opened fire. Cruz Cisneros died inside his truck from bullet wounds in his abdomen, thorax and face.

El Diario, Ciudad Juárez, February 28, 2008
FAMILY MEMBERS OF DISAPPEARED PERSONS SEARCH "NARCOFOSA"
After several bodies were found in a clandestine grave in the Cuernavaca neighborhood, family members of disappeared persons demanded information from the state and federal prosecutors' offices. Since last Monday, relatives of three missing persons voluntarily gave DNA samples in order to determine if any of the bodies found recently might be their loved ones.

El Paso Times, February 28, 2008
Jaime Hervella, founder of the Association of Relatives and Friends of Disappeared Persons, said an anonymous telephone tip led Mexican police to the house at 1847 Cocoyoc Street. "I received a phone call from an informer that at such and such a warehouse where they recently picked up marijuana, you will find some of the individuals on your list." Hervella's group maintains a list of about 200 men who disappeared in Juárez since the early 1990s and are believed to be victims of drug traffickers.

El Paso Times, February 29, 2008
FEDERAL CASE UNVEILS INNER WORKINGS OF AZTECA GANG
Barrio Azteca assists the Juárez drug cartel in the importation of drugs and with killings in exchange for narcotics at discounted prices, Assistant U.S. Attorney Margaret Leachman said. The gang also offers members sanctuary in Mexico from U.S. law enforcement.

In one of the strangest twists in this month's court hearings, it was revealed that the gang operates a drug rehabilitation center in Juárez for "la familia," a code name for its members, located a few blocks from the U.S. border.

The rehab center was necessary because the gang, which has dealt heroin on El Paso's streets, had some of its members fall prey to the highly addictive drug, gang enforcement officers said.

MARCH

El Diario, Ciudad Juárez, March 1, 2008
IN TWO MONTHS, 76 MURDERS
Yesterday, the last day of February, there were four murders in three different zones of the city.

El Paso Times, March 1, 2008
JUÁREZ—A body tossed off a cliff landed in the backyard of a home minutes before 3 A.M. Friday in the Felipe Angeles area of Juárez, police said.

The unidentified dead man's hands and feet were bound with tape, which was also wrapped around his head. He was wearing gray pants, a blue sweater with black stripes and black shoes.

El Diario, Ciudad Juárez, March 2, 2008
Elements of the Federal Police discovered three bodies in a clandestine grave in the Colonia La Cuesta. In total, 12 bodies have been exhumed in investigations during the last 10 days.

El Diario, Ciudad Juárez, March 2, 2008
Families of disappeared persons denounced the lack of information and of a place where they can provide facts to assist federal authorities to identify the bodies found recently in Colonia Cuernavaca.

"We are fighting, because after we have given so much information and help, they recover the bodies and take them away. They should have a place here where the people here could provide DNA and other information. A place where we could go and say, 'You know, we are family,'" said Patricia Garibay, member of the Association of Relatives and Friends of Disappeared Persons.

"There is no way, there is no one who wants to take our information. There are 200 people with files at hand, but we have no data bank, no one has given us any idea where we can go nor to whom we could speak."

Garibay was interviewed about the discovery of the remains of at least 9 persons buried in clandestine graves in the patio of a house in Colonia Cuernavaca. She said that the excavation revives the hopes that hundreds of family members feel, that finally, they could end the anguish at not knowing the whereabouts of their loved ones, the open wounds left by their loss.

And this week, she added, with the discovery of the remains of at least 9 persons in the house at Cocoyoc 1847 in Colonia Cuernavaca, the families renewed their search.

"You must realize that for us, it is like returning to the first day of the disappearance; yet again, they open up our wounds, and each time something like this happens, it pushes us to try to do something," she said.

El Diario, Ciudad Juárez, March 2, 2008

Ricardo Fuentes Garcia, 38, an infantry captain in the Mexican army, was assassinated in a hail of AK-47 gunfire by an armed commando in Ciudad Juárez, Sunday at 3:00 A.M. as he was driving a red Dodge Neon in Fray Junipero Street. Captain Fuentes Garcia was head of the Rural Defense Corps in the Valle de Juárez. So far the defense forces have lost 33 men across Mexico in 2008, the majority of them in states with a high level of organized crime.

Another murder. José de la Luz Arreola García, 42, died at the Clinica Santa Maria after being knifed several times.

El Diario, Ciudad Juárez, **March 3, 2008**
Due to increasing criminality, Juárez residents are converting their houses into fortresses. Sales of closed circuit systems, access controls and other protection systems for houses and businesses have increased 50% in the last three years.

Las Cruces Sun-News, **March 4, 2008**
JUÁREZ VIOLENCE CONTINUES AS 7 ARE KILLED IN 3 DAYS
On Monday night, three unidentified men were shot to death in a vehicle strafed by gunfire in a supermarket parking lot. On Sunday, Ricardo Fuentes Garcia, 38, possibly a Mexican army officer, was found fatally shot in the chest in a Dodge Neon at Paseo del Triunfo de la Republica and Fray Junipero. Fuentes had identification stating he was a Mexican army captain.

On Saturday, Luis Alonso Marrufo Armendariz, a 38-year-old officer with the Chihuahua State Investigative Agency, was shot in his police vehicle by people in a gray sports car on Manuel Cloutier Avenue. He died and another police officer traveling with him was wounded.

The body of Raymundo Martinez Alcantara, in his 30s, was found in a pickup truck Saturday on Tecnologico Avenue and Nayarit Street. He had been shot to death. José de la Luz Arreola Garcia, 42, was pronounced dead from stab wounds Saturday at Santa Maria clinic.

El Diario, Ciudad Juárez, **March 4, 2008**
Three men were killed in a hail of AK-47 gunfire in the parking lot of a mall in San Lorenzo. At the close of this edition, none of the dead had been identified. More than 100 shots were fired from a Windstar, Tacoma and Chevrolet Silverado that closed in on the Nissan Altima and fired at the occupants. The vehicles of the aggressors fled and could not be located despite police roadblocks. Minutes later, the Paseo Triunfo de la Republica, a main thoroughfare in the city, was completely closed causing traffic chaos.

ArrobaJuárez.com, Ciudad Juárez, **March 4, 2008**
Two of the three transit cops abducted Monday in San Lorenzo were found, injured and unable to speak. Identified unofficially only by their last names, Molina and Uribe were found abandoned near a house whose residents called an ambulance. The director of the Transit Police said, "We've found two of our men, but Lieutenant Z5 is still missing."

El Diario, Ciudad Juárez, **March 4, 2008**
Yesterday, two women accused the Mexican army of being responsible for the disappearance of their husbands. "I was talking on the phone [early last Saturday morning] with my husband when he said 'here come the soldiers' and he dropped the phone but it was still connected and I heard him scream and I heard them hit him and since then I haven't heard anything from him," said Julia Escobar. She and Maridani Lopez are from Novolato, Sinaloa, and they traveled to the border to look for their husbands, who remain missing. They first went to the military headquarters where no one met with them and afterward to the offices of the Federal Attorney General.

Unofficial sources report that the detained were sent directly to Mexico City as the case is being handled by the Special Prosecutor for Organized Crime Investigations, whose offices are in the capital.

El Diario, Ciudad Juárez, **March 4, 2008**
The Mexican army yesterday presented 4 individuals in their custody to the media, among them an ex-state policeman from Sinaloa. The detained include Jorge Ibarra García, 32, from Novolato, Sinaloa, who professed to having executed 20 persons in a two-year period and to belong to a criminal organization known as La Linea. They also presented José Ángel Pérez Ibarra, 25, from Culiacán, Sinaloa, who, according to the army, is an organized crime hit man who confessed to killing 21 persons since 2006.

New York Times, March 5, 2008

MEXICO: BACKYARD BODY COUNT AT 14

The federal attorney general's office said agents had uncovered 14 bodies buried in the backyard of a house in Ciudad Juárez, a city that has gained infamy for its gangland slayings and the unsolved murders of hundreds of women. The agents began digging at the house in the neighborhood of La Cuesta, across the border from El Paso, last month, after a drug raid. They first found the dismembered bodies of nine victims, some of whom died more than five years ago. Five more bodies were unearthed in the last week. Prosecutors have yet to determine why the victims were killed, but they noted that agents found 3,700 pounds of marijuana in the initial raid.

El Diario, Ciudad Juárez, March 5, 2008

PUERTO PALOMAS DE VILLA—Two people were found executed yesterday before dawn near the fence separating this border community from the neighboring country, their bodies riddled by multiple high-caliber bullet wounds to the head and thorax causing instantaneous death. The dead were identified as Luis Armando Murillo Ponce, alias "El Nalguitas (Little Butt)," 26, and Javier Pardo Soto, 22, alias "El Marciano (the Martian)." This new finding is added to the list of executions in the region in the last 2 weeks, including a municipal police official from Nuevo Casas Grandes.

Last week, this border community witnessed a fearful wave of violence that has caused the authorities of the neighboring country to guard hundreds of children who cross to attend school and have been endangered by executions on busy streets in broad daylight.

El Diario, Ciudad Juárez, March 5, 2008

WOMEN EXCUSE AGGRESSIVE SPOUSES; PREFER ECONOMIC SUPPORT

Many women pardon the violence committed by their husbands and avoid pressing charges against them because they need their economic support. "It is common that they refuse to denounce them because if their husbands go to jail, they will have no resources to survive," reported the Center for Prevention and Attention to Women and Children in Situations of Violence.

El Diario, Ciudad Juárez, **March 6, 2008**
Lieutenant Carlos Adrián de Anda Doncel appeared alive at 8:07 P.M. outside the San Lorenzo Bakery two days after he was abducted by an armed commando. He was immediately taken to the hospital, where he was reported in stable but delicate condition with wounds from beatings on various parts of his body as his abductors had tortured him to obtain information. He was reported to be hysterical. Gonzalo Díaz Rojero, director of the Municipal Transit Police, expressed gratitude to the kidnappers for freeing officer de Anda Doncel alive.

The officer had been abandoned with hands cuffed behind his back and his head covered by a hood at the entrance of the San Lorenzo Bakery. The bakery owner, Juán Rodriguez, said the man had asked for 3 favors: a glass of water, to call his wife and that he close the business so that his attackers would not return for him in the presence of his family and coworkers. Red Cross Ambulance 156 arrived and took him to the emergency room, under a heavy escort from fellow transit police.

Don Juán Rodriguez, the bakery owner, said that the man had been extremely terrified and after talking to his wife, he began to cry.

El Diario, Ciudad Juárez, **March 6, 2008**
Under heavy guard, Secretary of National Defense Guillermo Galván Galván made a stealth visit to Juárez yesterday for about 2 hours as part of a tour of the northern region of the country where a battle is under way against organized crime.

El Diario, Ciudad Juárez, **March 6, 2008**
According to statistics released by authorities, for every 5 victims of domestic violence, only one perpetrator receives therapy to prevent new attacks.

El Diario, Ciudad Chihuahua, March 8, 2008

A confrontation before dawn today in the Rosario neighborhood of Chihuahua City left 7 presumed narco-traffickers dead, 4 arrested, and 3 soldiers and one official of the Federal Police injured. The identities of the dead were not revealed by the military nor by the Federal Preventive Police.

El Diario, Ciudad Juárez, March 9, 2008

A man was found dead lying in a pool of blood in the northbound lane of the Casas Grandes highway, and another was taken to the hospital after both were apparently shot.

El Diario, Ciudad Juárez, March 10, 2008

MUNICIPAL POLICE OFFICERS HUNTED DOWN: 1 DEAD, 3 INJURED

Víctor Alejandro Gómez Márquez was killed; Mario Alberto Rodríguez Arámbula, Moises Casas Camargo and Commander Ismael Villegas Frausto were injured in an ambush in which 2 police patrol vehicles were chased, surrounded and then attacked by AK-47 rifle fire from gunmen in two other vehicles on Avenida Paseo de la Victoria. Villegas's name appeared on the list of police officers to be executed posted on January 26.

The attack took place at 8:40 A.M. as commander Villegas was being escorted under guard to a meeting with the Secretary of Public Security, Guillermo Prieto Quintana. The patrol vehicles crashed into a wall while the attackers continued to fire shots in an attempt to finish the job. The injured waited about 15 minutes for ambulances that transferred them to the hospital.

The body of Víctor Alejandro Gómez Márquez was left in the passenger seat until after 11:00 in the morning, when it was taken away by the Forensic Medical Service.

The hospital was placed under heavy security with armed police on all sides of the building.

El Diario, Ciudad Juárez, **March 10, 2008**

A newspaper vendor was killed yesterday around noon by a gunshot to the head, the motive as yet unknown. This killing brought yesterday's murder total to 17. The man was identified by relatives as Job Abdiel Acosta Medina, 24.

El Diario, Ciudad Juárez, **March 10, 2008**

A woman's body was found Sunday night in the passenger seat of a pickup truck, apparently dead from a laceration to her liver caused by a beating. She was identified as Rosa Lopez Moreno, 47.

According to witnesses, Lopez Moreno was traveling with her boyfriend, Catalino Mendez Ramirez, 35, and her daughter. The daughter reported that both adults had been drinking and began to argue. The girl went into a Laundromat and when she returned Mendez Ramirez told her that her mother had fallen asleep and drove to her home. The girl realized that the woman showed no signs of life and so she asked for help from the police and paramedics, who pronounced her dead. Mendez was detained for interrogation.

El Diario, Ciudad Juárez, **March 11, 2008**

The bodies of six gunmen killed Saturday in the shoot-out in Colonia Rosario may end up in a common grave as the state has not claimed the bodies, which remain under guard by the Mexican army.

El Diario, Ciudad Juárez, **March 11, 2008**

FALLEN MUNICIPAL POLICE OFFICER, VÍCTOR ALEJANDRO GÓMEZ MÁRQUEZ, TO BE BURIED WITH HONORS TODAY

"It is the most fearful pain anyone can feel, to lose a son is the most difficult," said the mother of the fallen officer. She said that her youngest son had lived here in her house with his wife and daughter, that he had an honest way of life, that he had not used his job to make money on the side, that he had not been able to afford his own house.

El Diario, Ciudad Juárez, March 11, 2008
Two Dead, One Injured in Separate Incidents

Juan Luis Ortega Herrera, 16, was shot to death at about 11:00 Monday night from a moving car near the corner of Francisco Martín López and Emiliano Zapata streets.

Jorge Soto Sandoval was killed at about 1:00 in the afternoon in the Colonia Torreon at Joe's Sandwich Shop, where he worked.

Daniel Huerta Carrillo, 17, was injured by gunfire at the corner of José María Pino Suárez and Pablo López streets. The victim was taken to the Santa Maria clinic and his condition was stable.

El Diario, Ciudad Juárez, March 11, 2008

Transit Police Lieutenant Carlos Adrián de Anda Doncel, freed the night of March 5 after being held and tortured for 48 hours by an armed commando, has left the city and his current whereabouts are unknown.

El Diario, Ciudad Juárez, March 12, 2008

Officer Víctor Alejandro Gómez Márquez, executed last Sunday in an ambush . . . was buried yesterday afternoon. . . . The Secretariat of Municipal Public Security had publicized the hour of the religious service, nevertheless, the family rejected the presence of the media for unknown motives.

El Diario, Ciudad Juárez, March 12, 2008

Blanca Edna Páez Orozco, 22, died and her brother, Abel Páez Orozco, 20, was injured yesterday afternoon in a house fire in the Finca Bonita neighborhood. The mentally disabled victims were tied to a bed when the fire broke out. Initial reports said that the sister and brother had been playing with matches. Their father, Abel Páez, 65, had tied the victims to the bed in the morning.

El Diario, Ciudad Juárez, March 13, 2008

The Secretariat of Municipal Public Security reported that three persons died violently yesterday in less than 5 hours in different areas of the city. Julio César Soltero, 20, was killed by gunfire in front of a house in Colonia Granjas de Chapultepec. At about 9:00 at night, a man of about 47 was shot and killed in his car in the Colonia Altavista. Residents of the area identified him as "El Bello" (Handsome) who lived near the place where he was shot. The third violent death happened about 15 minutes later, when a man identified as Juan Adrián García, 19, was murdered by four gunshots in the Colonia Aldama. According to initial reports, García was murdered by the ex-boyfriend of his girlfriend, identified only as Raul, who was angry at seeing the woman with García.

El Diario, Ciudad Juárez, March 13, 2008

Two men were assassinated this morning and their bodies left in the public right-of-way in the Ampliacion Aeropuerto neighborhood.

El Diario, Ciudad Juárez, March 13, 2008

At about 2:00 in the afternoon, an ex-municipal policeman was shot and killed by an armed commando at the intersection of Durango and Paseo Arboleda streets. Unofficial sources identified the ex-officer as Ricardo Eloy Yáñez Gómez, 32.

El Diario, Ciudad Juárez, March 14, 2008

NARCO-CEMETERY IN LA CUESTA YIELDS 33 CORPSES

The Federal Attorney General's Office reported that a total of 33 corpses have been found in a clandestine grave at a house in the Colonia La Cuesta.

A forensic anthropologist said that the recovered remains have been buried for approximately 5 years and only 3 of them are women.

El Diario, Ciudad Juárez, March 14, 2008

This afternoon, two men were assassinated at the intersection of Puerto Mexico and Puerto Alegre streets. The bodies remained in the cab of a Silverado pickup with Texas plates 92JPW4.

El Diario, Ciudad Chihuahua, March 14, 2008

CHIHUAHUA—Paulina Elizabeth Luján Morales, 16, the high school student missing since last Monday, was found dead yesterday morning. The girl died from a blow to the head and she had been sexually abused. The body was found in a vacant lot in the Colonia Valles de Chihuahua. Workers at a nearby farm found the body. They saw a bundle that they thought was clothes but when they approached, they realized that it was a woman and called the police. The body was dressed in gray pants, white T-shirt embroidered with the name of her school, black sports jacket with an orange hood, "Angelina" socks, a black belt and a key. The pants had black marks on them that looked like tire tracks. Family members came to the scene along with the father of Daniela Ivania Hernández Hernández, 13, missing since March 4.

El Diario, Ciudad Juárez, March 15, 2008

According to official and media reports, 64 execution victims have been found in narco-graves discovered in and around Ciudad Juárez in the last 8 years. In 1999, a mega-operation involving 500 Mexican soldiers as well as FBI agents excavated several ranches in a search for more than 100 bodies thought to be buried there. Despite the intense searching and worldwide media attention, only 9 bodies were found. In 2004, personnel from the Federal Attorney General's office exhumed 12 bodies from the patio of a house at 3633

Parsioneros Street in the Las Acequias neighborhood. Most of these victims had been assassinated on site by strangulation to avoid being noticed by neighbors. An informant working for U.S. authorities, identified as Jesús Contreras, "Lalo," Eduardo Ramírez or Guillermo Ramírez Peyro, participated in some of the killings that were carried out by a group of Chihuahua state judicial police under the command of Miguel Ángel Loya Gallegos, who is still a fugitive. So far in 2008, a total of 33 bodies have been found at two different sites in Juárez; none of the dead have been identified.

El Diario, Ciudad Juárez, **March 15, 2008**
Agrarian leader Armando Villareal Martha, founder of the organization Agrodinamica Nacional, was assassinated by AK-47 gunfire yesterday afternoon in Nuevo Casas Grandes. Villareal Martha was a well-known defender of the rights of farmers, especially in the struggle to obtain more affordable prices for fuel, electricity and other necessities in the countryside, and the murder was widely repudiated. The victim left his house accompanied by his son, who was driving the 2007 Dodge Ram pickup. The first shots were fired as they passed in front of a secondary school in the Colonia Centro. They tried to get away but the attackers caught up with them and fired directly at the agrarian leader, killing him and leaving his son uninjured.

According to an anonymous source, Villareal Martha was pursued last Thursday after arriving at the Juárez airport on a flight from Mexico City accompanied by two other members of Agrodinamica Nacional. They were followed along the road to the town of Ascensión, where Villareal was able to evade their pursuers.

El Diario, Ciudad Juárez, **March 15, 2008**
A municipal police lieutenant was assassinated last night after being "hunted down" by a group of armed men. The officer was identified as Mario Moraz of the Delicias district and his death leaves behind a young daughter.

Before the murder of Lieutenant Moraz in the same sector of the city, a police patrol discovered a bundle lying in the street. Upon inspection, they realized it was the body of a man as yet unidentified. In the pocket of his pants, they found a plastic bag containing a hypodermic needle. It appeared that the body had been thrown from a moving car and showed no evidence of bullet wounds. A few minutes later at about 10:30 P.M., another body was found in the Colonia Hidalgo and a source reported that this person also carried a hypodermic needle.

El Diario, Ciudad Juárez, **March 15, 2008**
RELATIVES SEEK IDENTITIES OF THE BURIED BODIES
Short of breath and almost sobbing, José Luis speaks hesitantly about the possibility of ending his family's long nightmare when 4 years ago, one of his loved ones "disappeared." "We believe that he will be among the victims. I can't tell you why, but we believe that our search may soon be over," said the man who asked that his identity be concealed. Their odyssey began in 2004, when a family member was captured and never heard from again. Each time narco-graves are discovered, they think they might find their missing relative. "Other times we have struggled a lot and this time also, but it's very likely he will be there as the dates coincide." As of yesterday, they had received no information on how to make an inquiry with the authorities on the process of identification. "And when you go there they look at you as if you are a criminal . . . but we are just relatives and we want to give him a Christian burial."

El Diario, Ciudad Juárez, **March 15, 2008**
Those living near the warehouse in La Cuesta, where 33 bodies were exhumed, were shaken up to find the clandestine cemetery in their neighborhood. "We never imagined they would find so many bodies." The federal organized crime investigators stayed at the scene for 13 days and then left as

silently as they came, taking with them the heavy equipment, forensic anthropologists and cadaver dogs.

Some of the neighbors interviewed said they had sometimes heard strange noises in the house that they attributed to tortured souls, but an older man living next door discarded this idea. "Look, here you have to be more afraid of the living than the dead."

Yesterday, several relatives of the disappeared went to the morgue to solicit information, but the state delegation of the Federal Attorney General released no information.

El Diario, Ciudad Juárez, March 15, 2008

Yesterday afternoon an armed commando executed three men in a 300C Chrysler in broad daylight and in the middle of one of the busiest intersections in the city. Municipal police at the scene said there were more than 200 bullets fired at the car. Witnesses said that the driver tried to continue after the gunfire stopped, but due to his mortal wounds, he lost control of the car, which crashed onto the sidewalk at high speed and finally stopped with the driver dead at the wheel.

El Diario, Ciudad Juárez, March 15, 2008

A woman remains unidentified more than 24 hours after her body was found on the Camino Real highway and police have not advanced the investigation. At about 5:00 P.M. last Friday, someone called Emergency 066 to report that they had seen several people toss a body out of a car. When police arrived, they found the female body on the sidewalk near a pile of rocks, face up with outstretched arms, two bullet wounds visible on her right cheek.

El Diario, Ciudad Juárez, March 16, 2008

The State Investigative Agency reported that three men were killed Saturday night. A double homicide took place in the Colonia Alvaro Obregon at about

10:35 P.M. The unidentified bodies showed no external signs of violence. One had a tattoo on his left arm of a mouse wearing a hat. The second had four tattoos: the word "Juareño," on the shoulder, an eagle devouring a snake on the back, "Hecho en Mexico" on the upper left arm, and "Xicotencatl" on the chest, indicating membership in the "Mexicles" gang.

At 11:58, in the Colonia Pancho Villa, Pedro Pablo García Colorado, 18, was murdered in a gang fight between "Los Chicos Trece" and the "Veteranos."

Agencia Reforma, Mexico City, March 16, 2008

The number of executions related to organized crime thus far in the administration of President Felipe Calderón has risen to 3,008. During 2008, the number of killings has risen by 30%. . . . Security expert Ernesto Mendieta says that the violence will continue because current government strategies do not attack the roots of the problem, nor are the killers arrested. "There is not a single intelligence investigation that will stop the groups doing the killing. If you want to kill someone, you kill them."

El Diario, Ciudad Juárez, March 16, 2008

The Federal Attorney General's Office announced today that three more bodies were exhumed from the property on Sierra Pedregal Street in Colonia La Cuesta, bringing the total to 36. The bodies were buried in 16 graves and the victims were murdered and buried by members of the Carrillo Fuentes cartel.

Present at the scene were the anthropologist who directed the recovery of the bodies and her 5 collaborators, 15 federal agents and "Rocco," a 2-year-old Belgian Malinois who participated in the work. The anthropologist, who asked that her name be withheld, demonstrated the recovery process for the reporters.

El Diario, Ciudad Juárez, March 17, 2008

Four people were assassinated and their bodies found this morning discarded around the city. A male, approximately 35, brown skin, thin beard and mustache was found in the Emiliano Zapata neighborhood, the word "Juárez" was tattooed across his stomach. A little later, three murdered men were found in the Colonia Papalote with multiple signs of beatings in different parts of their bodies.

El Diario, Ciudad Juárez, March 17, 2008
This morning three bodies were found in Colonia Papalote. Two of the unidentified victims are men, while the third is a woman. The bodies were found semi nude with visible signs of violence. According to neighbors, the victims were not from that area.

El Diario, Ciudad Juárez, March 17, 2008
This afternoon at about 2:00 a jeep was riddled with bullets by an armed commando in front of a mall at the intersection of Zaragoza Boulevard and Emiliano Zapata Avenue. One body was left inside the jeep and the occupant was taken by the attackers.

El Diario, Ciudad Juárez, March 17, 2008
Nine murders were reported in less than 12 hours in the city. Four bodies were discarded around the city, two were killed in gang fights, one was killed at a nightclub and two others were machine-gunned in public. These killings bring the total so far in March to 58, the highest monthly tally in the history of the city. Also, this month federal authorities recovered 45 bodies buried on the grounds of two houses in the city.

El Diario, Ciudad Juárez, March 17, 2008
Two men were assassinated yesterday at noon in the Colonia Galeana. One man tried to escape by boarding a city bus, causing panic among the passengers. He died from his wounds a few minutes later in a rear seat on the bus. Witnesses reported that a group of armed men attacked the two men, wounding them with multiple gunshots in the back. Neither man was identified.

Frontera Norte Sur, Las Cruces (N.Mex.), **March 18, 2008**

The unearthing of at least 48 murder victims from three properties in Ciudad Juárez and Chihuahua City during recent weeks grimly refocused attention on the persistence of torture and forced disappearance in Mexico. Since many—if not most—of the victims were presumably associated with illegal drug trafficking and other criminal activities, the popular wisdom is that common citizens who keep their noses out of trouble shouldn't be overly concerned by the discovery of mass horrors like the latest narco-graves.

Condemned by all human rights organizations, forced disappearance constitutes the silent side of Mexico's narco war. Much more visible, of course, are the inner city shoot-outs, streetside body dumpings and public executions that have jarred entire regions of the country. In Ciudad Juárez, for example, 9 people were reported slain gangland style on Monday, March 17, including one man who was shot to death inside the popular Willy's dance club in the city's Pronaf district.

Deming (N.Mex.) Headlight, **March 19, 2008**

COLUMBUS MAYOR EDDIE ESPINOZA WATCHES FROM CHAIR AS DENTIST IS ROBBED AT GUNPOINT

"I went down there to get some dental work done," Espinoza said. "I was in the chair, the dentist was doing a root canal. A couple of guys came in and robbed the dentist (Felipe Salazar)." That was at about 9:30 A.M., Sunday.

"They're getting brazen down there," said Espinoza, whose dental work was not finished, for obvious reasons. "I didn't have no fear about going to Palomas before. Now, I do."

El Diario, Ciudad Juárez, **March 19, 2008**

Juan Manuel Castro Ávila, 35, director of the transit police in Guadalupe, Bravos district, was wounded in an AK-47 attack at the entrance to his office in the Guadalupe Town Hall. The uniformed officer was shot by an armed commando from the inside of a vehicle as he arrived for his evening work shift at about 7:00 P.M. The armed attack caused terror among the residents of Guadalupe who at this hour were getting off work and walking around the central plaza. Castro Ávila was reported in serious but stable condition after being taken to the hospital in Juárez.

El Diario, Ciudad Juárez, **March 20, 2008**
A 30-year-old woman, identified by neighbors as Carolina, was killed by two gunshots when she opened the door to her house last night in the Hacienda de las Torres neighborhood. She was a housewife and mother of three small children, who were present when she was shot. Police report that a man knocked and then shot the woman at point-blank range when she opened the door. After hearing the shots, neighbors arrived to find the victim dead in the entrance to the house with two children crying beside her body. Minutes later, her husband returned from work to the tragic scene.

Also, last night police found an abandoned late-model Mercedes C-230 with broken front and rear windshields. Witnesses said that a woman and her daughter had been taken from the car after trying to escape from a violent situation in their home. Her husband pursued them in another vehicle, broke into the car and took them away to an unknown location.

El Diario, Ciudad Juárez, **March 20, 2008**
ASCENSIÓN—Three people have disappeared from this rural community in the last few hours, abducted by a group of heavily armed men. The identity of the missing is unknown. Another man is reported missing in the small town of Puerto Palomas.

El Diario, Ciudad Juárez, **March 21, 2008**
Two men were found dead last night in different areas of the city. Unofficial sources reveal that one of the dead men is a former agent of the Transit Police

who resigned about a year ago. The body was found wrapped in a plaid blanket with a plastic bag over the head. Another man was found about 9:30 in the Colonia Cuauhtemoc. Neighbors reported seeing the body thrown from a car and that the man lived for several minutes. He had been severely beaten and his face completely disfigured.

El Diario, Ciudad Juárez, **March 21, 2008**

State Attorney General Patricia Gonzalez Rodriguez is avoiding public events. She was at her offices in Ciudad Juárez yesterday under heavy guard, but refused to be interviewed. Unofficial sources said that Gonzalez Rodriguez met with business leaders who expressed their concern about the wave of executions and abductions in the city. On several occasions, the official has received funeral wreaths and some of her aides have been murdered or injured in organized crime shootings.

El Diario, Ciudad Juárez, **March 21, 2008**

PUERTO PALOMAS DE VILLA—The recent execution of two persons and the abduction of six others in this border community has provoked the resignation of the entire preventive police force of the village. At 6:00 P.M. Wednesday, the police found out that armed groups had abducted several people, and an hour later, Police Commander Emilio Pérez and six of his subordinates received death threats. They abandoned their posts, and their whereabouts are unknown. Yesterday, only two officers were present at the jail. "We can't do anything, we are alone here," said one of the officers, who did not give his name. He said that yesterday two bodies wrapped in blankets and tied with adhesive tape were found in separate locations on the outskirts of the town. Afterward the bodies were identified as Sergio Pérez, 55, and Rigoberto Muñoz Acosta, 21.

As of yesterday afternoon, Palomas was left with no preventive police. State authorities asked that soldiers from the army post south of Palomas patrol the urban area.

El Diario, Ciudad Juárez, March 21, 2008

Three men were shot by two armed men inside a nightclub after being involved in a fight. The incident took place at 4:30 in the morning in the La Mentira bar in the Colonia La Cuesta. The victims were identified as Arnulfo Loma, 24, who was found on the street outside the bar; Saúl Bernal and Ignacio Bermúdez, whose bodies remained inside. The killers were said to be well-known clients at the bar who escaped without being detained.

El Diario, Ciudad Juárez, March 21, 2008

Transit policeman Jorge Osorio was shot in the back this morning as he patrolled in the area of Vicente Guerrero Avenue and Paseo Triunfo de la Republica.

Las Cruces Sun-News, March 21, 2008

The embattled city of Palomas, Mexico, is now literally lawless. The Luna County Sheriff's Office and U.S. Border Patrol reported Thursday that the Palomas Chief of Police came to the Columbus Port of Entry late Tuesday night, requesting political asylum. The chief, identified as Emilio Pérez, reportedly told Immigration and Customs Enforcement his department's only two officers had fled and he had no idea where they are.

Dallas Morning News, March 21, 2008

CIUDAD JUÁREZ, Mexico—The killers arrived at the motel in the predawn gloom. Dressed in military-style uniforms and armed with automatic weapons, they forced the manager to hand over a guest list, then stormed from room to room, pointing their guns at the terrified occupants. In room 49 they opened fire on the man and woman inside. The woman's body was on the floor next to the bed, and the man was in the bathroom. At least 100 bullet casings were found, police said. The killers escaped in three late-model SUVs.

El Diario, Ciudad Juárez, March 21, 2008
At 7:10 P.M., another transit policeman was attacked and seriously injured after being shot by an armed commando. Minutes later, his motorcycle exploded and crashed. He was transferred to a hospital and dozens of policemen arrived to guard the medical institution.

El Diario, Ciudad Juárez, March 22, 2008
Despite intensive security operations this week by state and municipal authorities, 11 murders took place in a recent 12-hour period. The toll for March now stands at 77, an unprecedented number of homicides in one month in the history of the city. The recent rash of killings began Thursday night at about 7:00, when the body of a man was found adjacent to the Colinas de Juárez cemetery. At 9:30, another body was found on the sidewalk in the Colonia Cuauhtemoc. At about midnight, an individual was killed in the Colonia Municipio Libre when a group of men confronted him [and] shot him in the head. At 1:00 in the morning, another man was found wrapped in a blanket in the Colonia Lucio Blanco. At 4:30, 3 men were shot in the La Mentira bar. Then at about 5:30, a couple was killed in a room at the Motel Rio by a group of armed commandos who broke into every room until they found their targets. At about 8:00 two more people were found assassinated in a house in the Colonia Monterrey. In addition a transit policeman was shot inside his patrol car [and] managed to drive himself to the hospital, where he is reported in serious but stable condition.

El Diario, Ciudad Juárez, March 22, 2008
This morning the body of an unidentified man was found on the sidewalk a few meters from the Delicias police station.

Las Cruces Sun-News, March 22, 2008
TENSION HIGH IN BORDER VILLAGES OF COLUMBUS AND PALOMAS
COLUMBUS [N.Mex.]—Residents on both sides of the border are nervous after a month of border shootings, disappearances and at least two confirmed

murders allegedly sparked by drug-traffickers' turf wars in the Mexican town of Palomas. On Thursday, after reporting his two police officers had disappeared, Palomas Chief of Police Emilio Pérez fled to Columbus requesting political asylum. . . . On the same day the police chief fled, the bodies of two people were found wrapped in blankets and dumped along a road near Palomas. Several other people were seen taken hostage over the past few days by heavily armed men.

Norte de Ciudad Juárez, March 23, 2008
TEARFUL RELATIVES CONFIRM IDENTITY OF VICTIM KILLED IN THE MOTEL RIO
Who Was She? América Dayanara Maldonado Íñiguez, 27
    The State Attorney General's Office reported that América Dayanara Maldonado Íñiguez, 27, was identified by family members as the woman killed last Friday in the Motel Rio. At about 10:30 this morning, family and friends arrived at the morgue to officially identify América. At least 10 people accompanied a tearful young woman and helped to shield her from the press. The body had been found in room 49 of the Motel Rio on March 21 at 6:00 in the morning along with another body identified as Luis Martín Sánchez Loya, 35. Both died from multiple gunshot wounds to the neck and face. More than 90 bullets were recovered at the crime scene.

El Diario, Ciudad Juárez, March 23, 2008
Five men were shot to death yesterday and others were injured in three separate incidents. At a little after 9:00 P.M., the owner of the El Eje bar in the Colonia Constitución, his brother and an employee were killed; none have been identified but residents nearby said the proprietor was known as "Chuy." They said that Chuy "had already been sentenced" since last Thursday when his pickup was burned outside the bar. "It's a pity because you get to appreciate your neighbors, but who knows what they were up to, even though it doesn't

justify murder, but that's how these things are done," said another business-man.

In another incident, a man of about 50 was shot to death from a moving car as he walked along the street about 5:00 P.M. in the Colonia Melchior Ocampo. Others in the area hit the floor inside their houses to avoid being hit by stray bullets. The man who was dressed in cowboy-style clothes was left lying on the sidewalk with at least three bullet wounds visible. No one saw the killers' vehicle. Later, at about 5:20, Saturnino Acosta, 45, owner of a small store in the Oasis Revolución neighborhood was shot and killed at point-blank range. An employee, Facundo Bautista Hernández, was also injured in the attack.

El Diario, Ciudad Juárez, March 23, 2008

Four men were burned to death beyond recognition at the "Los Lamentos" ranch about 50 kilometers from Palomas. The fire and the deaths were reported to the state police at about 6:00 P.M. Friday by the owner of the ranch. The bodies were transferred to the Forensic Medical Service and the case is being investigated. Last Wednesday, armed groups abducted several people in the border community and public servants received death threats.

El Diario, Ciudad Juárez, March 23, 2008

CHIHUAHUA—Sergio Granados Pineda, secretary of government, rejected the idea that the state is ungovernable due to the wave of executions in Ciudad Juárez and the flight of the Palomas police force under death threats from narco-traffickers. He said that the state would not ever "throw in the towel" when it comes to public security.

El Diario, Ciudad Juárez, March 23, 2008

NUEVO CASAS GRANDES—The two men killed Friday night while driving in a Jeep Grand Cherokee with no plates were identified yesterday by the authorities as Hugo Rene Clemente Monarrez, 29, and José Martín Burgos García, 19. Police recovered a large quantity of AK-47 cartridges at the scene.

El Diario, Ciudad Juárez, March 23, 2008
A sergeant with the Technical Preventive Group (formerly Delta Group) was shot to death today at about 5:00 P.M. The victim, who was off-duty, was driving a dark green Dodge Neon when a commando attacked him several times.

El Diario, Ciudad Juárez, March 23, 2008
Three people were murdered yesterday in a two-hour period. José Uribe Roldán, 19, was shot in front of his house in the Infonavit Solidaridad neighborhood by members of the Sunside Park 04D gang. Neighbors reported that the victim belonged to the Los Cheros gang and that the killers had been chasing him. Minutes later, at about 1:30 P.M., a body was found in the Granjas Unidas neighborhood, lying face down with two bullet wounds in the back. He has not been identified. At 3:00 P.M., Nicolás Olivares García, 50, was killed outside of his house by a group of four armed men shooting from a late-model vehicle. His body was left where he fell in the patio of his house, where he made bricks. Unofficial sources said that the victim was a retail drug dealer.

El Diario, Ciudad Juárez, March 23, 2008
CHIHUAHUA—Two men from Juárez were shot to death yesterday when they left the El Cubo disco in the "Golden Zone" in Chihuahua City at about 2:00 A.M. Héctor García Pérez, 40, was dead at the scene, while José Luis Araiza Galindo, 22, died later at the regional hospital. The victims had apparently argued with their attacker inside the club and when they left, he shot them at point-blank range and then escaped in a black Jeep Cherokee.

El Diario, Ciudad Juárez, **March 23, 2008**

Two high-ranking municipal police officials were assassinated yesterday in separate incidents. Juan Manuel Ruiz Flores, operational commander of Delta Group, was killed by an armed commando around 5:15 P.M. as he drove on El Centenario Street. He was off work and driving a Dodge Neon when he was pursued by at least two other vehicles, but he was unable to outrun them. After Ruiz Flores was hit by the initial hail of gunfire, one of his attackers returned to finish him off with several shots at close range. The killers remained at the scene even as the ambulance and paramedics arrived and they were warned via their dispatcher to stay away from the scene until it was safe to approach.

Meanwhile, in Parral, Carlos Gómez Sáenz, subdirector of the municipal police of that city, was executed by a group of armed men as he left his home at 9:21 P.M., accompanied by his 10-year-old daughter, Karla Verónica Gómez Villa, who was shot in the back. She was reported in stable condition at the hospital, under heavy police guard.

El Diario, Ciudad Juárez, **March 23, 2008**

An unidentified man's partially nude body was found yesterday in Colonia Hidalgo near a pile of garbage bags. The body appeared to have multiple injuries caused by beating. He appeared to be between 40 and 45 years old and had a bulldog tattooed on his right arm.

El Diario, Ciudad Juárez, **March 23, 2008**

EL PASO—Javier Emilio Pérez Ortega, municipal police chief of Palomas, is in El Paso under the protection of Immigration and Customs Enforcement (ICE), after crossing the border at Columbus, New Mexico, to seek asylum in the United States.

El Diario, Ciudad Juárez, **March 23, 2008**

Secretary of Public Security, Guillermo Prieto Quintana, said that 180 new cadets will begin police training this Monday. The SSPM has offered the cadets a $750 monthly training stipend, and as new police officers, they will receive a salary of $980 per month. The secretary urged citizens to apply to join the new police force.

El Diario, Ciudad Juárez, March 23, 2008
The growing psychosis among security forces due to the recent assassinations of police officers is reflected in the collapse of vigilance in the city. Javier Aguirre Reyes, head of a small business association, said that uniformed police are more worried about watching their backs than protecting the citizens.

El Diario, Ciudad Juárez, March 24, 2008
The bodies of five men, strangled and showing signs of torture, were found discarded in different areas of the city during the past 10 hours. Unofficial sources indicate that the men were abducted, beaten and tortured with sharp objects, strangled and then dumped in open areas. The first victim was identified as Manuel Carranza Montoya, about 30–35. The second murdered man was found along the Juárez-Porvenir highway. He was about 35 and had several tattoos: the name "Herrera" on his upper back, "Mi Madre Alicia" and a heart pierced by a sword on his chest and the word "Juaritos" on his neck. Another victim, 20–30 years old, was found in another place along the Juárez-Porvenir road thrown into a vacant lot. Later, another body was found in the Colonia La Cuesta, his face partially covered by a black plastic bag. He was 45–50 years old with a partially gray beard. The fifth strangled body of a man 25–27 was found yesterday morning with a white electric cord tied around his neck. The bodies were all taken to the Forensic Medical Service, and it is hoped that their families will come to identify them and claim their remains.

El Paso Times, March 24, 2008
JUÁREZ COURTS TAKE HISTORIC LEAP IN ADOPTING LEGAL REFORM
For the first time, the prosecutor, the defense lawyer, the judge and the accused are in the same room and proceedings are open to the public. The

parties take turns presenting their case to the judge in the back-and-forth familiar to anyone watching televised courtroom dramas. Lorenzo Villar, a former lawyer and one of 12 newly minted judges, is an enthusiastic believer in the new way. "The biggest difference is the judge doesn't stay in his office and his assistants do all the work," he said. "Now the judge decides everything in a public manner. The prosecutor has to tell me about the case, then the defense lawyers and you get to know the victim and the suspect personally. All gets resolved in an hour."

There are no juries in Mexico. "There is more guarantee (against corruption) in this system. Before, there could be pressures," said defense lawyer Ulises Soteno Torres.

El Diario, Ciudad Juárez, March 24, 2008

Due to a lack of sufficient weapons, the SSPM has ruled that only command-level officers may carry their service weapons 24 hours per day. The spokesman said that it is impossible for all officers to retain their weapons when off duty and this privilege will be accorded only those at high risk. This decision was made despite the fact that the last 4 police officers executed were low-level street cops and were not on the "narco-list" of "executables."

"We are not allowed to keep our weapons, we have to turn them in when we go off duty so that there will be enough for the next shift. If you want to take it, you have to pay 200 pesos per week," said an officer who asked for anonymity.

El Diario, Ciudad Juárez, March 25, 2008

PUERTO PALOMAS DE VILLA—The body of a man was found yesterday in a garbage dump. He had been shot 18 times with a type of bullet used exclusively by the army. A man collecting recyclables found the body of a man about 22 years old, wearing an imitation goose down vest, army boots and a military-style haircut.

El Diario, Ciudad Juárez, **March 25, 2008**

FAMILIES OF FALLEN POLICE LEFT WITHOUT PENSIONS

Families of executed municipal police officers will not receive a government pension unless the officers were killed on duty, said Julio Gomez Alfaro, co-ordinator of the Commission on Labor and Social Protection. "The pension and retirement policy doesn't include executions. . . . " However, he added that the lives of all police and firemen are insured and that the families of the fallen officers will receive this economic support. As of yesterday afternoon, 8 municipal policemen had been assassinated so far this year, as well as 2 state police, two CIPOL agents and one army soldier.

Mario Campolla, brother of murdered officer Oscar Campolla, said that their relatives' bodies are sometimes robbed. "On top of the cowardly murders, they take your relatives' things. They stole my brother's watch, a ring and his salary. When they returned his wallet, all of the money he had in it was gone."

"Wives and children of the police have been abandoned. There are mothers who no longer receive their husbands' salaries because the men have disappeared. The corporation does nothing to search for the missing officers," said one relative.

El Diario, Ciudad Juárez, **March 25, 2008**

CHIHUAHUA—"All of the public security agencies are infiltrated—all of them, pure and simple—and we are not going to put our hands in the fire for any bad element," Governor José Reyes Baeza declared yesterday, concerning the narco-related assassinations and executions in Chihuahua in recent days. The governor explained that the state is facing an atypical situation over the last two months and he has confidence that in the next few weeks, Chihuahua will return to its prior condition of normalcy. Baeza Terrazas said that he had formally petitioned the federal government to send their elite forces to investigate, "and that they explain to us what is happening in Chihuahua." For his part, local representative Miguel Jurado

Contreras declared yesterday that the state is completely overrun by narco-trafficking.

El Diario, Ciudad Juárez, March 25, 2008

Daniel Antonio Hernández Enríquez was killed and another man was wounded yesterday when they were attacked by armed men as they walked along Yaqui Street. The dead man's mother arrived at the scene and identified the body.

Other recent victims identified and/or cause of death:

- Saturnino Acosta Herrera, 51, shot in the chest
- Israel Macías Navarro, 37, shock induced by gunshot to the abdomen
- Jesús Macías Navarro, 41, gunshot to the face
- Joel Tim Ríos, 43, bullet wound to the chest
- Unidentified man, Colonia Hidalgo, asphyxia by strangulation
- José Uribe Beltrán, 19, bullet wound to the head
- Unidentified man, Colonia Granjas Unidas, bullet wound to the head
- Nicolás Olivares García, shock induced by bullet wound to the chest

El Diario, Ciudad Juárez, March 25, 2008

Two men were shot to death in their pickup truck last night after being pursued by their killers, and two others were abandoned on the streets of the Colonia 16 de Septiembre. The two bodies were found about 3 blocks apart in the western area of the city, semi nude and showing signs of torture. The other two men were driving in a Chevrolet pickup in the Colonia Profesora Maria Martinez when an armed commando chased them down and shot them. Witnesses said that the dead men were known in the area by their nicknames "El Pelon" and El Tuercas" (Baldy and Nuts).

El Diario, Ciudad Juárez, March 25, 2008

CHIHUAHUA—Two months after suspending public activities due to a viral illness that caused partial facial paralysis, Governor Reyes Baeza Terrazas announced his return to public life, including travel outside the state. He reported that he had been treated with acupuncture which accelerated his recovery of mobility in the right side of his face.

El Diario, Ciudad Juárez, March 25, 2008

More than 40 unidentified bodies have been buried in a common grave, said Rosa Padilla Hernandez, coordinator of the Forensic Medical Service. "We are working at maximum capacity with 103 employees working three shifts, but this has been one of the most violent months ever and we cannot keep up," said forensics expert Hector Hawley. "When we arrive at a crime scene we can't work too fast, but in this month, there have been cases when we have barely arrived and we get calls about another event. . . . "

Frontera Norte Sur, Las Cruces (N.Mex.), March 25, 2008

No Easter Truce in 2008

Narco-violence in Mexico showed no let-up during the Easter holiday season. Press reports from just the three days between Holy Thursday, March 21, and Easter Sunday, March 23, registered at least 59 homicides connected to organized crime. By all accounts, Ciudad Juárez's citizens are terrified by the seemingly endless string of killings. Shootings have occurred on main streets, in front of commercial malls and other businesses and in bars and motels. As many as 218 executions were reported in Ciudad Juárez and different regions of Chihuahua from January 1 to March 25 of this year.

ArrobaJuárez.com, Ciudad Juárez, March 26, 2008

Hooded men in a pickup killed a man today in the Infonavit Juárez Nuevo neighborhood. Neighbors identified the victim as Joaquín, nickname "El Vino,"

22. He was shot more than 15 times, and his mother was present at the scene. The killers shot at her from the inside of the truck as they drove away.

El Diario, Ciudad Juárez, March 26, 2008

The number of homicides committed in March has risen to 103. This number is more than January (48) and February (45) combined, a toll unheard of in the history of the city. The latest victim, Joaquín Fernando González Arjón, 23, was shot multiple times by hooded men in a van. His mother was at the scene and tried to help him but he died in her arms and she collapsed in an emotional crisis. The victim had recently served time in prison for robbery and he was said to be a member of the Mexicles and Sorgueros gangs.

El Diario, Ciudad Juárez, March 26, 2008

"Why was he killed?" Family members and Delta Group companions of Juan Manuel Ruiz Flores gathered at his funeral to ask why there has been no progress in the investigation. "We don't know anything. He was a quiet person, he didn't mess with anyone and he lived a simple life."

El Paso Times, March 26, 2008

One of the men caught in El Paso trying to smuggle a .50-caliber semiautomatic rifle and other weapons into Mexico last week is the CEO of a religious charity, officials with the U.S. Bureau of Alcohol, Tobacco and Firearms confirmed Tuesday. Jonathan Lopez Gutierrez, 32, is the CEO of Emmanuel Ministries, a 40-year-old shelter for about 100 children in Juárez. Many Americans traveled to volunteer at Emmanuel Ministries, according to testimonies on the Web site.

Lopez, a Mexican citizen, was arrested March 19 on the Stanton Street bridge driving a white van. Inside the van were six .223-caliber rifles and the

.50-caliber semiautomatic weapon hidden under a load of roofing shingles, according to court documents. The van had been rented through Emmanuel Ministries, said ATF spokesman Tom Crowley in Dallas.

El Diario, Ciudad Juárez, March 26, 2008

A group of 59 men accused of beating their wives and partners will not go to jail, but will have the option of undergoing psychological therapy as part of a reform of the justice system.

El Diario, Ciudad Juárez, March 27, 2008

Elements of the Federal Preventive Police, CIPOL, Municipal Police and U.S. Border Patrol agents were deployed in a joint operation along the banks of the Rio Bravo from the Juárez Valley to Anapra with the objective of stopping illicit activities along the border including traffic of illegal immigrants, weapons and drugs. These actions were supplemented by Mexican army checkpoints in different areas of the city.

Dallas Morning News, March 27, 2008

CIUDAD JUÁREZ—Mexican President Felipe Calderón dispatched an estimated 2,000 soldiers and hundreds of federal police to Ciudad Juárez and outlying areas Thursday in response to the continued rise in violence here that has claimed the lives of nearly 200 people in the last three months. The crackdown comes as a senior U.S. law enforcement official across the border in El Paso cautioned that Juárez, much like Nuevo Laredo in the past, faces a prolonged drug war where the worst is yet to come, a war that's gradually spilling over into the Texas side of the border. Another 40 people have been killed about 100 miles to the west of Ciudad Juárez, in and around the town of Palomas, just across the border from Columbus, N.M.

El Diario, Ciudad Juárez, **March 27, 2008**
At the Security Summit celebrated at the Hotel Camino Real, "Joint Operation Chihuahua" was launched with the participation of the Secretary of National Defense and the Federal Police. The meeting was attended by Government Operations Secretary Juan Camilo Mourino, Defense Secretary General Guillermo Galván, Chihuahua Governor José Reyes Baeza, and Juárez Mayor José Reyes Ferriz. The preventive forces will include 2,026 army troops, 900 Federal Police and 300 state police.

El Diario, Ciudad Juárez, **March 27, 2008**
Polygraph tests will be a new tool for detecting bad elements in the police forces. Saúl Hernández, head of the Chihuahua Department of Preventive Operations (CIPOL), said that these kinds of controls are reliable and necessary so that the population can be sure that the police officers are honest.

El Diario, Ciudad Juárez, **March 27, 2008**
Yesterday the federal prosecutor released six police who had been detained for 36 hours by elements of the Mexican army after discrediting the charge that they carried illegal weapons. Military sources had also alleged that the municipal police officers were following an army convoy and radioing their movements to a group of narco-traffickers. Mayor José Reyes Ferriz said yesterday that he did not have enough information about the case. "As the governor has said, we know that all of the police forces have been infiltrated by bad elements and our job is to identify these persons and get them out of the municipal police," said the mayor in a press conference.

El Diario, Ciudad Juárez, **March 28, 2008**
"Joint Operation Chihuahua" is the fourth battle plan against organized crime to be implemented by the government of President Felipe Calderón. Other

operations have been launched in Michoacan, Tijuana, Guerrero and Nuevo León-Tamaulipas.

Las Cruces Sun-News, March 28, 2008

COLUMBUS [N.Mex.]—Palomas will receive 100 soldiers from the Mexican army as part of an indefinite operation to combat border violence. . . . Columbus Mayor Eddie Espinoza said he was cautiously optimistic about the news of the troop deployment. "I've got to see it to believe it," said Espinoza, after being notified of the deployment Thursday. "That's great. I think it's about time they stepped up."

Rick Moody, agent-in-charge of the Deming Border Patrol Station, said in recent weeks it's become common for agents to hear gunshots at night. In the past week, he said he was aware of at least nine violent incidents, including shootings and kidnappings, against targeted individuals. "These are special soldiers that have been deployed. Juárez also received a deployment. They're generally only deployed in situations like this, where the violence gets out of hand," Moody said. "There are two major criminal organizations attempting to control these corridors, these gateways into the U.S., and they use terrorist tactics and extreme forms of violence."

El Paso Times, March 28, 2008

JUÁREZ—A deployment of more than 2,000 soldiers is arriving in Juárez to take the city back from feuding drug traffickers—blamed for intensely violent murders that are causing concern on the U.S. side of the border. . . . The deployment is expected to spark more violence, but officials said they were prepared to meet any threat or attack. Officials did not say what kinds of weapons the soldiers would carry.

El Paso Times, March 29, 2008

JUÁREZ—While hundreds of Mexican soldiers armed with automatic rifles arrived in C-130 Hercules aircraft Friday to overpower warring drug gangs, the U.S. State Department reiterated its earlier advice that travelers should be careful when visiting Mexico.

Dallas Morning News, March 29, 2008
DRUG CARTELS OPERATE TRAINING CAMPS NEAR TEXAS BORDER
JUST INSIDE MEXICO
CAMARGO, Mexico—Mexican drug cartels have conducted military-style training camps in at least six such locations in northern Tamaulipas and Nuevo León states, some within a few miles of the Texas border, according to U.S. and Mexican authorities and the printed testimony of five protected witnesses who were trained in the camps.

El Diario, Ciudad Juárez, March 29, 2008
A patrol car from the Cuauhtemoc district was found abandoned in the Rincones de San Marcos neighborhood, just a few meters from the house on Plateros Street searched by the army yesterday. The officers assigned to the patrol car are missing.

El Diario, Ciudad Juárez, March 29, 2008
In two days, four cases of young children—aged 6, 11 and 13—raped by family members or teenaged acquaintances have been reported. In two of the cases, the accused rapists were 17 and 16 years old and were friends of the victims.

El Diario, Ciudad Juárez, March 30, 2008
Elements of the Mexican army detained 5 persons and confiscated more than a half ton of marijuana, 17 late-model vehicles, and two firearms in the Rincones de San Marcos and Colonia Ampliacion Aeropuerto after an anonymous tip. Those arrested are members of the criminal organization of Pedro Sanchez, operator for the Carrillo Fuentes cartel in the town of Villa Ahumada.

El Diario, Ciudad Juárez, March 30, 2008
A municipal policeman with 16 years of service joined another four agents who resigned on Friday after the inauguration of the Joint Operation Chihuahua. Forty-six agents have resigned for various reasons in the last month.

Las Cruces Sun-News, March 30, 2008
PALOMAS, Mexico—It's nothing compared to the violence a month ago, says American expatriate Georgie Flores, who gave this strange tour Saturday. "There's a cooling down, big time." The afternoon of Feb. 27, Javier Perez Mendiola, 41, also known as "El Indio," and Adrián Juárez Mendoza, 28, were shot to death at the Pemex gas station on Avenida 5 de Mayo, four blocks from the border. Just weeks earlier, Feb. 18, four men were shot in Palomas—two died. On March 18, Palomas' chief of police fled to Columbus [N.Mex.] after his two deputies left the department. Two days later, two bodies wrapped in blankets were found, dumped along a road near Palomas. This week, four burned bodies were found at a ranch south of town. Flores said he saw the Pemex shooting—for three solid minutes, the street was full of automatic-weapons fire—and the bodies: "There were 3(00), 400 shots. This guy didn't have no face no more."

El Diario, Ciudad Juárez, March 30, 2008
Despite the military presence, a man was shot to death yesterday outside of his recycling business in Loma Blanca in the Juárez Valley. The victim's body, not identified by the authorities, was found thrown into a parking lot.

El Diario, Ciudad Juárez, March 30, 2008
A man and woman were found murdered yesterday in adjacent houses in the Colonia Zaragoza, apparently beaten to death. . . . With these crimes, the total assassinations during March rises to 107. There were 48 in January and

45 in February, and in addition the discovery of 45 bodies in hidden graves, according to journalistic records based on official statistics.

El Diario, Ciudad Juárez, March 31, 2008

Four more municipal policemen were detained by elements of the Mexican army, causing the police assigned to the Babicora district to refuse to go out on patrol for fear of being arrested by the military. For more than 3 hours, officers coming on duty abstained from going out on patrol and demanded to speak to their superiors to express their fears. An agent with 17 years of service who has been recognized for heroism said, "If there are bad elements, they should pursue them but those of us who are doing a good job and trying to do the best we can for the citizens, we do not deserve to be detained or charged with crimes. It is not fair to us or to our families that we fear being arrested or killed."

The officers were especially concerned when they found out that the first four agents arrested by the army had been handcuffed, beaten and humiliated by military personnel.

El Paso Times, March 31, 2008

The Mexican army and federal police have taken over the 066 emergency telephone system in Juárez, city officials confirmed Monday. The hotline, which is the equivalent to 911 in the United States, will allow federal authorities to receive anonymous information about crime. . . . In related news, six Juárez police officers were arrested for being in possession of marijuana, officials said.

El Diario, Ciudad Juárez, March 31, 2008

Two men between the ages of 30 and 35 were found dead in different neighborhoods, their heads covered with plastic bags wrapped with brown tape and showing signs of torture.

APRIL

El Diario, Ciudad Juárez, April 1, 2008
10 MORE POLICE ARRESTED
Ten municipal police and two specialists with the state Public Justice Ministry were detained by the Mexican army and turned over to the federal prosecutor for possession of drugs and weapons.

El Diario, Ciudad Juárez, April 1, 2008
Faces distorted in pain and anguish, family members of municipal police officers arrested by the military gathered yesterday at the offices of the federal prosecutor.

"All I know is that it is not fair to hold him," said Carmen Lamas, wife of Arturo Roman Cruz. She contends that he was abducted Friday morning by the military.

El Diario, Ciudad Juárez, April 1, 2008
In an action unprecedented in the history of this border city, municipal police protested this morning against the Mexican army, refusing to work for fear of being arrested and accused of participation in organized crime.

El Diario, Ciudad Juárez, April 1, 2008
Municipal police officer César Gómez is fighting for his life in intensive care after being shot by elements of the Mexican army when his patrol car went through a military checkpoint. The military detained two other officers in the car, Arturo Sotelo and Raul Palacios.

El Diario, Ciudad Juárez, April 1, 2008
Members of the State Investigative Agency and CIPOL were disarmed this morning by the army and the federal prosecutor, after all personnel from both

agencies were summoned to the local headquarters of the State Office of Public Security. Masked military personnel armed with assault rifles sealed the building and army helicopters circled overhead during the operation.

El Diario, Ciudad Juárez, April 1, 2008
Three men were liberated before dawn today by the Mexican army, which said they had been held captive by the Juárez cartel for up to 41 days. The men said they had been abducted at different times and places by hooded men wearing uniforms of the Federal Investigative Police.

El Diario, Ciudad Juárez, April 2, 2008
Elements of the State Investigative Agency and the Police Intelligence Unit (CIPOL) were disarmed and forced to undergo different examinations of confidence under the authority of the army and the Federal Attorney General's Office. Some agents were identified as appearing in YouTube.com videos supposedly involved in narco-trafficking.

El Diario, Ciudad Juárez, April 2, 2008
Municipal police from the Babicora and Cuauhtemoc districts gathered in their stations and refused to patrol for three hours to protest the aggression against César Antonio Gómez (shot by the army at a checkpoint) and the arrest of two other officers. Yesterday morning, it was revealed that a female police officer had been the victim of sexual aggression by a group of soldiers and had required urgent medical attention. The attack was not confirmed but it generated a great deal of anger among the police, who warned of possible confrontations with the military.

El Diario, Ciudad Juárez, April 2, 2008
Municipal police and the army tell different stories regarding the attacks on police officers that resulted in one being shot and seriously injured.

El Diario, Ciudad Juárez, **April 2, 2008**

Police Burdened by a Dark History

The relationship between police and drugs is nothing new. Evidence of police complicity in narco-trafficking has occurred in every municipal administration. As recently as January 16 [2008] the ex-director of Municipal Public Security [2004–2007], Saulo Reyes Gamboa, was arrested in El Paso for narco-trafficking. Reyes Gamboa, an attorney and public accountant, served until the end of the administration of former Juárez mayor, Hector Murguia Lardizábal. . . . [article details police criminals back to 2002]

El Diario, Ciudad Juárez, **April 2, 2008**

The shriveled body of a woman was found yesterday afternoon in an unpopulated area southeast of the city. The body was found at the end of Avenida Manuel Talamas Camandari, where a new housing development is under construction. Authorities gave no estimation of the date of death of the unidentified victim, however, there was no flesh on the face and arms, and other parts of the body were desiccated.

El Paso Times, **April 2, 2008**

The Mexican army on Tuesday rescued three men, including an El Pasoan, who had been kidnapped and were being detained in a home in Juárez, Channel 26-KINT (Cable channel 2) reported. The men were found handcuffed inside a home in an upscale neighborhood during a military operation responding to an anonymous tip about narcotics activity.

El Diario, Ciudad Juárez, **April 2, 2008**

Due to fear of being attacked or detained by army soldiers, more than 50% of municipal police suspended patrols during the first shift and agreed to respond only to emergency calls.

El Diario, Ciudad Juárez, **April 2, 2008**

Fifteen state police officers detained last Tuesday by the military were turned over to the Federal Attorney General's Office to determine if they will be charged with any crimes.

El Diario, Ciudad Juárez, **April 3, 2008**

Municipal police testified yesterday in a court hearing that they had been tied, blindfolded, beaten and tortured with electric shocks by soldiers and federal police who detained them before turning them over to the federal prosecutor.

El Paso Times, **April 3, 2008**

Juárez city officials said Wednesday evening that they have developed contingency plans after rumors that some municipal police officers plan to go on a "labor stoppage" in protest of the Mexican army and federal police in the city. Mayor José Reyes Ferriz said plans are in place to make up for any stoppage and that residents should welcome the opportunity to eliminate bad officers.

El Diario, Ciudad Juárez, **April 3, 2008**

This morning, the Federal Prosecutor's Office released four women—Cinthya Cecilia Soto, Silvia Marcela Soto Alvídrez, Imelda Villegas and Yadhira Meza Ramírez—who had been detained for two days by the army. Unofficial sources said that more agents will be released later today.

El Diario, Ciudad Juárez, **April 3, 2008**

Two armed men assaulted a branch of Scotiabank, the 14th violent bank robbery this year.

El Diario, Ciudad Juárez, **April 3, 2008**

The Coordinating Business Council and the municipality today presented their proposal to the governor to establish a security network in the city with more than 3,000 video cameras in stores, banks and schools. "These strategies will be implemented in less than three weeks," said Mayor José Reyes Ferriz.

El Diario, Ciudad Juárez, **April 4, 2008**

"We are going to continue with the internal investigation of the public security forces until they are completely cleaned up and sanitized," said Governor José Reyes Baeza, during the third day of protests by human right activists and family members of the police agents arrested by the Mexican army. Reyes Baeza said that the special operation would decrease the problem of atypical violence in Juárez during the last two months and he dismissed the idea that "narco-trafficking rules in Chihuahua."

El Paso Times, **April 4, 2008**

The Mexican army has detained 22 employees of the Chihuahua state attorney general's office and the state public security office as part of operations targeting organized crime. The detainees were being questioned on Thursday about possible crimes.

El Paso Times, **April 4, 2008**

U.S. authorities have indicted a suspected Mexican drug cartel leader who officials believe was one of several men dressed in military uniforms during a high-profile border incident two years ago. Jose Rodolfo Escajeda is identified as one of several men appearing to be Mexican soldiers who had crossed the Rio Grande and were helping suspected drug smugglers elude U.S. law enforcement during a chase. He remains a fugitive. . . . According to DEA officials, the Escajedas, based in the village of Guadalupe across the Rio Grande near Tornillo, are believed to control a 120-mile corridor east of El Paso.

El Paso Times, **April 4, 2008**

The city of Juárez has unveiled a new official hymn for the city, "Ciudad Juárez, Valor de México," loosely translated as Juárez, Jewel of Mexico, city officials said. The song praises the work ethics and pioneering spirit of Juarenses and will be taught in elementary schools. The hymn opens with the line, "Juárez is our city, the best of the borders, because it was born with courage and built its history with great faith and hope."

El Diario, Ciudad Juárez, **April 4, 2008**

CHIHUAHUA—General Jorge Juárez Loera, commander of the 11th Military Region, was interviewed at the State Government Palace, accompanied by the Attorney General Patricia Gonzalez. The general issued a call to the media. "The media are very important to us. Tell the truth, say what you have to say, but say it with courage. And I know that the media are sometimes afraid of us, but they should not be afraid. I hope they will trust us. And I would like to see the reporters change their articles and where they say 'one more murder victim,' instead say, 'one less criminal.'" Army troops arrived early and took up their strategic positions around the government buildings, ready for action along Calle Libertad.

El Diario, Ciudad Juárez, **April 5, 2008**

Three state police officers, José Guadalupe Rivas González, Juan Ramón Durán Robles and Luis Carlos Aviña Corona, were apparently tortured by the military while held at the headquarters of the 20th Motorized Calvary Regiment. "We were surprised when we saw our three companions, they had been severely beaten, one was taken to the hospital as his legs were seriously injured," reported another police officer being held by the Federal Prosecutor's Office. He said that the women arrested were blindfolded and stripped for a supposed medical examination. "It was denigrating what they did to the women." The anonymous source said that most of his fellow officers who were detained will not talk to anyone for fear of being picked up again by the army.

El Diario, Ciudad Juárez, **April 5, 2008**
After a visit yesterday to the border, U.S. Ambassador Tony Garza expressed concern about the "narco-violence" here and that this insecurity may lead to raising the level of the travel alert to U.S. citizens in Chihuahua. "Obviously, we support the President Calderón's initiatives and we also take this criminal activity seriously. Narco-violence and crime affect the lives of the citizens on both sides of the border. . . . "

El Diario, Ciudad Juárez, **April 5, 2008**
Municipal police who joined the force last March 8 said that as of yesterday, they had not yet received their paychecks and that they were going out on patrol without firearms, due to a shortage.

El Diario, Ciudad Juárez, **April 5, 2008**
HIDALGO DEL PARRAL, Chihuahua—Gun battles in the area yesterday afternoon left at least 14 dead and 7 wounded, including two persons identified as Federal Investigative Police. The shoot-outs began in nearby Villa Matamoros, where an armed commando assassinated Francisco Barron. The armed forces later patrolled the city of Hidalgo del Parral, where businesses shut down as if under martial law. It is presumed that this bloody afternoon was caused by "the cockroach effect," after the launch of the Joint Chihuahua Operation last Monday in Juárez. Preliminary reports indicate that the confrontation broke out between gangs led by Tacho Puertas and Kiko Barba, both members of the Carrillo Fuentes cartel after the first week of the military operation. At press time, no official information had been released.

El Diario, Ciudad Juárez, **April 8, 2008**
The army and the State Attorney General's Office engaged in a "numbers war" concerning the number of deaths resulting from the confrontation between two criminal gangs last Saturday in the southern region of Chihuahua state. General Jorge Juárez Loera, chief of the 11th Military Region, said that all of those killed in the shoot-out were criminals, that the federal forces had suffered no losses. "In addition to the 'cockroach effect,' the operation is stimulating more violence because the criminals feel desperate. Before, they could act freely, kidnapping and collecting ransoms, but now they are forced into more violent acts." When asked whether the cartel leaders had left the state, he said, "Normally the majority leave because they don't like it much when the army gets here." He lashed out against the representatives of human rights groups, "And when are they going to issue a recommendation to the cartels not to execute and kill people?" He affirmed that the military is respectful of the human rights of the common people (*la gente*) of Mexico.

El Diario, Ciudad Juárez, **April 9, 2008**
The Secretary of National Defense said yesterday that the Carrillo Fuentes organization is trying to discredit the Mexican army by committing violent and criminal acts disguised in the uniforms and vehicles of the military. It was revealed recently that the cartel had begun a counteroffensive to the Chihuahua operation, paying people to attend protest marches against the military presence.

El Diario, Ciudad Juárez, **April 9, 2008**
More than 50 percent of adolescents in Ciudad Juárez between 15 and 17 years of age do not attend preparatory school either because they were rejected by state-funded schools because there was no room for them, or

because they needed to work to help support their families. Student Jacqueline Holguin said that for students who finish their education with secondary school, their only future is to become maquiladora workers.

El Diario, Ciudad Juárez, **April 9, 2008**
The Honor and Justice Commission will review today the desertion and dismissal of 19 officers of the municipal police who have not shown up for work in recent days and have not turned in their voluntary resignations. The firing of these officers includes some elements considered "dark cases." "The recent turnover is very high and it is part of the filtering process that will continue until the purification of the police is complete."

El Diario, Ciudad Juárez, **April 9, 2008**
Dozens of soldiers interrupted the service at the municipal cemetery in Villa Ahumada, where Gerardo Gallegos, 19, killed in Sunday's shoot-out in Parral, was going to be buried. Military vehicles interrupted the funeral procession and blocked entrances to the cemetery as two helicopters flew over the area. The order came from one of the helicopters to hit the ground, causing panic to break out. Soldiers forced about 200 people to the ground, including women and children, and detained an undetermined number of men. The municipal police on duty at the time did not want to make any comment about what had happened, for fear of reprisals, and the mayor of Villa Ahumada could not be found. Unofficially, it was determined that a military commando was looking for several members of a criminal organization. Residents, who asked not to be identified for fear of the military, said that the soldiers began to search the vehicles with no respect for the mourners and also opened the casket and searched it. Witnesses said that once the military forces had secured the area, they freed the children, who stayed outside the cemetery crying for their parents. The body of Gallegos

was finally buried at about 7:30 in the evening. His mother's neighbors were worried about her safety as soldiers had entered and searched her house; it was left empty, with the lights on, doors open and contents in disarray.

El Diario, Ciudad Juárez, **April 10, 2008**

Governor José Reyes Baeza said yesterday that the city is paying the price today with public insecurity for having welcomed with open arms thousands of migrants from other parts of the country to Juárez. "Thousands of Mexicans have found alternatives here on the border, but after all this time, we see the effects of this generosity, mainly the problem of insecurity.

"Today in Chihuahua, we have the presence of the Mexican army, an institution that we all believe in and trust. . . . The only thing I know about the narco-traffickers campaign to smear the army is what the army has said, but we have to believe it is the truth and we have to prevent these criminal groups from soiling the reputation of an institution like the Mexican army by committing criminal acts while dressed like soldiers in order to discredit Joint Operation Chihuahua."

El Diario, Ciudad Juárez, **April 10, 2008**

Of the 96 cases with 117 victims of homicide that occurred in March, more than 60% are related to violence between gangs and the sale of drugs on the retail market, according to the State Attorney General. The March murders set a new record for Juárez. Never before in this border region have there been more than 100 murders recorded in only one month. "Something very extraordinary has happened here, it is historical that there have been more than 100 victims, but we now have to carry out the role assigned to us: to fight impunity," said the State Attorney General, Patricia Gonzalez Rodriguez. In the first trimester of 2008, there were on average 2 murders per day.

ArrobaJuárez.com, Ciudad Juárez, **April 10, 2008**

More than 80 civil society organizations across Mexico protested today against persecution, torture and impunity in Juárez. In a declaration entitled "Respect for Human Dignity," addressed to the President of the Republic and to the Commander in Chief of the armed forces and other government leaders, dozens of individuals joined with organizations to protest the murder of campesino leader Armando Villareal Martha and the subsequent arrests of activists Carlos Chávez and Cipriana Jurado, and the federal arrests warrants issued against leaders of social organizations who participated in different protest events.

El Paso Times, **April 10, 2008**

JUÁREZ—Two men were found shot to death Wednesday evening next to a pickup with Texas plates at a ranch about nine miles from the village of Guadalupe Distrito Bravos across the border from Tornillo [Texas]. The men were identified as Javier Trejo, who was found on the ground, and Alejandro Peña Trejo, who was in the bed of the older-model Chevrolet truck at the Trejo's ranch.

In Juárez, a man was fatally shot while sitting at home, and pieces of a skull and other human remains were found in the desert near kilometer 28 of the Panamerican Highway.

El Diario, Ciudad Juárez, **April 12, 2008**

In a ceremony yesterday at the headquarters of the 20th Motorized Calvary, the Secretary of National Defense and the Federal Attorney General yesterday incinerated 8.4 tons of marijuana and 4.4 kilograms of cocaine confiscated in recent raids by Joint Operation Chihuahua. Two elementary school students set fire to the drugs using an electronic device.

El Diario, Ciudad Juárez, **April 12, 2008**

95.5% of Juárez residents believe that the majority of the police are involved in organized crime, according to a poll contracted by El Diario. In addition,

8 out of 10 polled think that the police arrested recently by the army were involved in suspicious activities and not framed by the army.

Excelsior, Special to El Diario, Ciudad Juárez, **April 14, 2008**
In 10 days, narco-traffickers paid more than $336,000 to operate and obtain protection in Juárez, according to a payroll ledger found in a house belonging to a cartel leader.

El Paso Times, **April 14, 2008**
The State Department updated its travel alert for Mexico to warn U.S. tourists of ongoing border violence, including the current drug war in Juárez. "Violent criminal activity fueled by a war between criminal organizations struggling for control of the lucrative narcotics trade continues along the U.S.-Mexico border," the alert reads. "Attacks are aimed primarily at members of drug trafficking organizations, Mexican police forces, criminal justice officials, and journalists. However, foreign visitors and residents, including Americans, have been among the victims of homicides and kidnappings in the border region."

El Diario, Ciudad Juárez, **April 15, 2008**
A payroll ledger found in the search of a Juárez cartel leader that confirmed municipal police collected $8,000 per month has spurred a federal investigation. The ledger used code names for those who received payment from the Vicente Carrillo Fuentes organization. Municipal police spokesman Jaime Torres said that "We know that there are good and bad elements in every group and the police are no exception. We are in the process of detecting these bad elements. . . . "

New York Times, **April 16, 2008**
DRUG WAR CAUSES WILD WEST BLOOD BATH, KILLING 210 IN A MEXICAN BORDER TOWN
CIUDAD JUÁREZ, Mexico—One sign of the desperation to end organized crime in this border town is that the good guy on the police recruitment

posters is not a clean-cut youth in a smart police cap, but a menacing soldier in a black mask and helmet carrying a heavy machine gun. "The mortuary is full of more than 50 unclaimed and unidentified bodies, proof that the soldiers in the underworld war come from other states," the mayor said.

El Diario, Ciudad Juárez, **April 16, 2008**

Juárez residents' greatest fear is to get caught in the crossfire during a gun battle in the streets, according to a recent poll. Two out of three residents say that it is "very easy" to get a marijuana cigarette, a dose of cocaine or ecstasy.

La Jornada, Mexico City, **April 17, 2008**

NUEVO LAREDO, Tamaulipas—Offering salaries in dollars, life insurance, houses and late-model cars, the Gulf Cartel is recruiting ex-soldiers, according to an announcement posted Thursday on the streets of Tampico. "Stop your suffering, ex-soldiers, federal police . . . join the ranks of the Gulf Cartel . . . here we pay in dollars, we offer benefits, life insurance, a house for your family in a good neighborhood, and pick your own new car or truck every year . . . What more could you ask for? Tamaulipas, Mexico and the United States—all Gulf Cartel territory!"

El Diario, Ciudad Juárez, **April 18, 2008**

Víctor Jesús Jiménez Soto, Benjamín Verdugo Villalobos and Alfonso Leyva Carrasco showed the marks of torture and violence on their bodies and said that the drugs and guns were planted by the Mexican army.

El Diario, Ciudad Juárez, **April 18, 2008**

The State Attorney General reported 21 homicides in the city during the first 18 days of April. Official statistics indicate 231 murders so far in 2008; 12 are women. In January there were 48 murders, 45 in February, and 117 in March.

El Diario, Ciudad Juárez, **April 19, 2008**

POLICEMAN AND 8-YEAR-OLD SON SHOT AND KILLED

Four people were shot and killed last night in separate organized-crime-style incidents. Municipal police captain Alejandro Martínez Casas and his 8-year-old son died at the medical center where they were taken after the attack. Martínez Casas's name had appeared in the list of targeted officers on the Police Monument on January 26. The attack occurred at about 9:15 P.M. while Martínez drove his late-model, double cabin Nissan Titan pickup with Mexican plates, number DS57696, registered in the State of Chihuahua. A group of masked, armed men opened fire with AK-47s. Numerous bullet holes could be seen in the front and on the passenger side of the pickup. The child, whose name was not released, received various bullet wounds and witnesses reported that one of his arms was nearly destroyed.

The other double homicide occurred when the still unidentified occupants of a 2002 Honda were shot after being chased by four men in two other vehicles. Another man was shot and wounded on the sidewalk in Colonia Galeana. As neighbors gave first aid, 6 men got out of a black pickup and threw the wounded man in the truck. The victim was not identified as the armed commando unit took him away.

El Diario, Ciudad Juárez, **April 19, 2008**

Four presumed Federal Police officers were arrested yesterday for public drunkenness, causing a scandal, molesting a woman and assaulting Preventive Police agents.

Frontera Norte Sur, Las Cruces (N.Mex.), **April 19, 2008**

MEXICAN JOURNALISTS STILL UNDER SIEGE IN 2008

Two young radio announcers from the southern state of Oaxaca are the latest journalists to suffer violent deaths. Felicitas Martínez, 22, and Teresa Bautista, 24, were shot to death in an ambush April 7 while on their way to cover a state meeting of indigenous peoples. Four others were wounded in the attack, including two children aged 2 and 3. As of April 19, no suspects had been arrested for the crimes. Martínez and Bautista allegedly suffered threats before their murders. "Some people think we are very young to know, but they should know we are very young to die," Martínez and Bautista reportedly said on the air shortly before their deaths.

El Diario, Ciudad Juárez, **April 19, 2008**
The death of young Alejandro Martínez Cruz, son of the municipal police officer executed Friday night, has caused pain and shock. Neighbors commented that although they barely knew the family, they regretted both deaths, especially that of the 8-year-old boy. "We don't know if the father was bad or if he deserved to die that way or not, but there was no reason to kill the boy, he was an innocent victim. He hardly ever went out to play but when he did he ran around a lot, like all kids, he was a healthy boy and good at sports."

El Diario, Ciudad Juárez, **April 19, 2008**
More than 250 bullets were fired at the municipal police captain and his son who died in the hospital minutes after the attack in the Colonia Margaritas. The victims were identified as Alejandro Martínez Casas, 32, and his son, Alejandro Martínez Cruz, 8. The officer's wife and mother of the child drove the wounded to the hospital in a private vehicle. State authorities reported that the officer received multiple bullet wounds on his left side, thorax, abdomen and legs. The boy was hit in the head and chest. At least 6 Mexican army tanks and dozens of soldiers disturbed the crime scene, kicking around the spent cartridges in the area.

Rockford (Ill.) Register Star, **April 19, 2008**
Norma Trosper doesn't remember growing up with machine guns, burgeoning gangs or drug wars sprawling through the streets of her native town,

Ciudad Juárez. That was then, in the late 1970s and early '80s. Today, it's a different story in the Mexican border town. "It's like a war zone," Trosper said of a recent visit. "I was so scared. I mean, you can feel it. It's in the air. You just don't know how many dead there will be for that day. You can almost smell death."

El Diario, Ciudad Juárez, April 20, 2008

Mexican army personnel yesterday rescued a man who had been held captive. When found, he was gagged and bound with brown-colored adhesive tape and had been tortured. The soldiers also confiscated an unknown quantity of drugs in the rear of a recent model Hummer H2 parked in the garage of the house where the victim was held. After being freed, the unidentified man said that he had been held for 3 days after being abducted by a group of men in green uniforms, similar to those worn by soldiers. After spending several hours at the house, the soldiers left with the rescued man. At press time, no official information had been released. In another incident, a motorcyclist was presumably abducted after being chased and shot by a group of men. Witnesses who asked for anonymity said that the motorcyclist had tried to hide in a nearby Dumpster but he was found and taken away by an unknown group of men.

Washington Post, April 20, 2008

PUERTO PALOMAS, Mexico—Javier Emilio Pérez Ortega, a workaholic Mexican police chief, showed up at the sleepy, two-lane border crossing here last month and asked U.S. authorities for political asylum. In the past year, at least 10 gunshot victims have been dumped at the border checkpoint—taken there by friends or colleagues who believed their only hope of survival lay across the border. In the calculus of U.S.-Mexican border relations, the living were rushed to medical treatment—sometimes with law enforcement escorts—but the dead were not allowed across.

Arizona Republic, April 21, 2008

MEXICO CITY—One of Mexico's biggest drug cartels has launched a bizarre recruiting campaign, putting up fliers and banners promising good pay, free cars and better chow to army soldiers who join the cartel's elite band of hit men. . . . The Mexican military has long had a problem with desertion. Between January and September 2007 alone, some 4,956 army soldiers deserted, about 2.5 percent of the force, according to the National Defense Secretariat.

Soldiers are facing more incentives to switch sides because of Calderón's decision to use troops against the drug traffickers. . . . An army private earns an average of $533 a month. . . . " . . . what's true is that there is enormous desertion in the Mexican army and police force. They should be worried about that and take action to offer better working conditions."

El Diario, Ciudad Juárez, April 21, 2008

A nine-year-old child appears to have committed suicide by hanging himself in his house yesterday afternoon. His mother, Maria Isabel Tello Cofi, 28, had gone to a nearby store. When she returned from shopping, she found her son hanging from a clothesline rope. In addition to police and forensic personnel, state investigators and Mexican army soldiers came to the scene causing great disturbance to the family and neighbors, who considered their presence excessive considering the nature of the tragedy.

El Diario, Ciudad Juárez, April 21, 2008

Algae Amaya Núñez, 29, a schoolteacher, was shot to death Sunday night in the Juárez Valley while traveling with her 3-year-old son who was uninjured and a man who has disappeared. She was the sister of the ex-mayor of Guadalupe, Omar Alberto Amaya Núñez, killed by an armed commando in this town on September 24, 2006. Her father, Apolonio Amaya Fierro, also a former mayor, was killed in February 2007. State police found Amaya Núñez's body inside a red 2007 Fusion with Texas plates. At the time of the shooting, her husband was driving the car and stopped to help the wounded woman, but he was apparently abducted by an armed commando, leaving the three-year-old boy in the car. Police rescued the boy, who was turned over to relatives who fled across the international bridge to the town of Fabens, where the dead woman had lived. The hit men chased the family along the Juárez-Porvenir highway, shooting at their car. Algae Amaya Núñez was a founder of a branch of the Cobach High School in Guadalupe. School director Adolfo Risser Ramos said, "She was an excellent teacher. . . . " Family members said that she had been living for several years in the U.S. but that she visited regularly.

El Diario, Ciudad Juárez, April 22, 2008

Andrés Barraza López, 43, rescued by the Mexican army, was the owner of the drugs and weapons found in the house. He had apparently been kidnapped to settle accounts between members of organized crime.

El Paso Times, April 22, 2008

Margarita Crispin, the Customs and Border Protection officer arrested for allowing loads of marijuana to pass through her bridge lanes unchecked for four years, pleaded guilty to drug charges Monday morning and was sentenced to 20 years in prison. Crispin, 32, also agreed to forfeit a 2002 GMC Denali, $16,000 in cash, jewelry and any other assets up to $5 million.

El Diario, Ciudad Juárez, April 22, 2008

Richard Raymond Medina Torres, identified as a member of the U.S. military, was detained yesterday on the Mexican side of the Free Bridge while driving a car with weapons and ammunition in his possession. Inside the car, police found an R-15 assault rifle with 13 clips and a .45-caliber pistol with 70 cartridges.

El Diario, Ciudad Juárez, **April 22, 2008**

"We are experiencing a spectacular lack of values and principles; the criminals no longer care if they kill children or if they are present at the scene of the crimes; our society is disintegrating around us," declared the PRI leader in the Chihuahua state legislature, Fernando Rodríguez Moreno.

El Diario, Ciudad Juárez, **April 22, 2008**

Three municipal police officers traveling in a gray Lincoln were shot at about 7:30 P.M. today in the parking lot of an auto parts store on Avenida 16 de Septiembre. Abraham Carrillo Carrillo, 25, died at the scene. Felipe Galindo Reyes, 36, and José Nabor Alarcón were injured. According to news archives, Captain Galindo "Z-5 Galindo" was on the list of police officers to be executed as "those who continue not believing."

Dallas Morning News, **April 24, 2008**

Mexican president Felipe Calderón said that it is vital that his country receives a $1.4 billion U.S. anti-drug assistance package. "I'm not asking the United States for a favor. I'm asking for responsibility. . . . This is a shared problem that requires a shared solution."

El Diario, Ciudad Juárez, **April 25, 2008**

In Ciudad Juárez, reported cases of domestic violence increased to 6 per day compared to last year, when there was one complaint every 3 days, according to Municipal Public Security Statistics.

MAY

El Diario, Ciudad Juárez, May 1, 2008

Roberto Velasco Bravo, the organized-crime-fighting chief of the Federal Police, was shot and critically wounded in Mexico City. It has not been established if the police chief resisted a robbery while driving his Ford Explorer or if it was an execution.

El Diario, Ciudad Juárez, May 1, 2008

MAZATLAN, Sinaloa—Three confrontations on Wednesday in Culiacán apparently between members of the Sinaloa and Juárez cartels, the Federal Police and the Mexican army left 5 dead, including State police agents Salvador Castellano Rivera and Jesús Martín Muñoz Cota.

El Diario, Ciudad Juárez, May 3, 2008

Even though murders in April decreased considerably compared to March, not a single perpetrator has been arrested. According to official statistics, there were 52 murders in April, 55% fewer than the 117 in March. In total, there have been 262 murders in the first four months of 2008. January—48 homicides, February—45, March—117, April 52.

El Diario, Ciudad Juárez, May 3, 2008

Ex-police captain, Sergio Lagarde Félix, 44, who served as bodyguard for the ex-municipal police director, Saulo Reyes, was shot to death yesterday in the Avenida Valle de Juárez. The victim had worked in several other state and Federal Police posts, most recently as chief warden of the local prison. He had resigned in January to administer a funeral business. Lagarde Félix was the second homicide in May. On May 1, Salvador Martínez Espinoza, 20, died after being shot six times near the Yáñez bridge on the Juárez-Porvenir highway.

El Diario, Ciudad Juárez, May 6, 2008

State police officer Berenice García Corral, 31, was shot 32 times by AK-47 rifle fire on the porch of her house at about 9:00 Monday night. Unofficial accounts say that the occupants of a red Dodge Ram pickup approached the house and called out. The officer was shot and killed as she opened the door of her house. The victim had worked for 7 years in the corporation and was currently assigned to the sex crimes unit of the state investigative police. So far this year, 15 security officers have been executed in Ciudad Juárez. Medical experts determined that the agent died from a brain laceration caused by gunshots to the head.

Ismael Maldonado, 20, died of gunshots received early Monday morning in the Colonia Durango. He had been walking with two others when he was shot from a white Lincoln.

Two others shot near the entrance of the State Public Security Agency were identified as Lorenzo Núñez Aguayo and Agustín Navarrete Damián. They were traveling in a gray Crown Victoria when they began to be pursued by an armed commando in a late-model white pickup and were shot by AK-47 rifle fire as the vehicles reached the installations of State Office of Public Security.

El Diario, Ciudad Juárez, May 6, 2008

13 HOMICIDES IN 5 DAYS

A man between 19 and 22 years of age was shot to death in the Colonia Durango, the 13th murder victim during the first 5 days of May. Salvador García Espinoza, 20, shot May 1 on the Juárez-Porvenir highway. Former municipal policeman, Sergio Antonio Lagarde Félix, shot in the head near the Sanctuary of San Lorenzo on May 2. Shriveled body of a woman found May 2 in the afternoon near the Campo del Tiro. That same night, Benjamín Gamboa Acosta, 28, shot to death in Colonia Revolucion Mexicana. Also that night, Eva Lorena Hernández, 34, killed by multiple gunshots at the Kit-Kat bar, where she worked. Saturday May 3, Alberto Hernández Pérez, alias "El Gordo," shot to death in the Colonia Benito Juárez. Later José Inés González Carrillo, shot to death in the Colonia Salvárcar. Sunday, May 4 before dawn, José Manuel Mijares Ortega, 55, assassinated outside his house in the Colonia Morelos III. Same day at 6:30 A.M., Valentín Quiñónez Ibáñez, intending to commit suicide, was shot by municipal police. That afternoon, Héctor Carrillo Soto, 21, shot in the back by Federal Police in the Valle de Juárez. Lorenzo Juárez Aguayo, 29, Agustín Damián Navarrete, 38, assassinated at the entrance of the State Office of Public Security headquarters. May 5, 3:00 A.M., an unidentified man shot to death in Colonia Durango.

El Diario, Ciudad Juárez, May 7, 2008

Municipal Public Security Captain Saúl Peña López was shot last night at about 8:30 and died this morning from his injuries.

Reuters, May 7, 2008

CIUDAD JUÁREZ—Mexican drug hit men killed a senior police officer in Ciudad Juárez despite a huge army deployment in the violent city across the border from El Paso, Texas. Gunmen with assault rifles on Tuesday night shot Saul Pena, who was due to be named one of city's five police commanders. "It seems they were waiting for him," said police spokesman Jaime Torres. "They shot him with AK-47s in the back, the stomach and the leg. He died in hospital this morning."

Associated Press, May 7, 2008

CHIHUAHUA—New Mexico Gov. Bill Richardson said Wednesday that he has seen an improvement in security along the U.S.-Mexico border. "In my opinion, there has been a dramatic improvement in the last two months," Richardson told reporters in Chihuahua, where he met with Chihuahua Gov. Jesus Reyes Baeza.

El Diario, Ciudad Juárez, May 8, 2008

Luis Alberto Mata Olivas, 37, was shot nine times inside of his house by four masked men. The gunmen forced Olivas's wife and three children upstairs before shooting the victim in the kitchen. . . . Their getaway vehicle, a green Chrysler Grand Cherokee, was found abandoned near the scene.

El Diario, Ciudad Juárez, May 8, 2008

Reynaldo Longoria Ruíz, 68, a shopkeeper in the Valle de Juárez, was shot to death by AK-47 rifle fire last night, inside his store in the village of Praxedis Guerrero. According to witnesses, 2 masked men entered his store, shot him and then fled the scene in a late-model brown and green Blazer. Unofficial sources said the victim had received death threats on at least 3 occasions. He was known in the Valle as "El Caiman"—Alligator. This case brings to 20 the number of homicides in the first 8 days of May.

Washington Post, May 8, 2008

Edgar Eusebio Millán Gómez, 41, head of Mexico's federal police force, was shot as he entered his apartment building in the Colonia Guerrero neighborhood, a poor section of Mexico City that associates say he chose because it was close to law enforcement offices. The killing of such a high-ranking official in Mexico's capital . . . seemed to suggest that almost no one is immune from the violence that has swept Mexico in recent months. Millán Gómez was hit by at least nine bullets and died at the hospital, a police spokesman said.

Los Angeles Times, May 9, 2008

The nation's top organized crime officer, Edgar Millán Gómez, is shot dead in his home, the third police killing in a week. Officials blame the Sinaloa drug cartel. The assassination came a week after Millán Gómez held a news conference in the capital of Sinaloa state to announce the arrests of a dozen suspected cartel hit men. Millán Gómez was shot eight times at point-blank range about 2:30 A.M. at his home in the Guerrero district of central Mexico City. Authorities said the assassin was waiting in the home when two bodyguards dropped him off after a long day at work.

El Diario, Ciudad Juárez, May 9, 2008

A shoot-out last night at about 10:30 on Av. Juárez 2 blocks from the Paso del Norte international bridge between municipal police and an armed commando left 2 dead and 4 wounded, including 3 bicycle cops. Armed men apparently tried to abduct several people from a nightclub. The victims were 2 taxi drivers, German and Oscar, known to the cigarette sellers and parking attendants in the area, their bodies left on the sidewalk and the pavement. A man waiting in his car to cross to El Paso was shot in the abdomen. The shoot-out caused panic along the Av. Juárez.

In another incident, a man between 30 and 35 was shot to death in his car, a 1988 Grand Marquis, in the San Lorenzo neighborhood.

El Diario, Ciudad Juárez, May 9, 2008

Three uniformed municipal police officers were shot this morning by an armed commando. They were traveling to Babicora station in patrol car No. 137. Fellow cops rescued them from the car that crashed into a post. The injured officers were treated at the Star Medica hospital, which was soon surrounded by dozens of police to protect against another confrontation.

El Diario, Ciudad Juárez, May 9, 2008

Sixteen police officers have been assassinated so far this year in Ciudad Juárez, surpassing the total of 14 in 2007, when killings claimed 6 municipal police, 3 transit police and 5 from the State Investigative Agency. In 2008, 11 victims are municipal police, 2 CIPOL (Chihuahua state investigative police), 2 Federal Investigative Police, and one Mexican army soldier. Chihuahua State Attorney General Patricia Gonzalez Rodriguez said no connection was found between any of these cases. The rash of killings began January 24, 2007: . . . Edgar Valencia Delgado, 37, shot to death outside of his house in Horizontes del Sur . . . March 11, lifeless body of Sergeant Adolfo Rios Corral found with two bullet wounds to the head inside a car near Cuatro Siglos Blvd. . . . May 10, 2007, body of municipal officer José Luis Delgado Monsiváis, found inside a white Honda Accord . . . May 29, 2007, municipal policeman Ismael Cháirez Hernández and state policeman Enrique Martínez Torres executed inside an official state vehicle near el Campestre . . . June 6, state investigative agents Moisés Pérez and Héctor Macías shot to death . . . July 30, state policeman Hugo Alejandro Barrón Rangel, 25, shot in the eye and killed, his body found in the trunk of a car parked at the central bus station . . . August 13, traffic cop Gerardo Lechuga Valenzuela, 38, shot to death at the corner of Joaquin Terrazas and Arteaga . . . September 24, preventive agent Horacio Sol Martínez assassinated by thieves who had just robbed the Dental Right office. . . . October 4, traffic police commander Héctor Osorio Hernández, 43, run down by several vehicles driven by hooded men at the corner of Mina and Mariscal . . . November 19, municipal policeman Jorge Arturo Baca Terrazas executed in a Telcel office in a shopping mall . . . December 16, Transit Commander Francisco González Solano, 44, assassinated by a shot to the forehead, his body found near a dike in the Colonia Luis Echeverria. . . . December 22, officer Víctor Hugo Caldera Flores, 40, beaten to death in Colonia Granjero. . . . 2008 first officer murdered . . . municipal police Captain Julián Cháirez Hernández, early Sunday morning January 20, in the Chamizal subdivision . . . January 21, Francisco Ledesma Salazar, 34, municipal police director, executed at the door of his house as he leaves for work . . . At night on the same day, Fernando Lozano Sandoval, state investigative police coordinator, survives a shooting on the Av. Paseo Triunfo de la Republica. . . . February 5, Luis Alfonso Rivera Villa, 35, second in command of CIPOL, and his bodyguard, Jesús García Rodríguez, 25, shot to death in the Third Burocrat neighborhood . . . February 27, José Guadalupe Cruz Cisneros of the mounted police, executed in Colonia Plutarco Elias Calles. . . . March 1, state police agent Luis Alonso Marrufo Armendáriz, riddled with AK-47 rifle fire . . . his partner Valentín Ramos Díaz injured but survives . . . March 2, Infantry Second Captain Ricardo Fuentes García, assassinated in his vehicle on the Av. Tecnologico. . . . March 9, municipal policeman Víctor Alejandro Gómez Márquez assassinated by an armed group. Commander Ismael Villegas Frausto and two bodyguards, Mario Alberto Arámbula Rodríguez and Moisés Casas Camargo, injured. . . . March 14, Lieutenant Mario Moraz Cevallos executed in his vehicle in the Colonia Bellavista after leaving work. . . . March 19, Luis Humberto Rivera Gamboa, 37, machine-gunned leaving work at the Av. De las Torres . . . March 20, municipal agent Oscar Campolla Saucedo, 37, executed within 150 meters of the Aldama Station. . . . March 23, municipal policeman Alejandro Martínez Casas and his 8-year-old son, Alejandro Martínez Cruz, executed in the Colonia Margaritas. . . . April 22, three municipal policemen shot at the Autozone store on Av. 16 de Septiembre but only Abraham Carrillo Carrillo, 25, dies . . . Commander Felipe Galindo Reyes, 35, and José Amador Alarcon Rodriguez, 25, survive the attack. May 5, state policewoman Berenice García Corral, 31, assassinated on her porch . . . May 6, municipal police Captain Mario Saúl Peña López, 39, shot to death in his vehicle near the Cuauhtemoc police station.

El Diario, Ciudad Juárez, May 10, 2008

Six homicides occurred between Thursday night and Friday afternoon, bringing to 29 the number of murders in the first 9 days of May. In addition, 3 municipal police agents, including the recently named director of Babicora station, were injured in an execution attempt. . . . The latest trail of murder begins after the assassination of two taxi drivers in the central city and a man in San Lorenzo, followed by Edgar Adalberto Ortega Cantu, 25, found dead in Av. Henequen, shot in his car at 9:50 P.M. Thursday after a traffic incident involving an armed commando, a 1997 Mitsubishi Montero and a 1993 Crown Victoria. . . . Edgar Adalberto . . . thought to be an innocent person had the bad luck to stray into the intersection as the shoot-out erupted. . . . Second homicide, Gustavo Carbajal, 40, 2:30 A.M. yesterday, shot six times by two masked men inside the La Finca bar . . . third incident, 12:00 yesterday at the Alonso butcher shop in Colonia Lomas de San José . . . two men entered the butcher shop to rob it and shot the Alonso brothers who had refused to turn over the money, injuring Ubaldo Alonso Trancoso, 45, and killing José Francisco, 40. At 12:30, another murder in the interior of a house on a private street in Vistas del Valle, unidentified victim shot 12 times, body found face down in the living room. At 12:55, Juan Nicolás Ríos Alderete, 26, assassinated in his car on the sidewalk in front of the primary school in Colonia Morelos after being "hunted" . . . at the scene members of the victim's family attacked photographer Salvador Hernandez. . . . At 5:41, Jesus Garcia, 30–35, found face down next to a white van for sale, near the corner of Jacinto Benavente and Gabriel Garcia Marquez streets, several bullet wounds to the head and face . . . he was a parking attendant and washed cars for a living.

El Paso Times, May 10, 2008

A gun battle on the Avenida Juárez tourist strip left two men dead and wounded five others, including three bicycle police officers, as part of a resurgence of violence in Juárez. After the shooting, a man with a gunshot wound to the torso stumbled to get medical help on the U.S. side of the international bridge.

The violence, possibly linked to a war between drug cartels and government forces across Mexico, continued Friday with a double homicide in the town of Palomas and an attempt on the life of a Juárez police commander and his bodyguards. In Juárez, there were five other separate homicides as of 8 P.M. Friday.

"The El Paso Convention and Visitors Bureau understands the recent events in neighboring Juárez are unsettling for some. However, it is important to note that historically there has been virtually no crime committed against tourists to El Paso or the city of Juárez," bureau spokesman Pifas Silva said in a statement.

Friday afternoon, a father and son were killed in a hail of 67 bullets along a street in Palomas, across the border from Columbus, N.M., Chihuahua state police said.

Arnoldo Carreon Renteria, 57, and his son Damian Arnoldo Carreon, 25, were getting into their pickup, with New Mexico plates, when they were shot.

Los Angeles Times/Associated Press, May 10, 2008

Mexico's Federal Police Chief Grilled His Killer

Millán Gómez was shot eight times at close range as bodyguards accompanied him to his home in Mexico City shortly after midnight Thursday. Mexican media reported Friday that authorities suspect that Millán Gómez was betrayed by someone who knew his plans and movements. Millán Gómez asked, "Who sent you? Who sent you to kill me?"

EXTENDED PHOTO CAPTIONS

1. Abandoned dormitory at the CIAD #8 Rehabilitation Center in Colonia 1st of September where an armed commando murdered eight inmates on August 13, 2008.

2. Manuel, an inmate of the Vision in Action asylum for the mentally ill in Ciudad Juárez, tried to kill his mother during an attack of schizophrenia. He lost his mind after years of drug abuse.

3. Patio of the House of Death where Mexican Federal Police unearthed 12 bodies in January 2004. An undercover informant for the U.S. Bureau of Immigration and Customs Enforcement (ICE) participated in some of the killings and apparently transmitted information to ICE agents in El Paso by a wire hidden on his body.

4. Pastor José Antonio Galván, right, and inmates at the Vision in Action asylum, celebrate a birthday.

5. Military patrol along Juárez Avenue after a triple execution took place a few meters from the border at the Paso del Norte/Santa Fe bridge on May 8, 2008.

6. The aftermath of an attack on prayer service at a drug rehabilitation clinic in Juárez that killed eight and wounded five. Witnesses said the attackers wore military-style uniforms.

7. La Esperanza rehabilitation center in Juárez where addicts, prostitutes, homosexuals, and homeless people gather daily for meals. The center closed after receiving constant threats that it would be attacked.

8. Weapons confiscated by the army from presumed narco-traffickers, June 29, 2009.

9. Fifty Juárez police officers protest arbitrary arrests and false drug possession charges against fellow officers by the army, March 31, 2008.

10. A double execution in the southeastern region of the city, June 25, 2009.

11. Gang members under arrest for shooting a rival, the blood still on their hands, March 23, 2008.

12. Physicians, dentists, nurses, veterinarians, X-ray specialists, and lab technicians protest kidnappings, extortions, armed assaults, and robberies against the medical community in Juárez. The police were ineffective in preventing the crimes and were also accused of being the perpetrators, December 12, 2008.

13. A pregnant woman who washed cars for a living is caught in the crossfire and murdered during a car chase and shooting, June 3, 2008.

14. Alejandro and Refugio Irigoyen (center), learn of the death of their son, 19-year-old Jaime Alejandro Irigoyen. On January 12, 2009, men dressed as soldiers abducted the university law student and baseball player at his home. His body was discovered on January 14 while family and friends were protesting against the Mexican Army at the entrance to the military base.

15. A woman arrives at the scene where her husband, an alleged drug pusher, was shot. The pregnant woman and her three children rushed to the hospital where the man died.

16. Students, academics, and activists protest the murder of university professor Manuel Arroyo at the Federal Attorney General's office in Juárez, May 29, 2009.

17. A man is shot at a gas station while putting air in his truck tires the night of February 25, 2009.

18. A mass grave at the San Rafael Cemetery. Hundreds of murder victims during 2008 and 2009 remain unidentified.

19. Anexo de Vida rehabilitation center. On the night of September 15, 2009, at least eight men armed with assault weapons entered the center and murdered ten addicts. A survivor of the massacre said that the center had not received any warning or threats.

20. A man sells roses in downtown Juárez.

THANKS

This listing of murders and other events was constructed by Molly Molloy until around May 10, when the torrent of death became overwhelming. She also provided the translations included in the text and keeps a digital file of more than one thousand untranslated articles as well as a small roomful of hard-copy Juárez newspapers that will eventually be archived at the New Mexico State University Library.

This fatigue with recording the deaths is a common experience. I remember my friend, photographer Julián Cardona, in early June after the machine-gunning of the twelve-year-old girl, telling me, "I can't do this anymore, it is hopeless." And so for a spell, he stopped taking photographs. And then, of course, resumed.

I kept a running file of newspaper stories until around May or June, when it hit fifteen hundred pages single-spaced. And I threw in the towel.

I crossed the bridge from Juárez to El Paso in June or early July swearing I would never return. But I did. And Julián Cardona and Molly Molloy also resumed their work.

I want to thank my friend El Pastor José Antonio Galvan, who showed me the insane underbelly of the city and whose work with the destroyed minds of Juárez touches my heart. He is also, he says, building a cell for me at his asylum, and I am grateful that I will never be homeless.

And I must thank Esther Chávez Cano, who stood up for the people of Juárez when the government of Juárez cowers and stands down.

I want to express my gratitude to the reporters of Juárez. They kept at it under impossible conditions. Armando Rodriguez, for example, filed more than three stories a day until he was executed on November 13.

What little record we have of this killing season is because of their work and their love of their besieged city.